OCLC #3965139

D0070228

MS
K56
1998

A Female Economy
Women's Work in a Prairie Province, 1870–1970

A Female Economy analyses a hundred years of women's work in Manitoba from the province's entry into Confederation in 1870 to the publication of the *Report of the Royal Commission on the Status of Women* in 1970. Mary Kinnear shows that women's work, whether unpaid in the household or on the farm or for wages in the industrial, service, and professional sectors, was undervalued.

Kinnear details how ordinary women – early pioneers, East European immigrants, First Nations women, and professional women – lived and provides insight into what they thought of the world of work, often telling their stories in their own words. She explores cultural and economic expectations for women and juxtaposes the activities society deemed suitable for women with what they actually did. Kinnear argues that a host of factors, such as class and ethnicity, differentiated their choices but that these women shared many common experiences.

While women's own views furnish the main theme, *A Female Economy* contributes to a developing debate in feminist economics. By focusing on women's experiences in the sexually segregated economy of a Canadian province at the geographic centre of Canada, Kinnear furnishes a paradigm for women's economic activity in most Western industrializing societies at the time.

MARY KINNEAR is professor of history, University of Manitoba.

A *Female* ECONOMY

Women's Work in a Prairie Province,

1870–1970

MARY KINNEAR

McGill-Queen's University Press
Montreal & Kingston · London · Ithaca

© McGill-Queen's University Press 1998
ISBN 0-7735-1734-0

Legal deposit fourth quarter 1998
Bibliothèque nationale du Québec

Printed in Canada on acid-free paper

This book has been published with the help of a
grant from the Humanities and Social Sciences
Federation of Canada, using funds provided
by the Social Sciences and Humanities Research
Council of Canada.

McGill-Queen's University Press acknowledges
the financial support of the Government of
Canada through the Book Publishing Industry
Development Program for its activities. We also
acknowledge the support of the Canada Council
for the Arts for our publishing program.

Canadian Cataloguing in Publication Data

Kinnear, Mary, 1942–
A female economy:
women's work in a Prairie Province, 1870–1970
Includes bibliographical references and index.
ISBN 0-7735-1734-0

1. Women–Employment–Manitoba–History.
2. Women–Manitoba–Social conditions.
3. Sexual division of labor–Manitoba–History.
I. Title.
HD6100.M35K55   1998
306.3'615'097127   C98-900861-4

This book was typeset by Typo Litho
Composition Inc. in 10/12 Sabon.

For my family,
past, present, and future

CONTENTS

$\mathcal{I}$LLUSTRATIONS

$\mathscr{P}$REFACE

A Female Economy represents a discovery both personal and professional. I arrived in Manitoba in 1965 and work became the dominant
feature of my life. For years I did not know what spare time was.
Although my understanding was not particularly sophisticated, it was
plain that my experience of work was not the same as a man's. Absorbed
by raising a family, establishing a career as a historian, and making new
friends, I wanted to know how other women had moved through these
same stages of life. How had previous generations of women coped?
How had they combined productive and reproductive, paid and unpaid
work? What had they thought about their working lives?

I looked at the history books to satisfy my curiosity, but they
revealed little. When a woman was mentioned, it was as an occasional
leading lady, usually judged to be noteworthy because of her relationship with a man. One remarkable exception was *The Woman Suffrage
Movement in Canada* by Catherine Cleverdon, a book which included
a vivid section on suffragists in Manitoba. Then in the 1970s there was
a sea change in the recording of history. Along with the resurgence of
women's politics in the fullest meaning of that word came a renais-
sance in women's history. Encouraged by male colleagues at the University of Manitoba – until the mid-1970s I had no female colleague in
the History Department – I prepared a history course which examined
the women of Western civilization. Urged to use local archival sources,
my students began to recreate the lives of ordinary women from the
diaries and memories of the women in their communities.

Their achievements led me to change professional direction – to
abandon the far-away archival resources of eighteenth-century politics
and instead to explore material closer to hand. The more I delved, the
more complicated historical research became. I found I was not, after

all, a pioneer. Others had been there before me, but their work had largely been overlooked in major historical publications. Moreover, I soon found that "women" was not a simple word. The women of Manitoba were far too diverse to be lumped together in a single category. Race distinguished First Nations women politically as well as economically; ethnicity loomed large, and class was significant; poor women had fewer resources than rich women and this materially affected how they spent their days. Religion too was important – many immigrants had come to Manitoba precisely because of persecution in Europe and had created settlements or settled in neighbourhoods in which religion was the central organizing principle of life. A comprehensive social history of women in Manitoba, to include all ethnic groups, all religions, and all economic classes of women – a truly multicultural history – has yet to be written. *A Female Economy* begins to chart this vast territory by focusing on women's work.

This project has been long in the making, partly because of diversions into other historical research whose appeal was irresistible. My biography, *Margaret McWilliams: An Interwar Feminist*, was written after I found McWilliams was an early historian not only of the province but of women in Manitoba as well. My study of professional women, *In Subordination*, was born when I could find few descriptions, and still fewer assessments, of these women even though they comprised a steady 10 to 20 per cent of the paid labour force from the 1880s on.

My first preparations for a study of women's work arose from a desire to use existing archival and statistical data. In 1982 Greg Mason of the University of Manitoba's Institute for Economic and Social Research, Beverley Tangri of the Department of Economics, and I collaborated in organizing a conference on the general topic of women and work. Sponsored by the Social Sciences and Humanities Research Council of Canada (SSHRCC), its agenda was to consider what resources would be necessary to support research into women and the Canadian economy. I was later awarded SSHRCC grants to support the historical investigation of women and work in Manitoba: in 1983 a strategic grant to generate historical statistics, and in 1984 a Canadian Studies Research Tools grant. Vera Fast and I published a collaborative annotated archival bibliography, *Planting the Garden*. A 1986 conference on the subject of women in history in Manitoba considered different aspects of women's work, and two publications resulted: an anthology in book form, *First Days, Fighting Days*, and a theme issue of the journal *Manitoba History*. I thank all who collaborated on these projects, including Kerry Abel, Marilyn Barber, Marie Bonin, Jennifer Brown, Carol Budnick, Sarah Carter, Angela Davis, Vera Fast, Sheila

Grover, Nancy Hall, Anne Hicks, Mary Horodyski, Susan Jackel, Brigitte Joyal, Linda Kealey, Annalee Lepp, David Millar, James Mochoruk, Donna Norell, Michèle Pujol, Sharon Reilly, Barbara Roberts, Sylvia Van Kirk, and Donna Webber. In the late 1980s I made more use of oral history. At first I worked with the large number of tapes deposited in various collections around the province. Then, for *In Subordination* I interviewed over two hundred women who had been involved in professional work, and this material substantially augmented the historical resources available. Another SSHRCC grant in 1991 supported the development of this book. I am very grateful to SSHRCC and its anonymous assessors for recognition and for the assistance, time, and material resources provided by grants.

Many of the debts I owe are to colleagues and students whose support and stimulation have encouraged me through frustrating as well as more productive times. It is a pleasure to thank the many people who have assisted me with help, advice, and research assistance. I thank colleagues in the Canadian Committee on Women's History, especially Margaret Conrad and Alison Prentice, for their friendly support over the years. In Manitoba I thank those who agreed to be interviewed, and I thank the many assistants who helped me shape the raw experience of other people into history: Daphne Andrews, Michael Bell, Cathy Carlson, Barbara Chatterly, Cathy Chatterly, Bonita Eastwood, Brigitte Joyal, Tamara Miller, Wendy Parker, Sherry Peters, Marcia Stenz, and Beverley Suderman. I thank Hrund Skulason for her translations from Icelandic, Marilyn Baker for her advice about paintings, and Patricia Dowdall for her editorial advice and encouragement. Sarah Carter and Laura Peers helped me with bibliographic advice on First Nations history. Thora Cook from the Western Canadian Pictorial Index and Elizabeth Blight and Lynn Champagne of the Provincial Archives of Manitoba were very helpful regarding photographs. Prabir Mitra and Heather Warkentin produced the map of Manitoba. I thank Patrick Wright and Carol Goodlow of St. John's College Library. Colleagues from non-historical disciplines as well as my own department have guided my forays into literature, economics, political studies, native studies, and art but must not be held to account for my interpretations. I would like to thank especially Barbara Angel, Jack Bumsted, the late Angela Davis, Vera Fast, Barry Ferguson, Gerald Friesen, Jean Friesen, John Kendle, Michael Kinnear, Debra Lindsay, Ken McVicar, Morris Mott, Ed Moulton, Karen Ogden, Kathryn Young, and Anthony Waterman. Editors from McGill-Queen's University Press, especially Joan Harcourt, Marion Magee, and Don Akenson, more than once provided just the right words for the occasion. It was a pleasure to work on this project while I was a visiting fellow in other universities.

I thank the Research School of Social Sciences at the Australian National University, Canberra, and the Fellows of Clare Hall in the University of Cambridge for their generosity and hospitality. Anonymous assessors for the press and for the Aid to Scholarly Publications programme of the Social Science Federation of Canada and the Canadian Federation for the Humanities gave valuable forthright criticism which brought about considerable improvements to the text.

Always I have paid attention to "ordinary" women. Such a common-sense concept founders in definitional quicksand. Despite the difficulties, I have tried to recapture the salient features of a mainstream majority whilst never losing sight of broader, inclusive visions. This type of study can only be pursued when there are time-series of comparable statistics and the extensive data generated by government agencies are an excellent resource. They provide the objective, quantitative bare bones of the female figures in *A Female Economy*. Painting in the details of flesh, clothing, and relations requires the use of more subjective, qualitative data. We must apply our imaginations to tap into women's consciousness, to understand their mentalities, to perceive their pains and pleasures as human beings, to comprehend their breathing, working lives. This necessarily involves risk, and a historian's surmise may turn out to be incomplete, or mistaken. Nevertheless our trade requires us to do more than describe; we must try to understand the past and explain it to the present.

Like so many women before me, I have reaped greater benefits from my unpaid work than from my paid job. I thank Michael, and David, Andrew, Sara, and Lucy for making my work so very rewarding, and I dedicate *A Female Economy* to my family: past, present, and future.

MK
St. John's College, University of Manitoba
July 1997

A Female Economy

Map of Manitoba

$\mathcal{P}$ARAMETERS

A Female Economy analyses how women disposed of their labour during the century from 1870 to 1970 in one of Canada's prairie provinces – Manitoba. It describes women's work both paid and unpaid, within the family and without. Although the book arises out of the work of women in a diverse community situated in the geographic centre of Canada, it allows us to see in miniature what women were doing in most Western industrializing economies from the mid-nineteenth century onwards. Naturally the history of Manitoba has some features peculiar to itself. A pre-industrial fur trade lingered into the twentieth century, and industrial-scale agriculture dominated the provincial economy for decades. Overall, however, women's work in Manitoba paralleled women's work inside and outside the home elsewhere. Numerous archives, oral as well as written, document women's work and allow us to see "minute particulars" in a local setting which mirror the larger picture of women's occupations in Western society generally.[1] Such a community study contributes to the search for "common themes and patterns in the organisation of work" and explores "the dominant ideologies shaping gender relations" in history.[2]

Early in the twentieth century a few historians recognized that women's working lives were different from men's, and more recently historical studies have chronicled women's experience in considerable detail.[3] *Manitoba 125*, the latest history of the province, exhibits this new awareness.[4] The first economists were slow to acknowledge the significance of women's work, but John Stuart Mill, benefiting from the conversations and writing of his future wife, Harriet Taylor, saw its importance. He looked to the household to discover how a nation should manage its resources. Women's work was his model for political economy, and his definition of domestic economy remains a useful starting point today in setting out the parameters for a study of women's work.

Domestic economy, wrote Mill in 1844, was an art: the "maxims of prudence for keeping the family regularly supplied with what its wants require, and securing, with any given amount of means, the greatest possible quantity of physical comfort and enjoyment." The most beneficent purpose of political economy, in turn, was "to accomplish for a nation something like what the most perfect domestic economy accomplishes for a single household."[5] It was women who managed the domestic economy, but by the nineteenth century women's work had spread beyond the confines of the home and it incorporated more than the servicing of family wants.

Nineteenth-century Manitoba, an agrarian frontier society with wide open spaces, was not the original context for Mill's thoughts, but his description of domestic economy nevertheless captures the major themes of women's work in the province at that time. Most women shared his belief that the "first call upon their exertions" was to see that their families were regularly supplied with the requirements for comfort and enjoyment, and they acted accordingly.[6] Mill argued that a woman should have access to paid work, which would allow her to be self-supporting. However he did not consider the possibility that after marriage, a family's financial support might be insufficient without the earnings of a wife. Wives ought not to be prevented from "obeying their vocation," but Mill did not concern himself with those groups in the population where the waged labour of all adults in a family – and sometimes of the children too – was necessary for the family's support.[7] Some families were not nuclear and some families had no male breadwinner. Moreover, Mill gave little consideration to women who lived outside the normal family, and none to women whose "given amount of means" was insufficient for livelihood. His thinking about women at work was not comprehensive.

However, the economists paid even less attention to women's activities. From Adam Smith on, economics was understood as any study having to do with the creation and distribution of the "necessities and conveniences of life." Women were intimately involved in this work, but their labour received little acknowledgement or analysis. Generally speaking, work has been narrowly interpreted by the economists as *paid* labour. Yet the sort of work most women mainly did was not merely a female version of men's work. The segregation by sex of women workers, both inside and outside the home, meant that women largely operated in a women's world in which much of their activity was not remunerated by money.[8] Consequently, just as women have been hidden from history, so have women not figured in economics.

Only recently have some economists begun to consider a new shape in their model-building: "femina economica," economic woman.[9] These economists are broadening the discipline, attempting to bring about "a cultural recognition of home, workplace and polity that recognizes the reproductive, productive and political aspects of most human activities in all institutional settings and in all social milieux."[10] Economist Marilyn Waring noted in 1988 that "the public policy implications of imputing women's work into the national accounts are vast," especially the sort of work traditionally performed without pay: "all caring services, subsistence production, and ... [a] vast range of life-enhancing work."[11] In this book, I have adopted Waring's definition of work, namely, "any activity culminating in a service or product, regardless of whether that activity is paid."[12] It comprehends farm work, child rearing, housework, and volunteer public service as well as the work measured by the orthodox criterion of payment. Women's work is rendered visible to the onlooker. Women themselves have long understood the value of their work for the well-being of their families. As Joy Parr showed in *The Gender of Breadwinners*, women were fully aware that "securing a subsistence and managing the complexities of social and economic existence have required deft balancing of these different kinds of activities."[13] *A Female Economy* is therefore a contribution towards a more balanced vision of the past.

Some terms used in this study need clarification, beginning with our subject, *women*. Nineteenth-century rhetoric often assumed that "woman" was a universal and eternal term. There was an implicit understanding that in essentials all women were the same and their functions were constant throughout history. In the twentieth century historians are more discriminating. It is recognized that besides differing from men, women also differ from each other. Just as class, ethnicity, and race reveal differences among men, so also do they distinguish one woman from another. Other differences such as age, religion, and place of residence compound the social, economic, and cultural divisions amongst women. While acknowledging that women share experiences of gender, we need simultaneously to recognize women's differences. The human condition is complicated.

For women, as for men, class position helped to determine how well they could secure the welfare of their families and themselves. But women did not experience class in the same way as men. They were not as free as men to choose among alternative occupations. Most women viewed themselves as the family of a man. Their status was derivative. Their class was determined, as was their livelihood, by their husbands. The occupation of an adult woman living on her own determined her class only for so long as she was single. At the time of marriage, her status tended to sink – or rise – to that of her husband.[14]

Women's life chances were affected by income level, which in turn had an impact on concrete matters such as the quality of housing, food, and clothing and the level of services available in emergencies such as sickness, unemployment, and death. Access to these benefits depended, in the first instance, on the livelihood of the wage earner and, more particularly, on the amount of money available for the wife to manage and the location of the family residence. In Manitoba, for example, there was a substantial gulf separating the living conditions available in the major urban areas – in Winnipeg especially – from the amenities common to the countryside.[15]

Class affected the prescribed role for women in several ways, but above all in the notion embraced by the trade unions, the declared protectors of working-class men, that it was desirable for a responsible man to earn a family wage.[16] In the trade union schema there was no place in the paid labour force for a married woman. A woman should work in the labour force only as a young single adult before marriage. The sole exceptions were if she remained single or if misfortune befell her husband. The proper place for a married woman was in the household, exclusively. In reality the role of a full-time housewife was possible only for a married woman in a household with an income above a certain threshold. Below that threshold, her earned income was necessary for the survival of the family. In farming families, the wife's labour was generally essential to the viability of the farm as a business. Still, the family wage ideology remained strong and was both reinforced and undermined in the years following the First World War. The notion was buttressed by the introduction of welfare legislation which promoted the state in the role of provider-husband, thereby reducing the need of widows or wives of unfortunate men to work for wages themselves. It was undermined by the spread of feminist ideas which treated the adult woman as an individual empowered to choose whether to earn her living regardless of her marital or maternal status or her class.

In Manitoba, *ethnicity* complicated the class structure. While research into the lives of First Nations women is beginning to document the experiences of the aboriginal population, most historical accounts focus on the white population. A comprehensive account of the importance of race and ethnicity in Manitoba remains to be written, but it is possible to see significant trends which emerged during the century 1870–1970. Immigrants of British origin from Ontario "controlled political and economic power," though this hegemony was slipping by 1970.[17] In rural Manitoba, Ontario-British people occupied much of the rich, productive arable land in the southwest. French speakers were settled along the Red River from Lake Winnipeg south to the United States border and were also found dispersed in Métis settlements mainly throughout the southeastern part of the province. St. Boniface, located opposite Winnipeg on the eastern bank of the Red, was the major French urban area.[18] The geographical division was mirrored in the capital city of

Winnipeg, which became "two distinct cities." The prosperous families of Ontario-British origin lived in the south and west of the city while the north end became "a noisy, crowded ghetto."[19] Such an ethnic division had obvious political and economic significance for men. The Ontario-British business élite was to be opposed in the early twentieth century by working-class newcomers from Britain together with East European immigrants and Jewish socialists. This urban split determined the provincial and municipal politics of the interwar years, beginning with the dramatic achievement of the Winnipeg General Strike in 1919, "one of the most massive and remarkable confrontations of capital and labour that the industrial age has seen anywhere."[20]

Economically, ethnicity was as much a determinant of survival strategy as previous education and work experience. Anti-Semitism was a common sentiment, but many of those outside the dominant Protestant Anglo-Saxon culture experienced barriers.[21] For Ukrainians, Poles, and Jews in 1931, "Winnipeg was far from being a city of 250,000 in which they ... were free to search for work. As much as two-thirds of it was barred and bolted against them."[22] For new immigrants, class and ethnicity tended at first to be directly related, but the connection grew looser in subsequent generations.[23] First Nations peoples, the original inhabitants of the area covered by Manitoba, experienced a rapid fall from a position of near partnership with the white population in 1870 to one of seriously disadvantaged subordination during the following century.[24]

Feminism is another term which requires clarification at the outset. *A Female Economy* is about women's work. Feminism has to do with beliefs about women, beliefs which in turn can influence behaviour. Some women were feminists, others were not. Insofar as much feminist analysis concerns women and work – access to, training for, prohibition from, progress in – it is relevant in an examination of the economics of women.

There is no single definition of feminism which attracts universal recognition: as Karen Offen has said: "Scholars have to invent their own definitions of feminism."[25] Mine draws on Nancy Cott's view that feminism is built on three core components: first, a belief in sex equality in the sense of a rejection of sex hierarchy; secondly, a presumption that women's condition is socially constructed, and changeable; thirdly, a notion of gender group identity in that women perceive of themselves as a social grouping sharing certain characteristics.[26] A person or policy described as feminist incorporates belief in equality with men, a conviction that gender roles are socially constructed, and a recognition of gender consciousness. This definition of feminism implies a sexual equality which at the same time permits sexual difference. Equality does not necessarily interpret "equal" as "identical." The definition allows comparisons between different time periods and countries and includes simultaneously the notion of a woman as an individual and as what Offen calls a "relational" human being, with responsibilities to and for human beings besides herself.[27]

Feminism understands emancipation to include the positive notion of autonomy: the freedom – and responsibility – to make decisions about one's own security and livelihood. A feminist world could be perceived only dimly in 1870, but over the century Manitoba writers created fictional women who reflected both the restraints of existing culture and the freedom of their creators' imaginations. The heroine of Francis Marion Beynon's *Aleta Dey* (1919) triumphantly allowed her love, and then her egalitarian principles, to sustain her, in the face of the conventions of pre-1917 society. Martha Ostenso's schoolteacher protagonist, Lind Archer, was one of several women in *Wild Geese* (1925) who flouted sexual convention yet prospered. Ostenso's book won a $13,500 prize in a field of 1,389 competitors; it remained in print into the 1990s. Margaret Laurence's female characters in her widely acclaimed novels set in the 1940s and 1950s were, like Morag Gunn in *The Diviners*, less cheerful but formidable in their strength. *April Raintree*, a novel by the Métis writer Beatrice Culleton which is set after the 1950s, showed the pain experienced by First Nations women but also their resilience. These women were all created by Manitobans and were no less real for being fictional.

In this book I take women who had historical lives and see how they experienced the past through their work. The women themselves are the centre of my analysis. I describe first who the women in Manitoba were and then the cultural economic expectations they were supposed to meet. I assess women's education and training, their domestic and farm work, their participation in the paid labour force, and their volunteer public service. Whenever possible, I let them tell their own story in their own words.

In *A Female Economy* each of the major forms of women's work, paid and unpaid, is considered as a topic in itself. This scheme raises organizational problems. In the world of women's work all the spheres are interlocking: work in the family provides preconditions for women's work in the labour market, for example. The interconnections amongst the various sorts of work are therefore noted in passing. Another problem arises from the lack of an explicit chronology. The technology of farm work, for instance, developed over time and indeed the structure of work in its many forms changed considerably. Neither farm work, nor homemaking, still less work outside the home, remained static over the century. Consequently, within each chapter some of the major changes are identified, but this book does not provide a dated inventory of "important" events, if by "important" we mean those happenings which traditionally have been assigned historical recognition. Rather, this book interrogates the meaning of "important" and returns always to the criterion of what was important for women. Recognizing that women were different from each other as well as from men, I place "work" on the shoulders and in the minds of the particular women concerned.

Importance is relative. No history of Manitoba can ignore completely events of epic proportion which contributed to the corporate identity of the community. Two grand events, in 1919 and 1950, punctuated the normal rhythm of Manitoba life and each was important for certain women. In the summer of 1919 the city of Winnipeg was virtually paralysed by a general strike for over four weeks. Many prominent citizens believed a socialist revolution along the lines of the Bolshevik Revolution in Russia was imminent.[28] A generation later, in 1950, the southern area of the province and Winnipeg were inundated by flood conditions described at the time as the most catastrophic ever seen in Canada. Flood water submerged an area seventy miles long and between five and thirty miles wide. Over 300,000 people were evacuated, and damages were estimated at over $50 million. In 1997 the province was able to cope with even worse flooding through better preparation, but 80,000 people still had to leave their homes.[29]

During the strike women were on both sides of the dispute, as strikers and scab labourers, rioters and demagogues. They made refreshments for striking workers and continued to care for their families under conditions of severe deprivation: "As mothers, wives, sisters and daughters of male strikers they gave their men support."[30] But they did more: they comprised 13 per cent of the strikers themselves.[31] During the 1950 and 1997 floods, women like men filled sandbags and constructed dikes, provided food and support service for other weary workers, and directed their volunteer organizations into relief operations.[32] Afterwards, women no less than men had anecdotes relating to their participation. The contributions of women to the events of a standard historical narrative must be recognized, but this is not the prime purpose of A Female Economy.

For women's lives during the century 1870–1970, the dominant narrative is driven by demography. Women are the mothers. Women's work has always incorporated the production of people together with their nurture. Consequently, women's work in the family, and for the family, has been a central fact of life. If there are events, and legislation, which matter to women, they are as much the technology relating to birth control, and the laws related directly and indirectly to marriage, as labour disputes and community catastrophe. Births, marriages, and deaths all have a direct impact on the size of the family and the work load of the mother, both inside and outside the household. Census data therefore allow us to do more than *describe* the female population of Manitoba. The figures which document demography also help to *explain* the connections between reproduction and production, between the number of people and the resources applied to their sustenance and comfort.

The story begins in 1870 and ends in 1970, two years which are somewhat arbitrary. As the proverb says, women's work is never done. However, a case can be made for framing an account with these dates. Manitoba entered the Canadian Confederation in 1870, a political decision which meant, among other things, that there was a more systematic collection of data. Statistics with respect to activities measured by the state became more comprehensive and accurate. One hundred years later, 1970 offered another political milestone with the report of the Canadian government's Royal Commission on the Status of Women. The state had come to recognize the importance of women in national life and signalled an intention to identify and remedy problems relating to their roles.

In 1995 a Winnipeg author, Carol Shields, won a Pulitzer Prize for her novel, *The Stone Diaries*, the story of an "ordinary woman" born in a Manitoba country town in 1905. Daisy Goodwill, daughter of a stone mason, becomes a housewife and mother and later in life writes a gardening column for a newspaper. The book contains a family photograph album but not one picture includes any likeness of Daisy Goodwill. Her life seems to be lived through others. Yet the reader gets to know the woman's toughness, her capacity to act within circumscribed situations, and her ability at times to reject conventional boundaries. As a writer, Shields has said her "life theme is either we're all ordinary, or none of us are."[33]

A Female Economy is the story of ordinary women. Our ability to see the features of their story would once have been considered extraordinary. Now we are better able to discern, and we can begin to assess, the historical dimensions of women's work: neither eternal nor unchanging but grounded in time and culture.

"FOREIGNERS ON SOMEONE ELSE'S GROUND"

Who were the women of Manitoba?

Manitoba in the late nineteenth century was a society undergoing kaleidoscopic change in size and composition. Even its geography was unstable. In 1870 it was a small southern rectangle of about 14,340 square miles, known as the "postage-stamp province." Not until 1912 were the boundaries fixed, extending up to Hudson Bay in the northeast and by then encompassing 250,000 square miles.[1] In 1870 the recorded population was 24,000, but by 1901 immigration had increased it tenfold. There were a few small towns and one major city, Winnipeg, with a population of almost 50,000. Immigrants continued to move in rapidly, and by 1911 the provincial population had risen to 461,394. The population in 1971 was almost one million: 988,245.[2]

ECONOMY AND CULTURE IN 1870

The first generations of immigrants joined a society which was mushrooming in size and heterogeneous in composition. Before the nineteenth century the fur trade prospered in Rupert's Land, a vast area of almost three million square miles drained by the rivers flowing into Hudson Bay, ceded by the British crown in 1670 to the Hudson's Bay Company. The company, with its headquarters in London, had sovereign power over the territory and a monopoly of trade and commerce carried out through a network of fortified trading stations. This empire did not go unchallenged by rival adventurers and traders from France and Montreal who in the 1780s joined together in the North West Company.

Both companies relied on the active co-operation of the men and women of the First Nations. Although the men provided most of the pelts, the women trapped smaller animals, like marten; they also served in intermediary roles as guides, interpreters, and diplomats; and as consumers they fuelled the demand for European goods such as knives, cloth, and axes. They manufactured many of the goods vital to wilderness survival, such as moccasins and snowshoes, and preserved food like pemmican and fish. They helped in the construction of birch-bark canoes and were employed to paddle and steer them. When land around the forts was planted for subsistence agriculture, women provided much of the labour. Many of these women married fur traders. At the beginning of the nineteenth century aboriginal and mixed-blood women performed valuable work in the dominant economy.[3]

The fur trade economy was altered irrevocably when the Earl of Selkirk sought to establish an agricultural colony and purchased from the Hudson's Bay Company a tract of 116,000 square miles along the Red and Assiniboine Rivers south of Lake Winnipeg. In 1811, the first party of Selkirk settlers from Scotland arrived at York Factory on Hudson Bay. In the spring of 1812 they travelled down the rivers and the length of Lake Winnipeg to the Red River. They were joined by a second party in 1813. Early hostility to settlement from some First Nations people and from the North West Company was resolved by warfare followed by the amalgamation of the two companies in 1825. The role women played in this new agricultural and ethnically mixed society was radically different from what it had been in the fur-trading community.

From early days missionaries and priests influenced the development of this new agrarian society. Clergy disapproved of local marriage customs ("à la façon du pays") and church weddings became widespread. The churches frowned on mixed-race unions and "were not in any way champions of miscegenation."[4] Native and mixed-blood wives were scorned in favour of white immigrant women. Incoming white women brought to their new home expectations of economic partnership in farm work gilded with aspirations of a more leisured existence graced by education and gentility. Schools for girls were established with a rapid turnover of schoolteachers who tended to retire on marriage. A community of Grey Nuns arrived to provide social services for the French and Roman Catholic community on the east side of the Red River, and on the west side English-speaking women created a welfare infrastructure through various charities. Women were valued as ornamental signs of modernity.[5]

Many former fur traders retired to the colony and there engaged in business. Despite the clergy's views, intermarriage between whites and those of aboriginal or mixed blood continued. Many of the men lived "by the hunt, the trapline, the fishery, the boat brigade or the cart line, 'wintering over' in Red River or in some camp out on the plains near the buffalo herds, perhaps practising a little desultory farming and cattle raising and, when opportunity offered, engaging in trade." Their wives performed "all the functions of a modern packing plant and tannery ... using traditional labour intensive methods." These women had access to modern living as well. They owned "kid gloves and hoop skirts, books and British periodicals, music and pianos."[6] They were under pervasive pressure to deny their own culture and to emphasize imported European "civilization," a cultural treachery which could lead to personal tragedy.[7] By 1870 Manitoba had become a society composed of First Nations peoples, families of the "principal settlers" from 1812, the officers of the Hudson's Bay Company, the merchants, and clergy of various denominations.

ETHNICITY

When Canada's prime minister, Sir John A. Macdonald, introduced legislation in 1870 to create the province of Manitoba, he declared that "fortunately the Indian languages of that section of the country give us a choice of euphonious names." Manitoba was an old Indian name meaning "the God who speaks – the speaking God."[8] In that year most of the women who lived in the province proper and in the land to the north belonged to one or other of the First Nations peoples. In the south were the Assiniboine, part of the Sioux nation; in the southern and western areas the Cree and some Dakota; in the central and eastern areas the Ojibwa (also known as the Saulteaux and Bungi); and in the north, the Chippewa. The Métis were concentrated mainly in the south.[9]

The historian Gerald Friesen notes that these peoples possessed a variety of cultural traditions. Plains Village people lived a relatively "sedentary culture rooted equally in the land and the field." Plains Woodland people, such as the Cree, "retained connections with the boreal forest while using plain and parkland as well," with the bison hunt less central to their economy. Plains Hunters relied more on the bison hunt, travelling great distances with skin tepees. Subarctic peoples like the Chippewa hunted the caribou which also involved considerable travelling. Some groups were more nomadic than others, but all lived in a travelling, trading, hunting society prepared to protect itself through its warriors.[10] Other scholars such as Laura Peers have pointed out that Plains cultural traditions were not in reality discrete: there was considerable shifting and adaptation amongst the various economies arising out of changing ecologies.[11] However, all groups, whatever their dominant economy, considered land to be their major

Indians, Garden Hill, 1940. (Western Canadian Pictorial Index A0255–08147)

resource. A possible influx of white immigrants threatened their ways of life precisely at the same time as a catastrophic decline in the numbers of the bison occurred. The Canadian government entered into negotiations with First Nations groups during the 1870s in order to clarify issues arising out of land ownership and residence.[12] The resulting numbered treaties of the 1870s created a new distribution of economic and political power amongst indigenous peoples and immigrants, and the newly confirmed entities of Canadian and provincial authorities.[13]

When Manitoba entered Confederation just over half its population was aboriginal or Métis. Forty years later the ethnic composition had become more complex.[14] White immigrants had been attracted by the prospect of land. In their wake came entrepreneurs eager to develop Winnipeg as a new Chicago, a centre for manufacturing, distributing, and financial services as well as for trade in grain and agricultural produce. People came to Manitoba from eastern Canada and from the United States in thousands, but they came in hundreds of thousands fom Europe, propelled by government agents who extolled the attractions of abundant and fertile land.

By 1911 the First Nations people formed only about 2 per cent of the population, according to the census, and the largest single cultural group, comprising slightly over half of the population, was British. The second large category was European. Labelling of groups frequently masked rather than revealed the real ethnic composition of the province. In the years before and after World War I many Manitobans were from parts of the Austro-Hungarian empire which along with Germany were nations considered international enemies of Canada. Ukrainians, Galicians, Slovenians, Poles, and Russians were not always finely distinguished in governmental sources. Still, it was possible to state that approximately 7 or 8 per cent of the population in 1911 was German in origin.

Two points can be made about the ethnic composition of the province over time. First, not since the early waves of immigration was there even a slight gender gap in ethnic groups: most groups emigrated, when they did, as family units and normally included a balance of the sexes. Secondly, the preponderance of immigrants of British origin diminished as the twentieth century progressed; "the prairies increasingly came to be peopled by those with no ties to other parts of Canada."[15] By 1971 42 per cent of the population were of British origin. The remaining 58 per cent had become even more diversified: 12 per cent German, 11 per cent Ukrainian, 8 per cent French, 3 per cent Dutch, and 3 per cent Scandinavian.

LANGUAGE

In 1870 English and French were the two official languages of the new province of Manitoba. But until the First World War there was a great mix of other languages in use as well as the languages of the First Nations people. Thereafter came an inexorable move towards English as the mother tongue.[16] In 1931 57 per cent of the female population said English was their mother tongue; by 1971 the proportion had grown to 67 per cent (66 per cent male). This trend was not particularly at the cost of the other official language, French: the percentage of those claiming it as their mother tongue remained the same from 1931 to 1971. Nor was it at the cost of German: 8 per cent of the female population in 1931 said German was their mother tongue, the same as in 1971. However, the Scandinavian languages fell off: from 3 per cent of females in 1931 to under 1 per cent in 1971; and so did Yiddish: from over 2 per cent of the female population in 1931 to 0.6 per cent in 1971. The single biggest decline was with Ukrainian. In

1931, 11 per cent of the female population spoke Ukrainian as their mother tongue; by 1971 this figure had dropped to 7 per cent.

The early multilingual character of Manitoba was thus soon lost. In the residential schools established in the 1880s, the use of aboriginal languages was prohibited and native language skills declined among First Nations people.[17] In 1916 English was made the sole language of instruction in all Manitoba schools. Although languages other than English continued to be used illicitly in the schools, the only legal way for children to learn and use their mother tongue was in their families and communities. Women as mothers and teachers were powerful transmitters of culture through language.[18]

POPULATION INCREASE:
IMMIGRATION AND MARRIAGE

The dominant population trend of the one hundred years from 1870 to 1970 was one of growth resulting – in large part – from immigration. The most spectacular jumps occurred in three decades. In both the 1870s and the 1880s the population more than doubled, and in the decade 1901–1911 it grew by 220 per cent.[19]

These waves of immigration were directly related to the land and transportation policies of the Canadian government. For a nominal fee of $10, the Dominion Lands Act of 1872 made a quarter-section of land (160 acres) available to any "person who is the sole head of a family" or to a man of 21 years of age. After three years that person could obtain title, provided a stipulated portion of the land had been prepared for cultivation and the building of a homestead begun. Technically, three categories of women were eligible to apply for such land: widows, divorcées, and, in certain cases, separated or deserted wives, always providing they had dependent children. Actually, few women fell into these categories.[20]

Immigrants arriving in western Canada at first came overland or by river, but in 1878 the railway arrived and travel became less onerous: Winnipeg was connected to the south with Minneapolis/St. Paul. In 1883 Winnipeg was linked directly to eastern Canada by the Canadian Pacific Railway. As a result of settlement and transportation developments, the population of Manitoba had quadrupled by 1885.[21] The next great wave of immigration was provoked by a combination of increased European demand for grain and the aggressive policy to attract new settlers pursued by the Canadian government after 1896.

The majority of settlers who came to Manitoba, especially those at the turn of the century, came in family groups. And for most of the century 1870–1970 the population was roughly balanced between men and women.[22] The proportion of women aged 20 to 44 years remained relatively constant, dropping only slightly from 33 per cent in 1881 to 31 per cent in 1971.[23] However, during the earlier periods of settlement fertility rates were high – higher indeed than elsewhere in Canada – and this trend contributed to the increase in population as did the fall in mortality among women and children that occurred after the middle of the nineteenth century.[24] The continuing increase in the population of Manitoba was interrupted in the Depression years, and with this slower rate of increase, the growth of Manitoba's population eventually converged with overall Canadian trends.[25]

Examining the marital status of women in Manitoba over the century, we find once again a remarkable stability. The percentage of women aged fifteen years and over who were married stood at 61 per cent in 1911 rising only slightly to 64 per cent in 1971.[26] Among the widowed, the proportion of widowers was always substantially lower than the number of widows: widowers were more likely to remarry and the mortality rate was greater for older men than older women.[27] The percentage of widowers over the period was relatively constant at between 2 and 3 per cent, but during the twentieth century the proportion of widows doubled from 5 per cent in 1911 to 11 per cent in 1971. Although the 1968 act which provided easier access to divorce would lead to substantial changes in the population profile in the decades after our period of study, the number of divorced persons in the years before 1971 was always less than one per cent of the adult population of Manitoba.[28]

RELIGION

Cultural differences were mirrored in religious affiliation.[29] In 1870 roughly half the population – primarily the French-speaking proportion – was Roman Catholic. The other, Protestant, half was either Anglican or Presbyterian. Religion in First Nations communities reflected the denominational Christianity of missionaries, whether Roman Catholic or Protestant. Methodists arrived with the influx of immigrants from Ontario. Immigrants, whether from North America or Europe, introduced denominational complexity at a time when society was becoming increasingly secularized. While many immigrants from Germany and eastern Europe were Roman Catholic, many Ukrainians were Russian Orthodox. The religious loyalty of Mennonites was divided amongst various sects. Lutherans were strongest in the Interlake region and other areas of German and Scandinavian settlement. In 1925 the Presbyterians and Methodists joined together in the United Church, which dominated the southwest part of the province.[30] By 1971 about a quarter of the population was Roman Catholic, the same proportion belonged to the United Church, about 10 per cent was Anglican, 6 per cent Lutheran, and 2 per cent Jewish. Within the churches, a gender gap was not obvious, except for a slight female preponderance in the United Church.

LOCATION OF RESIDENCE

Into the hunting, fishing, and agricultural society of pre-1870 Manitoba came more farmers – some experienced and others woefully ignorant – a few professionals, and lots of adventurer businessmen. The location of their new homes substantially influenced the work which the women who accompanied them would have to do. New communities tended to strive to re-create the societies they had left behind.

The more productive arable land was already occupied by the descendants of the Selkirk settlers and the Ontario-British immigrants. The French-speaking Métis descendants of North West Company fur traders had settled south of St Boniface along the east bank of the Red River and were augmented by French immigrants from the United States. Early in the 1870s group immigration, facilitated by the Canadian government, varied the general pattern of individual family settlement. Two tracts of land were "reserved" for Mennonites, pacifists displaced from their Russian farms by a demand for military service. Between 1874 and 1879, fourteen hundred families settled to the southwest and southeast of Winnipeg.[31] Also in the 1870s, Icelanders, driven from their homeland by poverty and catastrophic volcanic activity, settled on the shores of Lake Winnipeg just north of the then provincial border, where they could continue to work as fishermen. They named their principal town Gimli, or Paradise, and established their own republic for a few brief years.[32]

Larger in numbers than any other single group at the turn of the century were the Ukrainians (also called Galicians or Ruthenians). People from the same villages tended to emigrate together and, once they arrived in Manitoba, worked to re-create their old-country settlements. Rather than the wide open prairie with its rich fertile soil, they preferred the sort of land that was recognized as valuable at home: wood lots with access to streams. They chose settlements in the poplar belt and often laid out their farms with kin and neighbours in the same configuration as before.[33] Amongst this wave of emigrants were the Doukhobors, like the Mennonites and Jews in flight from religious persecution in Russia. Most went to Saskatchewan, the province to the west, but a community of about 1500 families settled on the Manitoba border near Swan River.[34] The Doukhobors, Mennonites, and

Ukrainians all came from Russia or the eastern Austro-Hungarian empire but were distinct in their religious, economic, and family structures.[35]

Location of residence was a factor in two other elements of the province's population profile: family size and age of marriage. Country families tended to be larger than those in the towns. The age at which individuals married was earlier in rural areas.[36] Over the century 1870–1970 people moved steadily away from the farms and thus away from these characteristics associated with rural living.[37] In 1871 96 per cent of the population was considered rural, but thereafter there was a trend towards urban living. The single most urbanizing decade was 1901–1911. In 1901 27 per cent of the total population lived in cities; by 1911, 43 per cent did. Slightly more women than men lived in towns or cities, reflecting the increased opportunites for paid employment for women in the towns as compared with the countryside.[38] By 1951 49 per cent of the population was urban, and by 1971 three-quarters of the urban population lived in Winnipeg.

WHAT WOMEN THOUGHT OF OTHER WOMEN

The immigrant woman in western Canada acquired mythical status with the publication in 1910 of *Janey Canuck in the West*. Its author was Emily Murphy, who went on to become a suffragist, the first woman magistrate in the British empire, a campaigner against drug trafficking and the white slave trade, and, in 1929, one of the five Alberta women who brought about the momentous ruling that women were persons. The adventures of Janey Canuck, a thinly disguised Emily Murphy, included encounters with other women.

Murphy's account of Doukhobor women, although more sympathetic than those of many others, showed as much about her own Ontario-British attitudes as about utopian Russian expectations of female behaviour. Murphy was disconcerted by the Doukhobors' own curiosity about her clothing and cooking: women were interested in the way other women looked and worked. She was anxious to dispel a common notion that Doukhobor women were oppressed. "Much has been made of the fact that the Doukhobor women perform the arduous work of harnessing themselves to the plough," she wrote, but "this is entirely at their own suggestion." Murphy, who later wrote *The Black Candle* (an exposé on opium and white slavery), admired Doukhobor moral rectitude: "They do not steal – or very seldom – fight, drink intoxicants, smoke or swear. Their lives are saturated with ideas of thrift and small economies. They hold themselves slaves of neither priest nor landlord." She envied the bright colours of the women's clothes, their avoidance of corsets, and their acceptance of the daily round of household and farm tasks. The Doukhobor woman knew who she was: "She is not expected, as our women are, to be a combination of Mary, Martha, Magdalen, Bridget, and the Queen of Sheba."[39]

From early times, women had interacted with women of other backgrounds, but not always with Janey Canuck's friendliness. White women immigrating into Red River introduced severe racial tension into the community and displaced the aboriginal and Métis women as its social leaders.[40] Describing uncomfortable encounters in the 1920s, Gabrielle Roy wrote of being made to feel different as a French Canadian by English-speaking store clerks in Winnipeg, but she also noted how she too was curious about others: "I'd often turned around myself to stare at some immigrant whose soft Slavic or Scandinavian accent I'd heard. I got so used to it eventually that I suppose I thought of it as natural for us all to feel more or less like foreigners on someone else's ground. That is, until I came around to thinking that if everyone was a foreigner, then none of us was."[41]

A COMPOSITE PICTURE

A demographic portrait of Manitoba's women, 1870–1970, would contain multiple moving images, shifting perpetually. A century ago, the entire population was more youthful: there were more girls and fewer older women. As more people lived longer, more women than men survived to an older age. Throughout the century, though, about a third of the female population at any time was between the ages of 20 and 44, that is, of normal child-bearing age. Even though the age at which most women married declined a little over time, the proportion of adult women who were married remained constant at about 60 per cent. Most of the women whose partners died remained widowed. Over time, the superior age of grooms declined, so that by 1971 the gap in marital ages was reduced to two-and-a-half years.

The work of a typical adult woman was primarily as a housewife, and over the century the number of people for whom she had to care declined. The number of children in her family fell, and after the Second World War almost all her babies stayed alive. In 1870 a woman was most likely to be a First Nations woman; yet by 1911 over half the province's women were of British origin and the rest were most likely to be of some other European origin. By 1971 the proportion of women whose ethnic background was neither British nor First Nations had increased even more. English was the mother tongue of about a half of the women earlier in the century, but of two-thirds by 1971. In 1870 half the women of Manitoba were Roman Catholic; by 1971, after some fluctuations, a quarter were. The percentage of women in the province who belonged to the United Church declined from about a third in 1921 to about a quarter in 1971.

Demographic data begin to identify the women of Manitoba, 1870–1970, and to provide a context for the stories which follow. Statistical measurement sets the scene of people's relations with each other and helps to assemble the skeleton of Manitoba's female population. Other sorts of evidence can help us see the human features of the women of Manitoba.

$\mathcal{P}$RESCRIPTIONS

"Women are educated for one single object, to gain their living by marrying," wrote Harriet Taylor in 1833.[1] Her future husband, John Stuart Mill, was therefore repeating a commonplace when he stated that financial dependency and household work were women's lot in life.[2] But the boundaries and structure of the household have not been constant through history. In the nineteenth century the work of richer men's wives involved substantial management responsibilities but few tasks of manual labour. In families with fewer resources, however, the wife often needed to earn cash in addition to looking after her family.

In the past, women's work often went unexamined by economists: "Women do not figure prominently in the writings of economists ... Their economic contribution through participation in wage work [was] ignored, and their fundamental role in reproducing the nation's 'human capital' [was] taken for granted."[3] Despite the absence of commentary about women in economic treatises, there are many texts where contemporaries wrote about the proper place of women's work. Professional pundits have long commented on the fluctuating frontiers of what sort of work women *ought* to do and where they should do it.

In 1870 Manitoba wanted settlers. Women were needed to help produce crops and goods, and they were needed to swell the population. Women were in the spotlight both as producers and reproducers. Immigration literature tried to attract women as well as men, and its language reveals contemporary assumptions about the work which women were supposed to do. Over the next century social workers, journalists, concerned citizens, and politicans all contributed their voices to a debate about the proper place of women's work in society. Newspapers and novels, pamphlets and polemics, swelled debate on the question.

The language of legislation also revealed the attitudes and intentions of law makers. In confirming or challenging social norms these voices referred both implicitly and explicitly to an emerging feminist critique which could draw nourishment from ancient texts.

A year after the tracks reached Winnipeg, the Canadian Pacific Railway used the experience of pioneering homesteaders in a public relations campaign to attract more immigrants. *What Women Say of the Canadian North West*, a pamphlet published in 1886, was based on a company survey of women who had recently settled in western Canada. The completed questionnaires, available for historical research, provide insight into prevailing attitudes towards women's work – both what women could expect as immigrants in the area and what might be expected of them.[4]

The pamphlet was arranged as a sequence of questions commonly asked by would-be immigrants. Each was followed by a selection of responses from women in Manitoba who were mainly, though not exclusively, engaged in farm work. Women expected to do hard labour and to provide manual energy in a business partnership. "Advice to newcomers" stressed this: "This is a splendid country for industrious people, but everyone coming here should know how to work ... Every housekeeper here learns to be a baker, laundress, tailoress, soap and candle maker, and dairy woman ... To women settling in the country [I] would suggest that they pay some attention to gardening, and bring seeds with them." The respondents, who were genuine new immigrants themselves, counselled against a rigid idea of feminine propriety: "Lend a helping hand to the men not supposing it is out of a woman's sphere as the first year brings lots of extra work on the men ... All should come with means enough to buy one or two cows and a few hens, which will soon bring in quite a portion of the living ... I think this is a good country for any person who is willing to work. One of our neighbours came here and had only 45 dollars (£9) when he landed in Winnipeg. He is now in a good position."[5]

Two sections considered these questions: "Can hard-working girls easily obtain situations at good wages on farms or households in the North West?" and "Are there openings for girls in trades, such as milliners, dressmakers etc?" The responses discussed the working conditions a girl could anticipate. The use of the term "girl" reflects the assumption that the paid working woman would be young and single, and several replies noted not only the wages but also the likely prospect of marriage: "As the country is largely settled with bachelors, good girls do not require to be long at service as they can soon get homes of their own."[6] Overall, the answers in this propaganda document gave a cheerful impression of contentment and prosperity rewarding the hard work of married women, who were working mainly as farm wives, and of single women working primarily as domestic servants and in the sewing trades.[7]

Twenty years later the Canadian Pacific Railway issued a sequel: *Women's Work in Western Canada*. As before, it was based on questionnaires, but this was a collection of success stories: women's "brave struggles against poverty ... and their bright hopes now abundantly realised." Again, the pamphlet dealt mainly with farm women, but one businesswoman was described, a native of New Brunswick who had settled in Winnipeg. She now had a son working for the Canadian Pacific Railway and a daughter who worked in an office. She herself kept a "large lodging house." Another family "came to Western Canada in 1891, bringing six children and ... $30 in cash." They settled in Dauphin, north of Brandon, and engaged in farming and the manufacture of furniture from "rough lumber." Their first income came not from the husband's labour but from the wife's garden and dairy produce.[8]

Farm women expected to work hard, and there was no serious challenge to this view either from them or from society. From time immemorial, the majority of women in any pre-industrial economy had expected no less. The "good wife" of the Old Testament was actively involved in the administration of the family fortunes. She directed the labour of indoor servants and also had the experience to determine whether to sell or buy land and produce. She dispensed charity and engaged in manual labour herself. Outside and in, she did not "eat the bread of idleness."[9] This model of a wife, "far more precious than jewels" in pre-industrial society, remained the norm for so long as agriculture dominated the economy. Some single women worked as servants in the households of others. Some women practised trades in towns. A few women lived and worked in religious communities with other women. But, as Barbara Hanawalt notes, "the domestic environment accommodated the vast majority of [women's] work experience" and insofar as manufacturing offered work, this too was organized to a large extent on a domestic system where women and men laboured in textiles, for example, with spinning wheels and looms in their own homes.[10] In such an economy women's work was essential for family survival and was valued, as the studies of Eileen Power, Alice Clark, and Ivy Pinchbeck emphasized.[11] They neglected to note, however, that the women could rarely be described as independent. Women's productive work, with few exceptions, garnered less remuneration than men's and was confined to the domestic hearth where, in law, the husband ruled. Women were undoubtedly economically useful but dependent nevertheless.[12]

Nellie McClung was a Manitoba writer who set her stories among farmers. Her first full-length novel, *Sowing Seeds in Danny*, written in 1908, sold over 100,000 copies. When she was a child her family, the Mooneys, migrated from Ontario to farmland in southern Manitoba and she qualified as a teacher while still a teenager. She found a kindred spirit in Mrs. Mark McClung, soon to become her mother-in-law, a supporter of the local Woman's Christian Temperance Union and an advocate of women's suffrage. A skilful public speaker as well as novelist and story teller, Nellie McClung displayed a comprehensive and far-reaching feminism. She infused her speeches with humour and a heart-felt measure of the Social Gospel, the early-twentieth-century movement which sought to "revive and develop Christian social insights and to apply them to the emerging forms of a collective society."[13] Highly influential in the Manitoba campaign for women's suffrage, McClung moved with her family after the outbreak of war to Alberta, where she continued to work for women's citizenship and also for the ordination of women in the United Church. Although feminism permeated all her writings, her single most focused work on women and society was *In Times Like These*, a collection of revised speeches published in 1914.

McClung's human beings, men as well as women, had the capacity to learn, change, and develop: she was no biological determinist. McClung wrote: "The time will come, we hope, when women will be economically free, and mentally and spiritually independent enough to refuse to have their food paid for by men; when women will receive equal pay for equal work, and have all avenues of activity open to them; and will be free to choose their own mates, without shame, or indelicacy; when men will not be afraid of marriage because of the financial burden, but free men and women will marry for love, and together work for the sustenance of their families."[14] In a later article for the mass circulation magazine, *Maclean's*, McClung asked: "Can a Woman Raise a Family and Have a Career?" – her reply was "whole-heartedly, YES!" McClung not only considered that women could and should, if they chose, do paid work, but that married women could do it too, if their families shared in housekeeping responsibilities.[15] McClung's paean to freedom echoed almost word for word the writing of August Bebel in his *Woman under Socialism*, a text which in turn greatly inspired the American writer, Charlotte Perkins Gilman.

Gilman published *Women and Economics* in 1898. She particularly addressed herself to the problems of married women's dependency and its cure. That cure, as she saw it, was paid work in the labour force. In this she developed the idea of Barbara Leigh Smith Bodichon of the Langham Place group, a group of educated English feminists who published the *Englishwoman's Journal*. In 1859 Bodichon claimed that "adult women must not be supported by men, if they are to stand as dignified, rational beings before God," and that all women, married as well as single, should have their own income, either inherited or earned.[16] Gilman, for her part, believed that paid work would render a woman independent: both she and society would benefit. She did not go so far as to advocate the abolition of marriage, but she believed it should be a relationship of equals bonded not by economic dependence but by love, affection, and common interests. She disputed the allegation that "motherhood renders a woman unfit for economic production" and believed that "human labor is an exercise of faculty, without which we should cease to be human." Bodichon's nobility of labour should be accessible to women. Aided by kindergartens and socialized household services, Gilman's new woman would be freed from private household drudgery and enabled to bestow on her children the benefits of a larger vision gained in the wider world. The new woman would not be dragged down by household chores. A "kitchenless house" would reflect the wife's reduced domestic burdens and "personal character and taste would flower as never before ... It is better for the world that women be economically independent."[17] Gilman's work was translated into half a dozen languages and was widely influential. In England the Fabians took up many of her ideas.[18]

Olive Schreiner similarly enjoyed a reputation as a voice of the New Woman through the novel which she wrote as a young woman in South Africa, *The Story of an African Farm*. Her later book, *Woman and Labour* (1911), was known as the "bible" of the women's movement: "a trumpet-call summoning the faithful to a vital crusade."[19] Schreiner's clarion call could be heard by all classes. Even more condemnatory of dependency than Gilman, her tone was less romantic and more down to earth.

Over half of *Woman and Labour* was a denunciation of "parasitism." Technological changes, "which we sum up under the compendious term 'modern civilisation' have tended to rob woman ... of the more valuable of her ancient domain of productive and social labour" and even in child rearing modern woman had less to do. Women of all classes were now reduced "to the passive exercise of her sex functions alone," dependent on men for their livelihood, a parasitism inevitably breeding moral degeneracy not only for women but for their descendants – "the race." All good people would benefit from women's re-entry into productive labour. The women's movement was "a great movement of the sexes towards each other ... towards common occupations, common interests, common ideals, and towards an emotional sympathy between the sexes more deeply founded and more indestructible than any the world has yet seen." Faint-hearted men who resisted this movement were those fearful for their own interests, anxious to maintain their status and power in the face of increased competition. Schreiner was a Darwinist who absorbed the notion of the survival of the fittest. She condemned reactionary behaviour and dismissed as hypocrisy the chivalry of men who claimed that women should be protected from inappropriate jobs. This response arose, she argued, only when women's presence undermined male comfort. "The smaller type of male" is "as a rule quite contented that the women of the race should labour for him, whether as tea-pickers or washerwomen, or toilers for the children he brings into the world, provided the reward they receive is not large, nor in such fields as he might himself at any time desire to enter."[20]

Both Gilman and Schreiner favoured certain principles: the right of all women to productive labour, and the benefits of such labour to them and society. They roundly condemned dependency, or parasitism, as ethically bad not only for individuals but for the human race. They had a concept of the common good and, like McClung, were committed to a notion of community.

Nellie McClung's novels were mainly about rural women, but she herself was also concerned about women working in factories in the cities and was prepared to support women who moved away from the domestic setting. The prospect of change alarmed conservatives and their voices, too, were heard in Manitoba. In an article condemning women's suffrage, an editor in *Le Manitoba*, a French-language, Roman Catholic newspaper, wrote that women appeared "beautiful and attractive" only in the context of the home, "far from the clamour of the street; at your hearth, in your living room, near to the cradles."[21] Another traditionalist, the Conservative premier of Manitoba, Rodmond Roblin, was uncomfortable with women working outside the home. About 1910 McClung and another Winnipeg feminist took Roblin on a visit to factories employing women in hopes of persuading him to appoint a woman factory inspector. Roblin expostulated that middle-class women ought not to be in contact with such "utterly disgusting things" as a sweatshop located in "an airless basement where ... the floor was littered with refuse of apple peelings and discarded clothing" and where the toilet's plumbing "had evidently gone wrong."

Yet Roblin's chivalry about women had limits. He agreed that it was necessary for working-class women to go out to work: "These young girls in the factories whom we thought were underpaid, no doubt they lived at home, and really worked because they wanted pin money. Anyway, working wouldn't hurt them, it would keep them off the streets ... Most of the women in the factories ... were from foreign countries ... It doesn't do women any harm to learn how money comes."[22] His assumption was that middle-class women should preside over the home and that working-class women should learn the value of money the hard way, by earning it.

The plight of the poor, and of poor women too, was already well known in Winnipeg through the activities of social workers like J.S. Woodsworth. He was superintendent of All Peoples' Mission, a Methodist agency with a staff of twenty full-time workers and over a hundred volunteers. Its social welfare services were designed to help the new immigrants assimilate, a programme fashioned after settlement houses like Jane Addams's Hull House.[23] In 1911 Woodsworth published My Neighbour, which he described as "a study of city conditions, a plea for social service."

Woodsworth regretted the conditions faced by a single woman living in a boarding house: "It tends to destroy her womanliness, to lower her ideals, to destroy her individuality and break down her health. It exposes her to severe temptations and makes her less anxious to assume the duties of wife and mother." Woodsworth sympathized with the problems of domestic service: "with long hours and inferior social status it is little wonder that girls are glad to escape from housework to the more independent if worse-paid work in shops and factories." He nevertheless implicitly approved the notion of dependency, for he deplored the need for a man's wage to be supplemented "by the earnings of the wife and children" which "means the sacrifice of the best things that home life should yield." He thought a mother should be "free to care for her home and children."[24] This respect for the full-time mother, fully committed to her home and family, was a tenet of turn-of-the-century maternalism and found widespread support even among those who were not able to fulfil this aspiration.

Jane Addams in the United States inspired extensive admiration, at least before her peace work during the Great War cast doubts on her patriotism. Suffragism and pacifism brought both respect and condemnation, but her work for the poor was universally appreciated. She worked within existing institutions and conventions to improve living and working conditions for the less powerful members of the expanding industrial urban society of Chicago at the end of the nineteenth century. Her work was remedial and reformist and pointed the way to structural change. She had used her own personal wealth to help found Hull House, the settlement in the slums of Chicago where a community of progressive social workers strove to improve life for the working and indigent poor. Her views on women's work were informed by direct experience of the conditions immigrants faced and their aspirations.

J.S. Woodsworth and Workers at All Peoples' Mission, 1914.
(Western Canadian Pictorial Index A0671–20598)

Like Schreiner, Addams noted how modern society had reduced the traditonal family role of women. The new involvement of the state in the well-being of the family through the provision of municipal and other government services meant, she argued, that women should be involved in political matters.[25] Ever practical, she recognized the double load of mothers who worked in the labour force and continued to be responsible for family life too. She also was aware that a middle-class woman generally chose either marriage or a career: "She could not have both apparently for two reasons. Men did not at first want to marry women of the new type, and women could not fulfill the two functions of profession and home-making until modern inventions had made a new type of housekeeping practicable, and perhaps one should add, until public opinion tolerated the double role."[26]

The ideas of Gilman and Schreiner and the social activist work of Addams were well known to university-educated women, and in 1914 the University Women's Club of Winnipeg investigated the situation of women and girls in the city's department stores with a view to improving their conditions of work.[27] Concern about the working conditions of women in the labour force fuelled a desire to legislate for a "living wage." Towards the end of the war the provincial government launched an enquiry into the desirability of introducing protective legislation for women in the form of a minimum wage. This was consistent with the notion of a family wage for men, for the assumption was that a single woman would live at home and her "living wage" would not need to be large enough to allow her to be completely independent – still less to be able to support dependents of her own.[28] The government's own survey concluded that "the earnings of women in industry ... are hardly enough for subsistence." Correspondents to the enquiry considered $10 a week as "the very lowest estimate" of a "living wage."[29]

A Minimum Wage Board was established: two labour and two employer representatives and an independent chair. Two women were among the five members appointed. During the first two years of operation the board reached agreement on a $12 minimum weekly wage for women over 18 and a lengthy (18-month) probationary period for new employees who, with minors, could be paid less. The board also determined limitations on hours of work and rules covering lighting and ventilation in a factory. Labour groups, employers, and the government all shared a common ideology which served to confirm not only the concept of the family wage but also the existing gender division of labour: this legislation applied only to women who were understood to be a "transitory and low-skilled" pool of labour.[30]

Protective legislation was intended to save women from the worst effects of employers' exploitation.[31] Such protective laws included minimum wage legislation, regulations concerning hours of work, rules governing the provision of certain services such as toilet facilities and factory inspectors, and even prohibitions on women's work altogether. Some feminists opposed protective legislation on the grounds that it strengthened the notion of women's dependency: rather, women should have equal treatment with men. Egalitarian feminists argued that neither husband, nor employer, nor state should consider woman in need of protection, for that way lay the notion of woman as a perpetual minor, always under tutelage, never to be autonomous and free to take responsibility for herself. Other feminists took another point of view. Beatrice Webb, a Fabian who in the 1890s was concerned to improve sweated conditions in the segregated factories and workshops where most women laboured, approved of protective legislation, which she thought could in time improve conditions for men as well as women. She was acerbic about middle-class feminists who opposed state protection. "Unfortunately," she wrote, "working women have less power to obtain legislation than middle-class women have to obstruct it."[32]

A generation later in the United States the issue of protective legislation became increasingly divisive. It was "a form of sex discrimination." Harriot Stanton Blatch was suspicious of both the motivation for, and the likely effects of, such law. Women had been pushed into the lower grades of work and had been limited in their earning capacity if not shut out of a trade entirely by "these so-called protective laws." The better strategy was "to compete with men in a fair field with no favor on either side." Other feminists disagreed. Increasing polarization led to division over the desirability of an equal rights amendment to the constitution. An officer of the National Women's Trade Union League thought that "only the elite who did not have to work at all or professionals whose conditions of work were unique could possibly denigrate the benefits of labor legislation for women."[33] In the interwar years all Western countries passed some protective legislation, often with the support of trade union men wishing to keep women out of their own occupations. It met a mixed reception from feminists.

Ideas about women and work were not only filtered through local interpreters. People could, and did, read the books for themselves and sometimes they heard theories straight from the horse's mouth. Emma Goldman, for instance, visited Winnipeg in 1908 and spoke to a gathering of fifteen hundred people.[34] Goldman was an anarchist and out-and-out libertarian. A Russian emigrant to the United States, she considered a woman's right to work as one element of a comprehensive right to individual liberty in all aspects of living, including sexual and emotional behaviour. Goldman was the embodiment of a New Woman who acknowledged no master – neither conventional behaviour nor a man. She inspired great curiosity and fear: "She was considered a monster, an exponent of free love and bombs." Her anarchism was "the philosophy of a new social order based on liberty unrestricted by man-made law; the theory that all forms of government rest on violence, and are therefore wrong and harmful, as well as unnecessary."[35]

Both conventional and challenging ideas about women's work were discussed in the press and in society. Margret Benedictsson was a writer and a political leader within the province's Icelandic Community. Between 1898 and 1910 she edited *Freyja*, a monthly Icelandic-language magazine. The title meant both "goddess" and "woman," and its first concern was "matters pertaining to the progress and rights of women." Benedictsson insisted on the value of women's work in the family: marriage was like a company, with two departments, "the domestic and the provision departments. Both are of equal worth to the company." At the same time she supported women's entry into middle-class professional and managerial work and was concerned for more menial workers, suggesting that domestic servants should be more equitably treated. Influential within the Icelandic-speaking community (over 6000 people at the turn of the century), she organized many local suffrage societies besides managing the publishing business she and her husband owned. Benedictsson printed translations from the work of

Margret Benedictsson. (Western Canadian Pictorial Index A0280–09020)

Gilman and Schreiner in her magazine.[36] Francis Marion Beynon, women's editor of the *Grain Growers' Guide*, was a journalist familiar with Olive Schreiner's *Woman and Labour* and wrote her own commentary in 1912, a couple of years before the appearance of McClung's *In Times Like These*.[37] Beynon shared Schreiner's respect for women's ability to do several tasks simultaneously and appreciated her condemnation of war.[38] Indeed, Beynon's pacifism during the First World War would prompt her to break with more patriotic feminists and leave Canada for the United States.[39]

In Winnipeg, middle-class women who wanted to keep their minds lively formed discussion groups. In the intimate setting of the Social Science Study Club, a small number of women met regularly to discuss current issues, including the proper place of women in society. In the 1914–15 season, under the general theme of "Education," Margaret McWilliams led the discussion on the woman at the university and for

Francis Marion Beynon.
(Provincial Archives of Manitoba N63687)

preliminary reading set Charlotte Perkins Gilman's *Women and Economics*.[40] These women were also members of the University Women's Club and other city women's organizations, including the Local Council of Women, and used these organizations to lobby for progressive reforms.

Members of the University Women's Club, as university graduates, considered themselves enlightened on the topic of women and work. It is therefore revealing that in 1920 this group went on record as disapproving the combination of paid work and marriage. The club held a debate on the motion that the professional life of women should continue after marriage. The discussion illuminates the mind-set and imagination

of highly educated women of the time. One speaker for the motion
"deplored the economic waste of the present system." She thought
women should continue to work after marriage. "The salaries of two
would aid the economic situation" and child care would be no problem
because "school hours practically correspond with professional hours."
She appeared to assume that a woman's "professional" life was synonymous with schoolteaching. In contrast, another speaker thought the
home required undivided attention: "Good food, close companionships,
maternal influence were dependent upon the mother's remaining in the
home." An egalitarian feminist alleged her opponents were raising "the
usual question of opposition to women's rights, which denied to women
the right to continue in their profession after marriage." Modern professions should be "open to women on an equal basis with men ... The
economic dependence which affects marriage would be eliminated." But
when the voted was counted, the university women of 1920 could not
see their way to supporting the idea of married women in the labour
force.[41]

For men and women of the working class, Woodsworth's All Peoples'
Mission scheduled weekly lectures, debates, and discussions in a peoples' forum at the Grand Theatre in the centre of Winnipeg. The forum's
programme in 1916–17 included the following topics: "The Girl Wage
Earner," "Laws Relating to Women and Children," "Professions and
Careers for Women," "The Challenge of the Franchise," and "The
Present Social Ferment in Western Canada." Speakers included the
female provincial factory inspector, an official of the Children's Aid Society, the superintendent of the Children's Hospital – all of them women –
and women suffragists, along with university professors and farmers'
association and labour officials.[42] Through live debate and the newspapers, as well as books, residents of Winnipeg could experience the
intellectual vitality of an "intensely political" city.[43]

In Manitoba at the time of the Great War, progressive thinkers were in
favour of various forms of protection for women. The same Liberal government which instituted protective legislation in the work place also
introduced a measure of state protection for the family. In 1916, in the
same session which enfranchised women, the Mothers' Allowances Act
was passed. The rules for eligibility developed over the years, but at first
they required mothers to be widows with two or more dependent children.[44] The bureaucrats who introduced this measure were undoubtedly
influenced by contemporary maternalist legislation in the United States
which sought to bestow state approval on certain sorts of single mothers:
those who through no fault of their own were raising children.[45]

Women in Manitoba were also influenced by trends in Great Britain.
Maternalism was one strand in the feminist thinking of Eleanor Rath-

bone who drew on a set of ideas first propagated in Britain in the Fabian Women's Group. One of these women, Mabel Atkinson, considered in 1914 that the state "endowment of motherhood" was the "ultimate ideal of the feminist movement."[46] By this Atkinson meant a temporary cash allowance payable to the mother while she was withdrawn from the labour market during childbirth and for a short time thereafter. Rathbone took a much broader view: a family cash allowance paid directly by the state to the mother, its size related to the number of children and their ages and sufficiently large to pay for most of the expenses incurred in their upkeep. At the same time, trade boards established by the state would regulate wages and institute equal pay for equal work. The justification for the "family wage" would be removed, for the cost of family support would be borne not by the wage earner but by the state. The mother would normally, but not necessarily, pursue motherhood as a full-time occupation.[47] Rathbone's enthusiasm for this scheme was based on intellectual analysis and on her experience as a social worker during the First World War when she observed how wisely the wives and widows of soldiers administered their cash relief funds.[48] By the time she published *The Disinherited Family* in 1924 she had formulated a comprehensive attack on the family wage and had framed a substitute in the twin notions of equal pay and family allowances.

In the labour force, Rathbone argued, men and women should earn equal pay for equal work, and the cost of raising children should be met by child allowances paid by the state to the mother. She expected that most mothers would be homemakers and that few would in fact remain in paid work. Her ideas were not universally welcomed.[49] While feminists generally were no supporters of the family wage, some were suspicious of the stereotyping of women as mothers and the conservative implications of institutionalizing women outside the labour market. Rathbone herself did not advocate the restriction of mothers to full-time motherhood, but her proposals implied that most married women would not work for pay. It was a scheme that could be supported by those eager to keep women out of the competition for jobs.

Just as the protection of women in the labour force served to divide feminists in the United States, so did the protection of motherhood divide feminists in Britain. In 1926 and 1927 the most influential feminist organization, the National Union of Societies for Equal Citizenship, over which Rathbone presided, was split. Those women unhappy with Rathbone's priority left the National Union to denounce protection and promote women's status as a "free and responsible human being."[50] In the circumstances, however, of a segregated labour market where women were concentrated in the low-skilled and ill paid jobs,

where haphazard social services only flimsily provided occasional insurance against sickness, unemployment, and old age, and where there
was no network of institutionalized child care, only a privileged few
could contemplate "a fair field with no favour."

Charlotte Whitton, the social worker commissioned by the Manitoba government to enquire into child welfare in 1928, justified mothers' allowances in a way consistent with Rathbone's views: "Every
child has a right to a mother's care" and a decent standard of living.
Whitton did not demand dependency from the mother. On the contrary, "encouragement is given to mothers and children to augment
their income to the point ... where they may become wholly self-
supporting, provided that the welfare of the children is not impaired
thereby ... If the mothers' allowances adminstration does not gradually prepare her to stand on her own feet, it fails in one of its objectives." Whitton went on to dignify the domestic work of the mother:
"mothers' aid is not generally regarded as relief or charity but as remuneration by the state to the mother for caring for her children."[51]

Mothers' allowances were cash payments made to the mother as
distinct from payments in kind which were provided to destitutes.
During the 1930s there was a rapid increase in the number of people
receiving relief in Manitoba owing to the particularly high level of
unemployment: "a relatively severe depression in the city of Winnipeg
as compared with other cities in Canada."[52] Those on relief included
unemployed women, a fact which puzzled civic authorities. The city of
Winnipeg's unemployment relief policy insisted that unemployed men
perform some sort of work before receiving their vouchers for rent,
food, clothing, and expenses, but "relief officials did not know what
to do with unemployed women."[53]

City officials were bewildered because commonplace ideology did
not tally with material conditions. These women on relief could not
count on male breadwinners. There was no work to support the women
in their supposed transition from father's house to husband's. Indeed, in
most instances, neither father nor husband existed. And in many cases,
they had their own dependents. The ideology of female dependence and
the family wage was shown to be wanting. Responding to this anomaly
was not thought to be an urgent matter, however, because unemployed
women "were not perceived to be as serious a threat to public order as
were both married and single men," but their numbers were not
small.[54] In 1931 in Manitoba, 11 per cent of female wage earners
(4,349 women) were not in work compared with 24 per cent of males
(31,916). By 1936, although the percentage of unemployed male wage
earners had declined slightly to 22 per cent (26,847 men), the figures
for women had risen – to 4,665 (12 per cent).[55] These numbers were an

uncomfortable reminder that there were women who did not conform
to the model of the woman worker as young, single, and transitory.

That was not news to Winnipeg women schoolteachers whose pay
was cut more than men's during the Depression. The response of the
women teachers to the policy whereby the "Biggest Part of Burden to be
on Women," according to a newspaper headline of 1933, was to form
their own organization, the Women Teachers' Association, apart from
the chapter of the province-wide teachers' federation.[56] During the following fifteen years they submitted separate reports to the school board,
thereby providing a remarkable discourse which challenged conventional notions of women's work.

Because the salaries of female teachers in the high schools were to be
reduced by an average of $355 per annum, whereas those of men in the
same jobs would be cut by only $100, the women – at this level older,
single, university educated, and expecting a lifelong career – felt bitterly
the injustice of differential pay schedules compounded by differential
cuts. They argued for equal pay for equal work, although "no one –
man or woman – wishes to bring down the salary of any individual or
groups of individuals." They pointed out that not all men had dependents and that many women teachers were responsible for their own
dependent relatives. Yet their even-handed attitude towards equal pay
did not extend towards access to jobs. For a while, these single career
women were not happy at the prospect of competition from married
women. When married women were explicitly barred from employment
as teachers in Winnipeg after 1930, no objection was heard from the
Women Teachers' Association. In 1946, when the board repealed the
policy, the association requested that the board replace married women
by single women "as soon as single women are available," but after six
months they dropped their opposition to married women in teaching
jobs. Even women teachers were not entirely free of the conventional
notion that a job should go only to one provider in each family.[57]

In her 1939 report for the provincial Economic Survey Board, *Employment of Women in Manitoba*, Asta Oddson held up Scandinavian
society as a more enlightened model. Her report, a mixture of description and prescription, offered the vision of a society practising "the
equality of the sexes." Oddson, herself of Icelandic stock, set up
"the Scandinavian woman" as an exemplar: "She engages in a variety
of activities outside the home, as well as being the equal of man with
regard to political, civil and family rights and responsibilities, and is
trained from childhood to exercise these rights. She also receives vocational training and learns by experience to take her place in the life of
the community, and to use the weapon of trade unionism to defend her
occupational interests, just as do her male associates."

Describing the actual situation of women in Manitoba during the Depression years, Oddson recognized the motivation of wage-earning women: "The subsidiary income derived from working women is shown as the last line of economic defence in many homes." Such "subsidiary income" was earned under conditions far from her ideal of Scandinavian equality. In 1931 in Canada and Manitoba "women received about 60% of men's wages and in Winnipeg slightly more than 50%." Like Eleanor Rathbone before her, Oddson deplored the lower wage rates for women, believing them to be likely to undercut men's wage rates as well as being intrinsically "unfair to the woman worker."[58] She was equally aware of other anomalies created by adhesion to the family wage including the problems of women with dependents.

Oddson's exposition of this issue was parallel to Rathbone's. "In fact, a family wage system has never been attempted in this country ... the unmarried man is not paid less than the family man because of his lack of dependents ... The argument used by employers who pay less than a living wage to women, that they employ only women who live at home and who therefore have few expenses, needs to be brought into the light of day by a factual survey." Oddson cited recent Canadian and American surveys to show that over a quarter of wage-earning women had financial responsibility for dependents. She considered that "it is as much the duty of the state to protect its citizens against industrial exploitation as against attack from a foreign foe." Oddson prescribed the duties of the state as ensuring that "employment is made available to all" and providing "vocational training on a scale hitherto undreamed of in this country." She also looked forward to a population enjoying "freedom from drudgery."[59]

During the Second World War the behaviour of thousands more women continued to confound the model of female dependency, this time moreover with official encouragement. After the war ended, however, such public approval was no longer forthcoming.[60] Nevertheless there was evidence of a developing feminist intrusion into public awareness. In 1943 Prime Minister Mackenzie King appointed a Subcommittee on the Post-War Problems of Women to his Advisory Committee on Reconstruction. Its chair was Margaret McWilliams, a Winnipeg alderman who had chaired the Unemployment Relief Commission during the 1930s. In 1940 her husband had been made lieutenant governor of the province, and although she resigned from civic politics, she maintained her role in public service.

McWilliams worked from the assumption that in postwar society women would be right to expect to be "full members of a free community." A survey conducted by the subcommittee revealed the prevalence of the opinion that "married women should not be allowed to work if their husbands have a good position and can keep the family and home comfortable." The subcommittee nevertheless refused to endorse this expression of public opinion obtained "from women employees in several war plants." Instead, it made a commitment to an individual woman's freedom of choice: to each woman, "the right to choose what occupation she will follow must be conceded as a right to which every citizen is entitled. She must also have the right to equality of remuneration, working conditions, and opportunity for advancement." Equal pay, working conditions, and opportunities should extend beyond the fields of work traditionally associated with women. Within occupations like domestic service, which had long furnished women with work, conditions should be improved and rendered more professional. The government should offer training programmes in technical and professional work previously inaccessible to women. The report welcomed the new government intent to embark on a programme of state welfare and insisted that women be integrated into the newly developing plans for social security.[61]

Here was one version of progressive feminist ideology on women's work, but there was no single consensus view. In 1944 the province of Manitoba appointed a committee to examine the need for postwar rehabilitation for women then in the armed services. This committee reiterated the McWilliams belief in an individual woman's right to choose but interpreted the field of choice much more traditionally. The Manitoba committee named "fields where many might be employed" and, in contrast to the McWilliams committee, identified occupations long stereotyped by gender in sector and level. It emphasized homemaking above all but ignored the elaborate suggestions made by the McWilliams committee for improving the training, pay, working conditions, and benefits for household workers.[62] Its report was a pedestrian contrast to the McWilliams report.

During World War II many ideas about the proper place of women were re-examined in the light of national imperatives. More women, many married and often with children, were recruited into the labour force. Countries experimented with social and fiscal policies designed to enable women to contribute directly to the war effort. After the war, however, there was some reversion to traditional attitudes. In an early systematic analysis of public opinion, Gallup polls conducted in Norway between 1946 and 1953 illustrated the continuation of old prescriptions about women's work into the postwar era. When asked if married women "ought" to work outside the home rather than "concentrate on the work in their home," only 24 per cent of the women and 13 per cent of the men thought they should; over three-quarters of the female respondents and almost nine-tenths of the men thought married women ought not to work outside the home.[63] One Canadian woman in 1955 was clear on this point: "As a married woman for fourteen years and a working wife for less than one year – the two don't go together. You can't be a success at both. So I decided to quit my job to save my marriage. You simply can't look after a home and go to the office too. I don't care who you are or how well organized you are, you can't be a good wife and mother, hostess and housekeeper and also do a good job for your employer all at the same time." [64]

The long campaign for equal pay, however, was bearing fruit. When Norwegians were asked if society should try to change social conditions in order that men and women should have more equal opportunities for choosing occupations and positions, a decisive majority (63 per cent) was against such change, with more women than men resisting it (68 per cent versus 59 per cent). There was also a consensus that certain occupations (those requiring heavy work, and jobs in the military and in the church) ought to remain restricted to men. But when Gallup asked whether men and women should get the same pay for the same work when they were equally competent, 90 per cent of the women and 85 per cent of the men were in favour of equal pay.[65]

In 1963 one American encapsulated the frustration of millions when she published *The Feminine Mystique*. Betty Friedan expressed discontent with the continuing dependency and apparent economic redundancy of adult women. Her own solution at that time was to favour the entry of women into the male-dominated – and validated – world of professions and business. Many years later, she would argue for the re-evaluation of women's work in the family.[66] The response of women to Friedan's identification of dissatisfaction with the status quo was one important impetus in the women's liberation movement. In Canada, that movement found its most comprehensive and formal expression in the establishment in 1967 of the Royal Commission on the Status of Women.

The commission's report, published in 1970, was the single most thorough examination of women in Canadian society in the twentieth century. The terms of reference showed the way in which government was prepared to think about women: the commission was to recommend "what steps might be taken by the Federal Government to ensure for women equal opportunities with men in all aspects of Canadian society." One hundred and sixty-seven recommendations were made in the report. Among them there were sixty-eight concerning women in the Canadian economy, twenty-eight about women in the family; eight on social welfare policy; thirty-three related to education.[67] Most of the report, therefore, concerned women's work in one form or another. It serves as a compendium of attitudes about women's work in the late 1960s and as a repository of hopes for the future.

One brief to the royal commission came from a remarkable volunteer committee of Manitoba women. Initiated by a woman minister in the provincial cabinet and comprised of representatives from a wide variety of women's organizations, the committee solicited advice from organizations and individuals in rural and urban areas all over the province. In five months it compiled research and formulated recommendations on many aspects of women's lives: women's participation in electoral politics and in the churches; their situation in the family, both as single mothers and as unpaid housewives; their situation with regard to taxation, pensions, and insurance; the relationship between women and the law; and opportunities and limitations for women in education and employment. Other provinces produced no comparable brief. Its very existence was a testimony to the breadth of women's community service in Manitoba as well as to a feminist consciousness among the province's women of their own second-class status. It also showed women's discontent that their informal authority did not translate into formal recognition and power.[68]

The general attitudes of the federal commissioners were announced at the outset of their report: "Women should be free to choose whether or not to take employment outside their homes ... The care of children is a responsibility to be shared by the mother, the father and society ... Society has a responsibility for women because of pregnancy and child birth, and special treatment related to maternity will always be necessary ... In certain areas women will for an interim period require special treatment to overcome the adverse effects of discriminatory practices." This was an ideology which looked forward to "a new society equally enjoyed and maintained by both sexes."[69]

The society into which the report was launched remained, however, an amalgam of contradictory attitudes, many of which refused to go away after 1970. The prescriptions dominant a century earlier remained paramount, muted only by a modification of the insistence that the work of the married woman normally be confined to the household. Public opinion was beginning to "tolerate," in Jane Addams's word, the combination of marriage and paid work for adult women. Yet public opinion continued to expect, as John Stuart Mill had put it, that family care would be the "first call upon [women's] exertions." If in 1870 there had been a consensus that it was acceptable for single women to work, by 1970 there was consensus that single women ought to work. However, the notion of female dependency died hard. In practical terms, neither the free market nor legislation obliged employers to give women pay equal to men's, partly because when women were in the labour force, they were concentrated in low-paying, unskilled jobs where most of their co-workers were other women.[70] The slogan "equal pay for equal work" was meaningless when few men were in that particular work. The concept of "equal pay for work of equal value" – then in its infancy – received majority, but not unanimous, support in the *Report on the Status of Women*.[71]

The economy of Manitoba when the province entered Confederation in 1870 was a commixture of fur trade, farm, and factory. Industrialization had already transferred production away from the household and into factories and workshops. Instead of making their own food, clothing, and household utensils, or producing surplus for sale, families bought goods. The family was a unit of consumption.[72] In cash-poor families, however – on the First Nations reserves and in farm and new immigrant communities around the turn of the century and then during the Depression years of the 1930s – there was little consumer activity.

The family wage which could sustain a full-time housewife exercised a powerful hold on the imagination, and the behaviour, of women as well as men.[73] But it was not the only prescription for women's work. Over time, the prescription of separate spheres, of a man earning a family wage in the public world of trade, commerce, and factories and of a woman feathering the domestic nest in the private world of the family, was challenged. The dependence of the adult woman was contested. Official propagandists, local novelists, journalists, economists, social workers, and politicians all mediated the messages expressing both the conventional commonplaces and their challengers. By 1970 a more nuanced ideology of sexual equality was under formulation.

It is always difficult to determine the diversity, and the intensity, of assumptions held by groups in a pluralistic society. The century 1870–1970 saw shifts in the ideas of the sort of work women might do in Western society and about the conditions under which they should do it. Prescriptions regarding women's work were multiple. Public opinion was in favour of single women working in the labour market, but there were contradictory messages regarding the paid labour of mothers. Motherhood by itself was regarded as a disqualification for paid work, certainly until the Second World War and even afterwards by some. Whereas equal pay for equal work enjoyed considerable support, there was a substantial body of opinion which maintained that women's interests as well as men's were better served by a wage paid only to male breadwinners. Protective legislation for women was both supported and opposed by feminists. Economists and governments increasingly drew on these various and occasionally contradictory assumptions to fashion social policy, the more so as the century saw an exponential increase in the involvement of the state in the lives of ordinary people. The extent to which women actually conformed to the rules and protocols laid down for their economic behaviour is a separate question.

$\mathcal{E}$DUCATION AND TRAINING

Formal education provided the foundation for a woman's future work. Successive generations of girls enjoyed varied education opportunities over the century 1870–1970. The quantity and quality of a girl's schooling depended much on her native wit and proximity to trained teachers. Other important factors in the early years of the period were her ethnic origin, her family's religion and form of livelihood, and how long she had lived in the province. Education was also related to the dominant approach of provincial governments. The issue of equal opportunty in education for boys and girls was rarely raised publicly before 1970.

One milestone in Manitoba education which substantially altered opportunities available to children and young people came in 1916. Compulsory education, along with English as the single language of instruction, was made law. Another significant step was curriculum development during the interwar years. A third significant trend could be seen in the post–World War II tendencies towards more accessibility and greater standardization of educational opportunity across the province. If at the beginning of the period class and race were highly significant in influencing a child's chances, during the interwar years gender became increasingly important. By the end of the period education at the primary, secondary, and higher levels was becoming more, but by no means completely, homogenized.

When Manitoba entered Confederation in 1870, the province's legislature was empowered, in accordance with the British North America Act of 1867, to make laws in relation to education, but one qualifying provision read: "Nothing in any such laws shall prejudicially affect any right or privilege with respect to Denominational Schools which any class of persons have by law or practice in the Province at the Union." At the time the practice was various.[1]

In 1871 the provincial legislature passed an act establishing a system of public education. Control of education was under a government-appointed board, half of whose members were to be Roman Catholic and half Protestant, reflecting the religious balance in the population at the time. One member of each section was named superintendent of each group of denominational schools, and much evidence about education during the next generation comes from the annual reports of these superintendents. Underlying the legislation was the principle that public money, jointly raised by the provincial government and the local districts, of which there were initially twenty-four, would support denominational schools. Each local district school board could determine its own language of instruction, English or French.[2] On the whole Roman Catholic schools opted for French as the language of instruction while Protestant schools chose English.

Symmetry between Protestant and Roman Catholic, and between English and French, was soon lost. Immigration distorted the parities, and the increasingly dominant political group of Protestant English speakers was concerned to reinforce its emerging supremacy with a more monolithic education system.[3] Following 1870, there was a finer delineation of secondary and primary education, and the establishment of a university. Teacher training also was instituted. Informed opinion was split between those who thought education should be under the control of religious authorities and those who favoured secular education. Increasingly, the English-speaking élite was concerned to reinforce its culture, including language, in a policy to "Canadianize" the ever more ethnically diverse population.[4]

First Nations children were dealt with outside the provincial educational system. When the federal government signed a series of treaties with Indians in order to extinguish their land rights, the settlement included a federal responsibility for education.[5] After 1880 the Department of Indian Affairs began to implement a policy favouring industrial residential schools established away from reserves, but there were also day schools located within communities.[6] Both boarding and day schools were operated under cost-sharing arrangements with the Roman Catholic, Methodist, and Anglican churches. The residential schools suffered from low enrolment and the day schools from low attendance.[7] After 1951 Indian Affairs policy shifted towards the integration of First Nations children into local public schools. For most of the century 1870–1970, however, First Nations girls were subject to a different education structure from other Manitoban girls.

Assimilation to white society was a paramount goal of the federally controlled First Nations education system, but not on equal terms. The schools were designed "to prepare pupils for their expected future existence on the lower fringes of the dominant society."[8] The use of aboriginal languages was forbidden.[9] In the industrial schools, the academic programme "never took up more than three hours a day."[10] Although the schools were co-educational, boys and girls were rigidly divided with respect to vocationally oriented instruction and in the service and maintenance work they did outside classes. Girls worked in the kitchen and laundry and did most of the cleaning.[11] "The student population had almost no contact with their parents throughout the school year," and children could spend years away from their families.[12] "At that time, the children never came home," said Mary Redhead, a Cree from northern Manitoba. "Nobody came home until they completed their full education." The students were often very lonely.[13]

Until the 1950s the girls' practical education followed the pattern of domestic duties established at the outset, described in the 1895 annual report of the Washakada Indian Home in Elkhorn, Manitoba:

There is a resident dressmaker on the premises from whom they receive instruction in the cutting out and other necessary branches. Knitting and crochet work are encouraged in every way as a substitute for idle hours. The kitchen girls are taught their work thoroughly and completely, while in the laundry is done all the washing, ironing and clear starching for both the children and the staff. During meals, selected girls wait on the several tables and afterwards attend to the cleaning and scouring of the utensils used. All the cleaning, dusting and scrubbing ... is done by them.[14]

The principal explicitly disavowed "fine accomplishments or high scholarship." His desire was to "fit the girls to become good wives and good mothers."[15] At a school reunion of 1990, one woman, who as a girl had tried to run away, acknowledged she had "some fond memories ... I remember the handicrafts we were taught at a young age. When I was about 12 years old I knew how to knit and to do intricate embroidery and sewing. We were also taught many domestic things such as cooking, cleaning, ironing, and basic housekeeping skills."[16]

The curriculum of the provincial education system aimed to provide educational opportunities for all students, but city children generally fared better than those in the country. Actual learning conditions in western Manitoba were described in two community studies conducted in the summer of 1914. In the vanguard of new social planning ideas, the Methodist and Presbyterian churches collaborated in a wide-ranging investigation of the social conditions of two rural communities, Turtle Mountain and Swan River, studies which revealed much about their educational practices.[17]

Turtle Mountain was south of Brandon, near the United States border, in an area originally settled by people of primarily Ontario-British origin. In 1914 only 12 per cent of its population was not classified as

English, Irish, or Scotch, and the community had escaped the impact of the dramatic influx of immigrants between 1901 and 1911, for its population had risen by only 8 per cent.[18] Swan River, where "Janey Canuck" arrived in 1903, was on the Saskatchewan border and had not been settled until after the Canadian Northern Railway was routed through Dauphin at the turn of the century. Like Turtle Mountain, the majority of its population was from Ontario (57 per cent), but there was greater ethnic variety (including Russians, Icelanders, and Swedes). Its population had increased by 120 per cent between 1901 and 1911.[19] Taken together, these two communities were typical of the more prosperous, stable, and dominant Ontario-British part of Manitoba's population, which on the eve of World War I represented approximately 58 per cent of the inhabitants.[20] These settled, confident communities probably provided as favourable an educational environment for their youth as anywhere in the province outside the cities of Winnipeg, Brandon, and Portage la Prairie.

Yet, in buildings, equipment, and service, neither community met the minimum standards set by the superintendent of Turtle Mountain. He required a fenced, two-acre site with a garden and well-screened outhouses; a schoolhouse "well-lighted (from the left)" with attractive decorations, blackboards, and adequate heating and ventilation; sufficient desks, a good bookcase with books, a map, a globe, and a dictionary; and a sanitary water supply. He wanted the school open for at least 200 days in the year, and some simple record-keeping. The ideal teacher should be well trained, regularly inspected, and committed: someone who attended conventions and read teachers' journals.[21]

In both communities, the vast majority of schools were rural, and almost all had only one room. Half of Swan River's 33 schools met the two-acre plot requirement, but most made do with less and, moreover, neglected their grounds. In Swan River, 68 per cent of the schools had libraries. About 80 per cent of schools in both communities had maps. Few of Turtle Mountain's 36 schools had wells: "Water usually is carried by the children from a well on a nearby farm." In Swan River, 43 per cent had wells, but many were unfit for use. On the whole, the schools were neither clean nor hygienic.[22]

Each enquiry reported on school enrolment and attendance. In Turtle Mountain the investigators noted the population of school age and then the average number attending school in three categories. In the town schools, attendance averaged 71 per cent, in the consolidated country schools (which drew students from several communities), it was 64 per cent, and in the small country schools it was 48 per cent. In the province at large, attendance in the one-room country schools was 48 per cent in 1912–13, but rose to 55 per cent in 1913–14, after the passage of a new Truancy Act. In Swan River, only 40 per cent of the enrolled students were in attendance for 120 days or more. Added to "this shameful irregularity in attendance" was the problem in both districts of non-enrolment, estimated to be at least 11 per cent of the school-age population.[23]

The Swan River report attributed non-enrolment and non-attendance to sickness, poverty, distance, and, overwhelmingly, to "the children having to work." The Turtle Mountain report additionally blamed parents: "The average pupil lives less than 1 3/4 miles from the school, and in wet or stormy weather most of the parents are in a position to drive their children." The writer called on the school district, municipality, and province to work together to see "educational opportunity for every child, and every child taking advantage of that opportunity."[24]

Until 1916, when legislation was passed making school attendance compulsory, all schools throughout the rapidly expanding province experienced low attendance rates. In 1882 the average attendance in organized Protestant school districts was 3,285 out of 9,641 boys and girls of school age (5–15 years). That is, on average, each child of school age attended school for only one-third of a school year. Many children hardly attended at all. The 30-per-cent attendance rate had improved by 1886 to about 50 per cent: 8,611 out of a school population of 16,834. By 1912 the overall attendance rate was about 75 per cent. Absences were not always due to pressures from the family economy, with parents demanding that children help on the farm or in the household. In many fledgling school districts education was offered intermittently or not at all: schools "were unable to pay a teacher for more than a few months each year." There was only a slight difference in the attendance of boys and girls. In 1885 there were more boys in school than girls: 9,041 as compared with 7,885, but the gap was not so marked in later years. By 1901 the total number of female pupils in Manitoba was 21,304 and of male pupils, 22,256. Twenty years later, after compulsory attendance had been introduced and enforcement was more routine, attendance was roughly equal: 45,721 girls and 46,464 boys, and this balance remained true in succeeding decades.[25] Turtle Mountain and Swan River were both among the province's more prosperous communities, and the vast majority of their inhabitants was English-speaking. How much greater difficulty therefore must have been experienced by children in communities where the social infrastructure was less stable, which were frequently on poorer agricultural land and consequently had a smaller funding base, and in which English speakers were a minority.

One exception to this general picture of poor schooling among immigrant groups was the Icelandic community. The Icelanders who arrived in Manitoba in the autumn of 1875 came from a culture where literacy was high and each family was acquainted with poems and literature dating back to the ancient sagas. During their first winter in Gimli, "many of the people devoted much time to reading." Even though they were "lacking most other things, the people had brought their cherished books with them."[26] Visitors noted that despite the primitive houses, often furnished with only bare necessities, each Icelandic household had thirty or forty books. A young woman journalist for the *Toronto Globe*, who visited these Icelandic communities in 1890, described the Icelanders as "an intellectual race and very fond of education." She reported: "In the library of one farmer was found a copy of Byron, Whittier, Scott's *Rob Roy*, Huxley's Physiology, Dr. Cope's *Natural History* and a Webster's Unabridged Dictionary. He was asked if when reading English he used the dictionary often. 'No, except when I read scientific works,' was the rather startling answer."[27]

Immediately on arrival the Icelanders had declared their intention to establish a school. By Christmas 1875 about 30 students were in attendance, and a year later the enrolment was 63. English was the language of instruction.[28] In the Interlake region, where most Icelanders lived, the community supported a large variety of cultural activities despite much poverty. Girls as well as boys were encouraged in their education. Women's suffrage societies flourished from the 1890s, and the Icelandic-language monthly journal, *Freyja*, "devoted to Woman's Economical, Political and Social Rights" was published in Selkirk.[29]

In contrast to the Icelandic attitude, neither girls nor boys in early Mennonite communities expected education to be a priority.[30] In 1977 Mrs Agatha (Peters) Wiedeman, then aged seventy-six, was interviewed about her youth. Born on the Mennonite Western Reserve, near Plum Coulee, she had a brother and a sister, two other siblings having died in infancy. The interviewer describes her remembrance of school in this way:

She attended a private school ... They usually walked to school which was a few miles from their home ... The farmers in this area sent their children to private schools because they were too poor to pay for teachers. Usually, in these private schools the teacher was a grown-up child.

Because these schools had no educated teacher, their subjects were a little different from public schools. They had no history or arithmetic like they had in public schools. These private schools consisted mainly of Bible courses ... [Agatha] started school at the age of seven and went to school off and on until the age of thirteen.[31]

Poverty was not the only reason for such private schools. As D.S. Woods notes: "Sections of the Mennonite Colony, because of religious connections, refused to identify themselves with the school system, believing it incompatible with their religion to take part in the election of trustees, collect taxes through municipal officers, or even accept the Legislative grant."[32] However not all Mennonites took this view. Helena (Penner) Hiebert, born in 1874, was the daughter of Erdman Penner who established the first Mennonite store in Manitoba, a business which quickly expanded to six general stores in various southern Mennonite communities. For her grandchildren, Hiebert wrote "Granny Stories" and there described her early formal and informal education. While she, like Agatha Wiedeman, attended private, religiously oriented schools as a little girl, her father helped to establish secondary education in the district and Hiebert attended the Gretna Mennonite Collegiate Institute before going on to be one of the first women to attend Wesley College in Winnipeg. She later had a distinguised career in volunteer public service and served as a school trustee in Winnipeg during the 1930s.[33]

One large wave of Ukrainian immigrants arrived in Manitoba between 1896 and 1914. They settled in areas which at that time were still undeveloped and devoted much energy to clearing the land and building dwellings before turning their attention to education.[34] In the early years it was difficult for them to acquire any education at all. Speaking of the first decade of the twentieth century, one child whose family settled in the Shoal Lake area noted that "many pioneer areas that organized schools were not able to get teachers. Those teachers who came were only high school students who taught during the summer holidays." Another Shoal Lake child "grew up in the bush helping the best way I could, but did not go to school until I was nine years old. Going to school presented problems: there were no roads and we did not have proper clothes to wear." In the same area, one girl was twelve years old when her family arrived in 1907: "I attended school for a year and was placed in Grade III ... I went to work when I was fifteen years old ... I was seventeen years old when I got married."[35]

A woman who grew up in the Tolstoi area south of Winnipeg remembered that in 1897, "since there was no school in the district, I had to depend on what I learned in the Old Country ... even in my native village of Senkiw I could not get much education." Another girl in the same district attended school, but only "when there was a teacher": "I stopped school early and started to help at home, mostly going into the bush to help cut cordwood. We needed to sell many cords of wood to support the family of eleven children." When she was seventeen, this girl received a proposal from a man aged thirty-eight and hesitated, but: "My mother said to me: 'Barbara, for whom are you going to wait here in the bush? Have you not had enough of cutting cordwood?'" So Barbara Nabozniak got married.[36]

Cutting wood was a common way of eking out a living in the poplar belt. In the Interlake area, "things improved in 1910 when the CPR reached Arborg. It was then possible to take a cord of green poplar to the stores there and trade it for supplies needed ... While father hauled the wood to Arborg, I, though only ten years old, went into the bush with Mother to cut wood. I did not go to school until I was about twelve years old – there was no school. I was fortunate to get a year in school ... and that was all. I learned Ukrainian at home, and improved my English when I went to work in the city."[37]

Many young women had to rely on the little education they had had in Ukraine. Looking back, a nonagenarian defended her choice to marry at seventeen by reference to her alternatives: "Sure, I was rather young, but what would a girl do in the bush [in the Shoal Lake district in 1901] ... True, I had finished grade four in the Old Country and knew Ukrainian and Polish, but that was of little help – I didn't know English (I learned English from my children) ... I was lucky to have learned to read. I used to write letters to my children and to relatives in the Old Country – in Ukrainian, of course, and I used to read to my children." One girl who arrived at Gardenton, near Tolstoi, in 1903 at the age of eight attended no school, but after her marriage taught herself to read: "One winter when my husband was away from home, I learned to read – I learned all by myself by reading the Bible. My husband used to go to work in the bush during winter and I would be alone at home. I don't know how many children we had at that time, but after I put the children to bed I was very lonesome so I wanted to read."[38]

Between 1897 and 1916 legislation permitted schools to use a language other than English for instruction where at least ten pupils had another language as their mother tongue. From 1905 to 1916 the provincial government ran a normal school to train Ukrainian-speaking teachers, and once a supply of bilingual teachers was available, Ukrainian settlers were more interested in establishing schools in the country districts. In Winnipeg, however, superintendents resisted Ukrainian-language schooling.[39] In the city before the First World War, as in the entire province after 1916, English-language instruction was the norm.

Girls of all ethnic backgrounds who had access to grade school education before the First World War tended to remember more of the atmosphere and less of their actual lessons. At Gladstone, northwest of Portage la Prairie, Margaret Galloway remembered "no trimmings." This meant slates rather than exercise books, no playground equipment, and strict discipline.

The boys dipped your braids in the inkwells, untied your ribbons, jabbed your shins or where you sat down with pins stuck in the toe of their boots, put little dead garter snakes or live toads in your desk, or let an odd gopher loose from their pocket when school was in. In winter they carried pocketfuls of snow in to toss around or tuck down your neck when teacher wasn't looking. In spring they pockmarked the ceiling with mud picked off their boots, rolled into little balls well lubricated with spit and flipped off the end of a ruler to stick on the ceiling like a modern water sprinkler system.

The girls were patterned alike in frilled, starched cotton "pinnys" and cotton half sleeves, hair in knobs on the top of their heads or braided into two side braids (Y-ing into a single braid if your hair were thick and straggling). Mine never did achieve the two braids my sister wore.

Galloway's school would have been approved by the writers of the Turtle Mountain and Swan River reports, who strongly promoted the use of school premises for community activities. At the time of the South African War a Grand Patriotic Concert was held, which showed "what hardy specimens we were": "Imagine if you can a concert today with twenty-eight numbers, many of them encored and encored! Imagine if you can an audience with sufficient stamina to last it out!"[40]

Only a minority of students stayed at school until the age of 16 or more. The size of that minority varied: in 1914 at Turtle Mountain about a third of the student enrolment did so, but at the newer community of Swan River, less than 20 per cent did.[41] An incentive for these scholars was to gain a Third Class Certificate, which entitled the holder to teach in Manitoba schools.[42] Mamie Louise (Pickering) Thomson was a girl of twelve in July 1892, living in Portage la Prairie. She had already moved from "standard eight to the senior room." Her teacher then presented her as a candidate for the Third Class Certificate. Mamie fell ill and so did not write the exam then, but did so two years later, at the age of fourteen. She then went on to study for her Second Class Certificate at a collegiate level school. This certificate she gained in 1895. At the age of sixteen – her birthday was in August – she entered the Winnipeg Normal School.[43]

The Normal School, for teacher training, was one of the two categories of post-secondary education in Manitoba. The other was university-level instruction offered by the colleges and institutions of the University of Manitoba. Of the few women who achieved any education beyond grade school before World War I, the vast majority took Mamie Pickering's route and attended the Normal School.

There were two ways to acquire the Normal School qualifications of professional certificates. The regular way was to attend the school for a ten-week session, but credentials could also be earned by attendance at sessions of a few days each year offered in most towns of the province. Pickering wrote to her mother in September 1895: "I don't like the Normal much and I have made no chums. The people there are nearly all much older than I am." By early 1896 Pickering had cheered up, performed a considerable amount of supervised teaching in various city schools, passed her exams for the Third Class Professional Certificate, and was the incumbent teacher in the town of Austin, west of Portage la Prairie on the way to Brandon.[44]

Thirty years later a university graduate, Sybil Shack, decided she wanted to be a lawyer but realistically concluded: "I had only three career choices: nursing, stenography and teaching."[45] She therefore attended the Normal School in a class of other graduates, nine men and thirty-two women, with a view to teaching high school: "The majority of women were, like me, on the way to becoming teachers because there seemed no other reasonable way of becoming independent." Unlike some of her classmates, who did not value the teacher training course, Shack valued both the practical instruction and the idealistic atmosphere, echoed in the 1929–30 yearbook, which described "those long hot arguments that fill the room with the rumble of thunder and the flash of lightning. Then are life and death, and school, and women's clothes weighed in the balance of our criticism, and thought springs to life under the stimulus of thought, and word smites word in defiant combat."[46]

As Shack pointed out, other young women sought vocational training to be a nurse. In the period before 1913 most of such training was on the job, as an apprentice, in training programmes started in the first hospitals.

The Grey Nuns who arrived in 1844 were the pioneer health workers in Red River. They vaccinated hundreds against smallpox. They visited the sick, not only in St. Boniface and in the other areas of French-language settlement but also in the First Nations settlements in the province, and Sister Thérèse became known as "our Sister-Doctor." Sister Thérèse set up the first four-bed hospital, in 1871, on the top floor of the Grey Nuns' laundry; not until 1877 was a larger house acquired and made into a regular hospital. On the west bank of the Red River several doctors were in practice, but the sick had to remain in their own homes. Fear of typhoid, spread by the unsanitary river which doubled as the source of drinking water and as sewer, led to the establishment of a makeshift hospital, and after "the ladies of the Province … persevered with characteristic energy … and accumulated by concerts, bazaars etc. the handsome sum of $1345.80," a new building was erected at a cost of $1,818 in October 1875.[47] This was the Winnipeg General Hospital.

Twenty patients could be accommodated. Nursing was initially provided by men stewards assisted by convalescent patients. Only after 1882 did the board employ one woman as head nurse. In 1884 a new hospital, for 72 patients, was constructed, again after a substantial contribution from the "Women's Aid Society for the Winnipeg General Hospital." The staff then included five female nurses, four recruited from hospitals in eastern Canada and one from the Leeds Infirmary, England. They received room and board, and a salary of fifteen to twenty dollars a month. Shortly after the establishment in 1883 of the Manitoba Medical College for doctors' training, the hospital admitted women for nurses' training, and this was formalized in 1887.[48]

For at least the next generation nurses-in-training were exploited by many hospitals, large and small around the province, as a source of cheap labour while they received a minimum of instruction. The nurses were turned out "after a varying period of time to practise on a confiding public as trained nurses."[49] At the Winnipeg General Hospital, however, there were some formal requirements. In 1887 the rules and regulations governing its training school required a nurse to be examined in reading, writing, simple arithmetic, and plain sewing during her first month as a probationer. She then undertook to stay for a two-year training period during which "regular lectures will be delivered and practical instruction given in the wards and at the bedside. Practical instruction in cooking for the sick will also be given."[50] One of those first student nurses, Mary Ellen Birtles, described the "regular" lectures: "sometimes we had one a week and sometimes two, two bones by way of illustration in anatomy – a rib and a femur – until some doctor lent us a skull."[51] Up to the end of the nineteeth century, nurses in Manitoba bore the cultural millstone of the pre-Florence Nightingale era and could still be regarded as much as domestic servants as serious professionals.

The nurses made a strong effort to establish their work as a profession. Those who graduated soon created organizations whose social function was augmented by the promotion of professional standards. The Nurses' Alumnae Association of the Winnipeg General Hospital was formed in 1904 and one of its objectives was "to place the profession of nursing on the highest possible plane."[52] The following year the Manitoba Association of Graduate Nurses was formed and through its federal parent body became a member of the International Association of Nurses in 1911. Drawing inspiration from the international scene, and particularly from the examples of nursing organizations in the eastern United States and in the United Kingdom, the Manitoba organizations worked during the next few years to institute state registration as the basic qualification for a nurse.

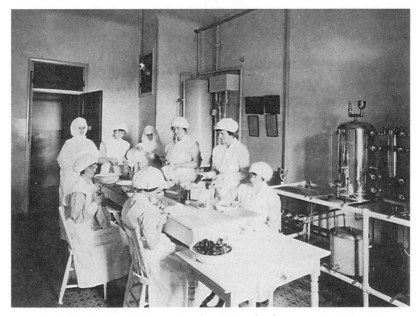

Nurses, 1922. (Western Canadian Pictorial Index A0259–08270)

Registration meant "legal recognition of the nursing profession, and the establishment of uniform qualifications for graduates of all the diverse training schools."[53] Supporters considered it an essential step towards the establishment of professional standards and self-regulation by nurses. The Manitoba Association of Graduate Nurses spearheaded the campaign and the cause attracted much prestigious support from Miss Frederica Wilson, the lady superintendent of the Winnipeg General Hospital, and the sister superior of St. Boniface Hospital as well as from some prominent doctors, including Dr. Jasper Halpenny, medical superintendent of the Winnipeg General Hospital. Not surprisingly, the major opposition came from smaller rural hospitals which were already under attack from people such as nursing activist Ethel Johns for having insufficient resources to give adequate training.[54]

When the legislation establishing registration was finally passed in 1913, one of the association's major objectives, the establishment of a uniform external standard for state registered nurses, was achieved. The control of registration was to be removed from the direct influence of the doctors: all examinations were to be conducted by the University of Manitoba. Nevertheless the nurses regarded the legislation as weak because hospitals with a mere five beds were still permitted to have a nurse training school. It was almost inevitable that nurses-in-training in such institutions received rudimentary and haphazard instruction and continued to be exploited as very low paid labour. Nurses who graduated from hospital training schools exceeded the number who were able to qualify as state registered nurses.[55] The Manitoba Association of Registered Nurses – the 1930 descendant of the Graduate Nurses organization – continued to lobby for improvements and was helped by a Canada-wide report on nurses' training produced in 1931. Education standards were climbing slowly.[56]

If teaching and nursing were fledgling professions which welcomed women, medicine and the law were at least accessible, if not hospitable, to women before the First World War. A university degree was a prerequisite.

The University of Manitoba was formed in 1877 by a federation of three existing church colleges: St. Boniface (Roman Catholic), St. John's (Anglican), and Manitoba (Presbyterian). Initially an examining and degree-granting body, the university soon offered instruction as well. A fourth college, Wesley, with a Methodist tradition, affiliated in 1888. Early women university students were a small group. Wesley College admitted women from the start, and Manitoba College admitted them beginning in 1886. Some women applied to St. John's but Archbishop Machray "with his Cambridge background was definitely opposed to granting such a privilege." Women could not attend the Anglican college until 1890 when Dora Fortin, the daughter of an archdeacon, was admitted.[57]

Few women, however, graduated before World War I. In the professions, the first woman to graduate in medicine was Harriet (Foxton) Clark, in 1892. Three additional women became doctors before 1914. The first women to graduate with a degree in law did so in 1917, although two women were admitted to the Manitoba Bar in 1915 after serving an apprenticeship as articling students. The first women to graduate in science were Annie Norrington in 1917 and Margaret Gow in 1918.[58]

Women students appreciated their privileges. When a professor from Edinburgh was to speak, Lillian (Ponton) Saul (B.A. 1893) remembered: "There was an uncertainty as to whether women students would be expected. Prof. Hart told us to come, and be ready in our gowns, but not to be disappointed if we were not admitted. You may imagine our joy when word came that we might come down." Saul's women contemporaries all "took the Modern Language course."[59] Most accepted that after graduation, if they worked for pay, they would work as schoolteachers. Like Saul, Jessie (Holmes) Munro, the first woman graduate (1889), and Alice Maud (Williams) Young (B.A. 1891) could "think of nothing for women but teaching school," and many of the graduates went on to the Normal School.[60] Looking back from 1937,

Edith (Sutherland) Clark (B.A. 1894) commented on the employment prospects for early graduates: "The teaching profession afforded employment to a very large number of the early graduates. Before Alberta and Saskatchewan had founded their universities these provinces employed many Manitoban students as teachers in summer schools. The various opportunities now afforded women did not exist then. A comparatively small number was to be found in stenography or secretarial positions. The number entering the hospitals to train as nurses had not made itself noticed."[61]

By 1894 thirteen women had graduated from the University of Manitoba, all with a bachelor of arts degree except for the single doctor, Harriet (Foxton) Clark.[62] Not all the students were supported by wealthy families. Nellie Hislop was the daughter of homesteaders from Ontario who came to Manitoba in 1883 when she was eleven. At the age of sixteen she passed her Second Class Certificate and taught school over the winter for $30 per month. Returning to her home in May, "I found a copy of the daily *Free Press* that some train passenger had discarded out of a window. A prominent feature in the paper gave the results of the annual university examinations. As I scanned the list of honours students and prize winners, I saw it included female names. Girls were attending university and winning prizes! It was a revelation to me and the awakening of a desire."[63]

Hislop did not have the resources to attend university immediately, so she spent five months at the Normal School and took a job as teacher at Plympton, just east of Winnipeg. Then in 1890 she started on her university quest. She financed her studies through teaching school in the summer and intended to return to college but had to help her family, now residing in Winnipeg. She did not graduate until 1895: "A total of thirty-seven students graduated in Arts at that convocation ... [My] brother Johnnie was fond of saying thereafter that the Hislops started a new trend: we proved that a working man's children could go to college and win a degree. At that time most college students (except those in theology) were the children of the wealthy or of well-paid professional people, such as lawyers, judges, and medical doctors." Hislop then took a Winnipeg teaching job, earning the "princely amount" of $50 a month for ten months.[64]

In the years before 1916, schooling could be offered in languages other than English under certain conditions: "When ten of the pupils of any school speak the French language, or any language other than English as their native language, the teaching of such pupils shall be conducted in French or such other language, and English, upon the bilingual system." The Mennonite, French, Ukrainian, and Polish communities had adopted this option. The clause was repealed in 1916, in the same legislation which introduced compulsory education for all children aged 6 to 14 years of age.[65]

The decision to make English the sole language of instruction was bitterly resented by some groups, especially the Ukrainians and the French, who devised ways of non-compliance. In "most" Ukrainian school districts after 1916 teachers "were required to teach Ukrainian after school hours in addition to their regular duties" but the enthusiasm for this practice waned in the 1930s.[66] Myths grew up relating stories of languages other than English being used during the regular school day. Certainly in the French communities there was substance to this.[67] Gabrielle Roy was proud to point out that "despite the law that allowed only an hour a day for the teaching of French in public schools in French-speaking neighbourhoods, it seems to me that the French we spoke was every bit as good as in Quebec, in the same period and for similar social strata."[68] Roy attributed this "miraculous situation" mainly to the "zeal and tenacity of our school-teachers, mostly nuns but also some lay teachers, who used to give extra, unpaid time to the teaching of French despite already onerous schedules":

A few used to take quite brazen liberties with the law ... When the provocation was not too visible, the Department of Education closed its eyes. As long as the children were able to show they were learning some English when the inspector came, the rest was more or less accepted ... The standing order at the time was that if the investigator or indeed anyone from the school board appeared unexpectedly, all our French textbooks were to be hidden, evidence of lessons in French erased from blackboards, and our English books prominently displayed. No doubt there were tense moments of that kind in some schools and perhaps even in mine before my time, but personally I was never aware of any such dramatic visit. Yet the danger was quite real and it galvanized us.[69]

The 1916 legislation proved to be a watershed for education in Manitoba. The interwar period marked a substantial increase in school enrolment even if attendance in rural districts continued to be a problem. Most girls, whatever their ethnic background, were likely to acquire elementary education. With respect to options beyond the basics for girls and women, there were significant curriculum changes which served both to expand and to limit female opportunities. Moreover, women acquired the franchise in 1916, and women's organizations and other groups looked to the schools to help educate girls as citizens. High on their agenda was the inculcation of nationalism and Christianity, preferably in its Protestant form, in an effort to "Canadianize" the youth of the country. Organizations in Manitoba like the Women's Institutes and the United Farm Women of Manitoba, together with the

Local Council of Women, echoed the educational goals of the newly formed National Council of Education which wished to see "national aspirations ... national manners and customs ... national contributions to civilisation" included in textbooks and the inclusion "in prescribed literature of a generous number of Scripture selections."[70]

Another emphasis was the move towards vocational training, and for girls this largely translated into an initiative to professionalize housewifery. In 1910 a Department of Household Science had been established in the University of Manitoba and women's groups wished to introduce instruction into the schools.[71] The Depression in the 1930s sharpened concerns about girls leaving school "without sufficient training and opportunity to secure gainful employment."[72]

Underlying these interwar developments was the continuing assumption that a girl would marry and that her education should equip her for the proper discharge of her duties as a homemaker and citizen. Some were also concerned that in the event she had no male provider, a woman would be able to fend for herself. But there was no unanimity on this: some social welfare policy of the interwar period saw the development of the state as a substitute provider for a delinquent or absent husband. Education was supposed to equip a girl for her future life.

In 1917 the National Council of Women, holding its annual general meeting for the first time in Winnipeg, called for "adequate technical training for both girls and boys" and "vocational training ... such training for girls to include household service and the care of children."[73] The Women's Institutes, which promoted talks and classes on home economics through their own rural branches, also campaigned to have the subject taught in the schools. This was a cause which attracted both progressive reformers and the conservative minded. Some reformers like Mary Speechly of Winnipeg wished to give women's family responsibilities due public recognition by elevating the status of housewifery and motherhood.[74] Home economics, they thought, would professionalize work in the home and would serve as a training parallel to the training for paid professional work in the labour force.[75] More conservative supporters wished to strengthen the family against what was perceived as a threat from newly enfranchised and educated women and hoped to channel women into traditional occupations.[76] In fact actual instruction in the schools developed slowly largely because of the costs of providing special equipment and instruction. As a 1938 report noted: "Although reasonably wide provisions have been made in the programme of studies for home economics, industrial arts and agriculture, to date little advantage has been taken of these courses apart from the city of Winnipeg."[77]

Whatever the motivation of the proposers, the Department of Education had included home economics in its programme of electives, but in fact this had little effect, either progressive or conservative, on the education of most girls in the province. What probably had more impact, serving to further the notion that women were less scientifically minded than men, was the existence of the "woman's option." The programme of studies for the secondary schools of Manitoba issued in 1919 outlined the Grade 12 curriculum which was a necessary preliminary to university entrance. There were four papers in English, three in mathematics, two in science, and one in history. However, it stated that "women students who do not wish to take all the mathematics prescribed may take … in lieu thereof" a review of the Grade 11 mathematics, and two additional papers in either English or French literature. This provision remained into the 1930s.[78] Graduates of the "woman's option" would therefore be able to leave high school without grade 12 mathematics and would in turn be formally unqualified to teach that subject at the grade 12 level in the event they became schoolteachers.

During the 1920s, in an attempt to provide education directly related to job prospects, the Department of Education permitted business courses – shorthand, typing, and bookkeeping – to be taught. With the increase in office work, such training was beneficial. There were also training schemes outside the public school system offered by commercial business colleges. They were often attended in the evening by women who had a regular day job. Such a person was Clara (Taylor) Shames who was born in Kiev in 1903 and arrived with her family in Winnipeg in 1914. When she was fourteen she sewed in a factory during the day and learned typing and shorthand at Pitman's in the evening. However, "when she went to look for office work, she found that factory work was better paid," so stayed at the factory.[79]

In the years after World War I, women gradually entered the university in increasing numbers.[80] Amidst the pleasures of intellectual learning they also encountered difficulties. Sexual harassment did not have a name but was nevertheless present. An indication of the atmosphere women might encounter is given by H.S. Ferns who was first a student and then a teacher at the University of Manitoba. Writing in his memoirs about Noel Fieldhouse, head of the History Department and a "great teacher," Ferns recounts:

It was in the lectures on English history that there occurred what seemed to me the best example of Fieldhouse's style. There were twenty or thirty students in the class, and he was discussing the activities and views of some English

aristocratic politician whose name I cannot now recall. "And he admired
and appreciated equally," Fieldhouse said, "the beautiful limbs of horses and
women." In Manitoba in 1934 this was a bold, risqué remark to make in the
presence of a mixed audience. Fieldhouse paused momentarily and without
the suggestion of a leer or of any feeling at all he allowed his eyes to scan the
form of the most beautiful girl in the class sitting with her wonderfully attractive legs crossed in the front row. She blushed, and Fieldhouse went on as
coolly as ever.[81]

It was only after World War II that large numbers of women began to
pursue higher education. Some women who had served in the armed
forces enrolled in university with support from the federal government.[82] By 1955 women students at the University of Manitoba, undergraduate and graduate, formed just under a quarter of the total number.
By 1970 37 per cent of all students, 38 per cent of undergraduate students, and 20 per cent of the graduate students were women. Substantial differences were still apparent in the subjects chosen by women and
men. In arts and science together, women were 36 per cent of the undergraduate enrolment in 1970. Other fields were dominated by one sex
or the other. The ratio of women to men in agriculture was 1 to 13; in
commerce, 1 to 8; in medicine, 1 to 7; in law, 1 to 12. In these faculties,
key training grounds for the economic and professional élite, the trend
was towards an increasing participation by women, but in 1970 men
were decidedly more numerous. Outside these faculties, women continued to be concentrated in fields of study hitherto dominated by women,
fields in which no trend towards sexual integration was visible: education, where women outnumbered men by 2 to 1; fine arts (2 to 1); nursing (over 200 to 1); and home economics (over 300 to 1).[83]

By 1970, formal barriers to women's education and training were
dissolving. There was, however, little evidence to suggest that women
were training themselves for the same kind of work as men. Some were,
and the fact that women could train as professionals was testament to
their own determination and to the persistence of other women during
the previous ninety years. Most were not in line for professional or
commercial work, and the reason was not far to seek. Education and
training continued to be directly related to the work women expected
to do as adults.

For a woman born in south Winnipeg in 1939, the educational
experience of most girls after the Second World War fitted them for a
life indistinguishable from their mothers'. After high school, girls went
to university or got a job. Then, as Melinda McCracken observed in
1975:

To be married, with a home and a family, was the next thing in life to do. The girls, those from the new postwar houses in Winnipeg, are now almost without exception full-time moms at home raising their children, just as their own mothers were. In fact, high school graduates have reproduced their parents' way of life almost perfectly. They curl, play bridge, raise their kids and build their home together. They use their parents' terms, like "home" for house, "chap" for fellow at the office, "gal" for girlfriend, and "my first" for their first child. The man earns money, and the woman stays home and raises the children. Family life gives them happiness and satisfaction, and there is no barrier between them and their parents ... they are upwardly mobile and ... are often now very prosperous ... They just went on being their parents, because that's what they were supposed to to, and everybody else was doing it.[84]

Most women expected to be primarily responsible for family work in adult life. Generally speaking, only single women expected to work for pay, at least before the 1950s. It was not easy to imagine the combination of motherhood with full-time paid work. Girls and women in the paid labour force tended to train for jobs from which they could retire, at least for a period of years, when their children were small and needed constant supervision. Many – women as well as men – believed it to be unprofitable to invest time and money in training women for professions which they might later abandon. Until motherhood and paid work could realistically be combined, such a calculation frequently served to confine a woman to the kind of training which would fit her for relatively unskilled and low-level, non-managerial work. In the early 1970s, an increasing number of women put forward the view that paid work and motherhood could be pursued at the same time and sought to put this into practice. They were encouraged by the appeals of the women's liberation movement to self-fulfilment and justice and were influenced by other factors, including the expansion of governmental social services and economic inflation, which made two-income families more widespread. But in 1970, such ideas were still confined to a few.

$\mathcal{H}$OMEMAKING

Domestic economy for John Stuart Mill meant "keeping the family regularly supplied with what its wants require, and securing, with any given amount of means, the greatest possible quantity of physical comfort and enjoyment."[1] Making a home for her family was the first call on the labour of the typical adult woman. As the Winnipeg alderman, Margaret McWilliams, declared in 1934: "A married woman's first job is to run her house and family, and not until she has learned to do that so smoothly that her absence for a meal does not upset the comfort of the home, should she take an outside job."[2] Almost all women, rural and urban, rich and poor, accepted homemaking as women's work. By the 1950s, however, a critique of the social and economic conditions surrounding women's homemaking work was confidently emerging.

Precisely because the primacy of homemaking was taken for granted, it is difficult for the historian to dissect and analyse. Work in the home was almost universally performed by women and must therefore take central place in an account of women's work. However, the census did not record the dimensions of homemaking, nor did women themselves normally enumerate their chores systematically. No national accounting system included "all caring services, subsistence production, and [a] vast range of life-enhancing work."[3] Economists are only now beginning to reconsider their previous exclusion of household work from their analyses.[4]

One textual source which can throw light on woman as homemaker and on the expectations governing her status as wife and mother is provincial legislation. Marriage itself was a public and legal act. For marriages in Manitoba in 1870, as in the rest of English Canada, the general common law principle applied: "the husband and wife are one person in law; that is, the very being, or legal existence of a woman is suspended during marriage, or ... incorporated and consolidated into that of the husband, under whose wing, protection and cover she performs everything."[5] Through "coverture" a married woman was "covered" by her husband who was responsible for her maintenance. The husband's responsibility and power also extended to children. The wife and mother had no independent rights within marriage. In rural areas, Manitoba farm women were particularly seriously disadvantaged by the absence of dower before 1918 (see below, pp. 86–7). In the towns and cities, a wife's insecurity related to her inability to own either her own home or her wages. Feminists had already begun to make inroads on the common law, however, with specific legislation designed to ensure a woman's security within marriage. A series of Married Women's Property Acts passed in Manitoba between 1871 and 1900 paralleled reforms elsewhere in common law countries which extended to married women the same property rights as single women possessed.[6]

Support for divorce legislation was slower to develop. Indeed, divorce was almost impossible in the nineteenth century. A marriage could be dissolved only through a private act of parliament. In 1913 the cost "without legal fees is about five hundred dollars – with legal fees it amounts to about a thousand dollars" – at a time when a woman's industrial wage was no higher than $500 a year.[7] In 1920 a bill to create a uniform divorce law for all Canada save Quebec was defeated. In 1925 a reform gave women equal access to divorce in the sense that the grounds were now the same for women as for men: adultery. Divorce remained difficult until 1969 when the grounds were augmented, most notably by a three-year separation provision. That law was based on the concept of no-fault marital breakdown and was welcomed by the *Report* of the Royal Commission on the Status of Women. The commission recommended that the three years be reduced to one, and this change was eventually incorporated into law in 1986.[8]

Bolstered by maternal sentiment, reforms were introduced in the 1870s to assign a share of guardianship and custody rights over children to the mother, and a woman's status as mother gradually improved. A father was considered to be the rightful guardian of his child, and only under certain abnormal circumstances were others afforded custody. This patriarchal assumption came to be eroded not only by feminists wishing mothers to share authority over children but also by childhood experts advocating the interests of the child.

Guardianship and custody over children became an issue at the death of the father, if a married couple separated, or on the rare occasions when they divorced. In Manitoba in 1878 a mother was allowed to petition court for custody of a child under twelve years of age, and in 1900 could apply for the custody of children under sixteen. Child custody, however, was related to morally respectable behaviour. If a woman had committed adultery, she was disqualified as a guardian. Moreover, if a women was the guardian of her child or children, after 1900 she was also liable for their maintenance. The adultery clause did not, of course, apply to unmarried mothers, who were by definition fornicators if not adulteresses. After 1912 a mother was permitted to sue the father of an illegitimate child for financial support. Most of the separate legislation governing child custody was consolidated in the Child Welfare Act of 1922 which gave equal custody rights to both parents and eliminated the adultery clause for women.

The writers of the Manitoba brief presented to the Royal Commission in 1968 were highly concerned with the support of wives and children who lived apart from a husband, either through desertion, separation, or divorce. Husbands still had a legal obligation to support dependents, but the legislation lacked satisfactory enforcement apparatus.[9] In 1970, the legislation still adhered to the concept of woman as dependent, but a divorced wife could not be sure that a husband would continue to maintain her, nor could she assume an equal division of marital property in the event of marriage dissolution.

Legislation also regulated the legal situation of single mothers – many of whom were, in the Victorian lexicon, "fallen" women and thus not entitled to the protection of conventional society. Two sorts of provincial law referred to them: laws delineating their obligations towards their children, and social policy affording some sort of maintenance in the absence of a husband.

The 1900 provision that made a single mother liable for the maintenance of her child created a new problem. Without her own male protector, and with minimal access to employment paying sufficient wages to support dependents, she was vulnerable to the power of a new authority: the state in the guise of protector of children. The authority of the new Children's Aid Society was clarified by legislation in 1900. The state could apprehend children and place them in care, either in a family or an institution, in the event of parental neglect or abuse.

An important new direction was taken in 1916 when Manitoba was the first province in Canada to establish a social programme to help the small group of single mothers whose practical difficulties in raising their children were considered to result from no fault of their own. The mothers' allowances programme provided monthly payments to mothers who were widowed or whose husbands were permanently disabled. The principle behind the scheme was to pay the mother a sufficient income to permit her to remain at home and care for her children. Grandiose rhetorical claims were made for the principle: "as the child is the chief asset of the State it is the duty of the State to provide for his maintenance," declared the Local Council of Women in 1915.[10] However, this did not supersede the duty of the husband to provide for maintenance when he could, and not all children with absent fathers qualified for assistance. Those whose mothers were unmarried were definitely ineligible.

Until the programme was discontinued at the end of the Second World War, mothers' allowances served as an exemplar of the idea that it was right for the state to serve as a substitute husband.[11] A comprehensive bureaucracy was instituted to ensure that the province could be confident of "assisting the proper type of woman to bring up its future citizens." The province must be sure that the allowance was "being used to the best advantage in the work of bringing up happy children, mentally and physically efficient and morally sound." During 1918, about 175 families received benefits; in 1919, 295 families did, and in 1923, 722 families. Regular reports continued to express the public consensus on motherhood and its obligations as well as the moral didacticism of the state: "Adequate food should be provided to enable them to grow up with strong and healthy bodies. The mother should not be away from home at work at any time when her children need her, nor do work that is beyond her physical strength. The care and training that a mother gives her children should be the greatest service she can render."[12]

After the Second World War, most welfare legislation was under federal or joint federal-provincial jurisdiction, and each province had fewer programmes peculiar to itself. Between 1916 and 1944, under initiatives taken primarily by provincial civil servants, promoted by the progressive Liberal government of T.C. Norris, and strongly supported by local women's organizations, Manitoba had taken the lead in providing public funds for the support of mothers blameless of immorality.[13] Motherhood was supported with money.

Provincial legislation reflected the maternalism of progressive social reformers of the first half of the twentieth century. Laws concerning women consistently embodied two principles. The law must enforce social morality so that a young single woman's prospects of marriage were not harmed by assaults on her sexuality or reputation. A woman's future maternity must also be protected, if necessary by labour legislation which prohibited certain occupations and certain practices, such as standing up all day, because they were thought to be dangerous to the reproductive system. The other constant theory was the dependency of a married woman. When Manitoba entered Confederation, such dependency was in legal terms almost absolute. After reform came with the Married Women's Property Acts, a woman was still in theory entitled to protection in the form of maintenance, even in the 1968 divorce reform provisions. In practice this was a modified protection, as little was done to enforce maintenance and support payments through the courts for separated and divorced wives. Under certain circumstances, the state could substitute for the husband as breadwinner. The mothers' allowances programme exemplified this principle. Along with the money came control. The state established a thoroughgoing investigative machinery to ensure its money was going to the right type of mother.

Just as the relationships of white women with legislation and the state changed over the century, so also were there significant changes in the connections between the state and First Nations women which had a considerable effect on these women's work for their families. The late nineteenth-century goal of the Dominion of Canada was to "restructure the domestic economy" of Indian women, in an effort to promote the protection, civilization, and assimilation of the First Nations peoples. State policies towards First Nations women, expressed in 1869 and persisting with only slight changes until 1951, had as their aim nothing less than the complete transformation of these women's economic roles.[14]

First Nations female economy on the Prairies before white settlement conformed to John Stuart Mill's description: women looked after their families' physical comfort and enjoyment within their traditional environment of a hunting and gathering economy. Women constructed the housing: "Female family members often worked together to construct a winter wigwam. They cut saplings from the woods to form the lodge frame, covered it with rolled sheets of birch bark sewn together and with woven rush mats made anew each fall. Together, the women could construct a comfortable and inviting winter dwelling in a matter of a few hours."[15] Women also managed the food supply. Despite the conventional emphasis on the consumption of large animals hunted by men, such as bison, moose, and deer, the aboriginal diet, except for feasts, included high proportions of smaller game, fish, and plant food traditionally trapped, cultivated, harvested, and processed by women. Traditionally, rabbit and partridge were snared by women and were generally available whereas big game was not. Wild rice was a risky crop, possibly successful only about one year in three, but it was the women who managed the rice fields when there was a harvest. The prairie turnip, a root vegetable available through the summer and autumn but preservable in various ways for year-round consumption, was harvested by women. In the Red and Assiniboine river valleys, women looked after cultivated corn and potatoes during the summer growing season. Women also harvested sap from maples and other trees and made it into syrup and sugar.[16] This diverse food supply, produced as well as cooked and stored by women, was dependent on a semi-nomadic way of life.

In 1874, with the extension of the 1869 Indian Act to Manitoba, the federal government sought to change this whole structure of life. A pass system, enforced by the Department of Indian Affairs after 1885, limited women's mobility and reduced travelling from site to site.[17] The objective of government policy was to substitute a settled life on lands specifically reserved for First Nations peoples and "train Indian women to behave in a domestic economy in a manner similar to the white European women who were settling nearby the reserves."[18] Consequently, the Indian agents expected the white schoolteachers, wives of ministers, women in religious orders, and wives of farming instructors on the reserves to instruct Indian women in conventional European homemaking skills.[19] For this, the white women were not paid. As well, formal instruction in domestic science was a major feature of the residential schools to which Indian girls were sent.

The state may have had a deliberate policy, but enforcement was always a different issue. The roles of First Nations women were indeed altered and somewhat diminished as a result of government policy, but their work was still critical for the family. In the late nineteenth century, "when the disappearance of the buffalo coincided with settlement on reserves and efforts to establish agriculture produced little in the way of an edible or marketable produce, women made a vital contribution to the cultural and physical survival of their communities." Noting that the evidence "rarely provides the first-hand voices of the women of this era," historian Sarah Carter has used the oral testimony of First Nations prairie women to add to the written record. In the late 1880s, the older women in these communities kept people's spirits up at a time of upheaval and poverty. "Their cheerfulness could not help but be infectious, thus everyone was soon striving to do his share, and the Crees were able to look on the bright side of things," wrote a Cree man about the Onion Lake Reserve in the 1880s. Well into the twentieth century, women went on communal walking expeditions for wild rhubarb, say, or to hunt gophers and ducks. The food was later shared, and sometimes sold: seneca roots, for instance, had market value for medicinal purposes. Women remembered the practical ways in which traditional food was harvested. Prairie turnip was eaten in many ways: "uncooked, boiled, roasted, in soups ... or ... dried, crushed into a powder and stored in skin bags for the winter." Old habits could not be stamped out.[20]

While the old ways continued, women on reserves also responded to the opportunities introduced by the Indian agents. They were taught to "knit, sew, mend, card and spin wool. They were instructed how to make butter and bread as well as the housecleaning skills of scrubbing, sweeping and washing." Geographer Pamela White has laid bare the ideological, as well as the economic, motivation behind this European-izing policy. For example, the Department of Indian Affairs went to great lengths to banish the baking of bannock and substitute yeasted bread. Bread did require less flour, but bannock, a mixture of flour, salt, and water easily cooked over an open fire with a minimum of equipment, was also a symbol of the traditional nomadic life.[21]

Despite fewer resources of housing, appliances, and tools, and a lower income than neighbouring white women, First Nations women were frequently criticized in departmental reports for failing to meet the agents' standards of housewifery. Moreover, they were blamed directly for the endemic tuberculosis which was over ten times more prevalent among the aboriginal population than among Canadians in general.[22] In 1907 when the chief medical officer for the department attempted to spread the blame beyond women's housekeeping habits to implicate as well the poor housing stock, lack of medical attention, and the role of residential schools as a breeding ground for the disease, he was dismissed.[23] The department clung to an image of First Nations women as failed white homemakers. Women were politically a useful scapegoat for the failure of the state's policies of restriction and coer-cion in the name of protection and assimilation.

First Nations people had a more considered and respectful judgement of women's versatility: "The women carried water, chopped wood, and also went and got the wood ... That's what the women did. In the winter they'd haul snow and melt it for water. The woman didn't waste any time. She was alway working, doing things around the house, in-side and outside." As a Cree woman remembered, "You put the child in the cradle, stand it up, and do whatever work you're doing."[24]

Sarah Carter noted evidence for the economic resilience and strength of First Nations women, but "for every story of the successful circum-vention of policy, regulations, and the authority of the Indian agent, there are many more that attest to the formidable yoke of oppression that characterized reserve life well into the twentieth century."[25] Part of that oppression was the intrusive role of the state in so many areas of women's lives, even in their selection of food for the family. This invasion of "private" life by "public" policy and attitudes among First Nations women may alert us to other instances of the significance of government in the lives of *all* women.

As we have seen, the language of law provides evidence of official attitudes towards women as mothers. The "mother-work"[26] experience of women can be recovered from other sorts of data as well – statistics, surveys, and individual accounts preserved in memoirs and letters. But first, the *definition* of homemaking should be clarified.

In *The New Day Recalled*, an account of English-speaking girls and women in interwar Canada, Veronica Strong-Boag posited four basic categories of homemaking: housework, reproduction and child care, the care of working adults, and the care of dependent adults.[27] To these could be added a fifth sort of work for the housewife: paid work within the home.[28] The last permitted a woman to earn money while performing family-related tasks in the home.

Women received advice about their housekeeping from all sides. In Manitoba the growing application of scientific principles to house-wifery, reflected in the establishment in 1910 of a Department of Household Science at the University of Manitoba, was designed to train the future wives of male university graduates in the modern ways of housekeeping.[29] The same motivation prompted the formation of home economics associations and the work of Women's Institutes in rural communities throughout the province. They were to promote "the improvement of individual homes in Manitoba" through the discussion of "subjects directly concerned with the general well-being of the family and the affairs of the home."[30] No woman could afford to ignore the tasks for her reputation as a housekeeper was at risk, and widespread public recognition, often arch, fulsome, or facetious, was accorded homemaking.[31]

The material conditions under which a woman laboured had a critical effect on her work load. The first major factor was the size and composition of her family group. Babies, old people, and invalids demanded more care than teenage children who might be expected to help with the chores. While more children could provide more labour, they also had to be fed, clothed, and cared for. A second important factor was the size and nature of the dwelling, particularly as these matters related to family size. Finally, the tools and facilities available to a woman mattered. If she had piped water, this eliminated the time taken in fetching water from a well. If she had a furnace rather than a wood stove, this affected her cleaning chores. Other labour-saving devices also influenced her work load. After World War II plumbing and heating facilities were modernized and electricity became widely available even in rural areas. Access to electricity could revolutionize a woman's schedule.

In the century 1870–1970 there were changes in these material conditions. Families became smaller. The number of live births per 1,000 population, the birth rate, declined. In 1921 it was 30.3; by 1971, 18.2. Infant mortality declined as well, so women did not need to give birth to as many children to have a certain number reach adulthood.[32] For an individual family, this decline in infant mortality meant that whereas a family in 1870, on average, contained 4.8 children, by 1970 the average family contained under two.[33]

The dwellings of new immigrants were usually small, whether in the countryside or in the town. On the prairie, poor settlers had to construct their first house from material at hand. The Duck Mountain district, north of Dauphin, was settled at the end of the 1890s by Ukrainians. The Hryhorczuks' first homestead was "a large hut which looked like some garage or a root cellar that one sees in some farmyards today":

The hut was built in a manner the highlanders of Ukraine employed to erect temporary shelter. First, the tops of two trees, some sixteen feet apart, were cut off, leaving suitable crotches. A pole was set in these crotches joining them. Short poles were then leaned against this pole to form a roof-like structure, which was covered with hay and large pieces of bark. A small window which my father bought in Dauphin was set in the gable over the aperture which served as a door. This opening was screened by a blanket.

We spent the summer in this hut and when it rained often, the roof would leak. Several times during heavy rains, the water also came in at the ground level and our belongings got wet. We, however, did not have many chattels as two of our trunks which carried mother's linen and our best clothing had been lost.[34]

For winter dwellings, log cabins were constructed and sod placed over the frame.

Some immigrant families could afford to purchase lumber. Nellie Hislop's Ontario family had sold a farm in Simcoe County and brought to Manitoba in 1883 cash, cattle, and modest household effects:

two bedsteads complete with bedding, which meant a good supply of woollen blankets, many homemade quilts, bedticks filled with goose feathers, and pillows; a chest of drawers, complete with swinging mirror, and a kitchen cupboard, both made of butternut wood (her mother's wedding presents); dishes, cooking utensils, and cutlery; the family pictures, some of which had come from Scotland; the big Bible, in which was written the family records; father's everyday Bible; a few chosen books representing the works of Bunyan, Shakespeare, Byron, Tennyson, Burns … as well as a good medical book and all our school books. Except for trunks of clothing, [Mother] packed little else – not a chair, sofa, or rug, no curtains, not a game or toy.

The Hislops were doubly fortunate in that they moved onto a homestead where there already was a house: "two small rooms: one for beds, the other a combination living-dining room and kitchen containing only a small rusty stove and a long plank table and benches." For insulation, the exterior was sodded to the roof, and they soon constructed a cattle

Nellie Hislop. (E.W. Nuffield, *With the West in Her Eyes.* Winnipeg: Hyperion Press 1987)

barn, a milk house, a granary, and a pig pen, partly with lumber purchased in Winnipeg. Three years later they moved into the city.[35]

In the country districts, small, roughly constructed dwellings remained the commonest form of housing for several generations. The Swan River rural survey of 1914 divided the population's housing into three categories: "log and pioneer," "frame," and "brick, stone, cement." The survey examined conditions in Swan River itself and in surrounding rural districts. By 1914, 62 per cent of all families still lived in "log and pioneer" homes, and 37 per cent lived in frame houses.[36] The companion survey of the longer established community of Turtle Mountain found fewer (43 per cent) in the log and pioneer category, and 30 per cent living in frame houses. At Turtle Moutain, almost 16 per cent lived in their top category, of "brick, stone, cement."[37] At the time of the First World War, therefore, the pioneer dwelling was still very much a part of rural life. A decade later, when the United Farm Women of Manitoba conducted a survey among their members to determine the work load of farm women, 20 per cent of their 307 respondents still lived in a house of four rooms or fewer, even though United Farm Women came from the more prosperous sections of the rural population.[38]

If early twentieth century rural housing in Manitoba was character-ized by "older settlements with old, damp and dark houses, usually overcrowded, and very new settlements with small crowded houses,"[39] the situation in the city of Winnipeg was much the same. The Hislops were among the more fortunate when they moved to Winnipeg in 1882:

The house was typical for the times: most streets had them. A terrace usually consisted of seven to ten houses with similar floor plans, built on thirty foot lots. The house measured twenty by thirty feet. It stood a story and a half high, the gabled end facing the street. A small entry hall led on the right to a parlour with bay window. The parlour and a large dining room at the rear were con-nected by an archway. An addition behind this contained a twelve foot by twelve foot kitchen with a bedroom built above it ... The house had no bath-room, no basement, and no running water. The front, both up and down, was heated with a coal and wood stove placed in the dining room. The bedroom above the kitchen depended on the heat given off by the cookstove pipes. Each bedroom was planned to hold a double bed, a bureau, and a washstand with the usual crockery set. Few bedrooms had closets.[40]

Nellie Hislop's house was luxurious compared with the situation dur-ing the massive immigration of the decade 1901–11: "In 1906, at the peak of immigration into Winnipeg, the North End, which comprised less than one third of the city's geographical area contained 43% of the population," accommodated in "overcrowded houses and tenements, lack of sanitary installations, dirty back yards, muddy, foul smelling streets, and poor lighting conditions."[41] J.S. Woodsworth graphically described families of five or more occupying just one room. His annual report of 1907–8 for the All Peoples' Mission described a family living in one room, which "contained no less than fourteen souls, men, women and children indiscriminately mixed. We thought it right to compel a reduction in the number; the family unable alone to pay the rent of this fairly large room moved, and we found them a few days later, the family of eight in a room 9 x 11 feet. The two beds, the cook-stove and the barrel comprising the effects occupied all the floor. The two doors had been lifted off their hinges, and in full gaze of a number of single men occupying the adjoining room the family lived its life. Really they were better off when living 14 in a room."[42]

Women with large families and little space, with little money for food, still less for cleaning and cooking equipment, had their work cut out for them. At the other end of the scale, some women were better off. Edith McColl came to Winnipeg on her marriage to a civil engineer, and they bought a house in the Wolseley district: "three rooms downstairs, and three up – besides the bath." The cost of this was $4400, and her husband's annual income in 1918 was just over $1200,[43] – not a particularly high salary for the time. Woodsworth estimated that in 1913 a family of five needed $1,216 per year for a minimally satisfactory standard of living, but the families he was writing about, in the North End, often received less than $600 per annum.[44] Certainly women with few resources had greater difficulty than women like McColl, who also had the benefit of household help: not a live-in maid, in her case, but a woman who worked for 20 cents an hour.[45] Even the economically secure women faced much hard drudgery, as a 1922 survey demonstrated.

The main purpose of this survey, conducted by the United Farm Women, was to discover how many women had "labour saving devices" to assist their work and to argue for greater accessibility to such devices. Respondents to the survey were among the more prosperous of the rural population which still outnumbered the urban population at this time. Sixty per cent of them had their homes heated by wood stoves, requiring "wood to carry in, ashes to carry out, and the never-ending muss to sweep up." Most houses were lit by coal oil lamps. Few had piped water. Two-thirds had no water in the kitchen; 82 per cent had no bath; only 27 per cent had an indoor toilet. Most got their water from a well, whose average distance from the house was over seventy metres. Over half had no "machine power" and even those who did rarely used household machinery. If the farm had electricity, it usually came not from power lines but from a generator and was used almost exclusively to operate farm machinery.[46]

The work load of most town women would be facilitated by piped water, not necessarily to their houses, but to a communal street tap outside, and by indoor plumbing. By 1914 the number of outside toilets in Winnipeg had been reduced to 666 from over 6000 in 1905.[47] Moreover, many town houses were heated by a furnace rather than a wood stove. Rural women did have one advantage over town dwellers: their large vegetable gardens. Many could preserve a considerable amount of their food for their families. This would reduce their expenses, but added to their work load.[48] Later, during the Depression, access to wild food through hunting and gathering in the bush might make all the difference for families without a regular income.[49]

Rural living conditions remained difficult for poor families in Manitoba into the 1960s. A 1965 survey reported that in the Interlake district, "28% had three rooms or less, yet 36% of the households contained five persons or more." Even then, three-quarters of the homes in the district were without running water or flush toilets compared with about half for other predominantly rural areas.[50]

The housewife's domestic work was described systematically by Meg Luxton in *More Than a Labour of Love*. In 1976 she did a study of Flin Flon, a northern Manitoba mining community with a population of approximately 10,000. Through carefully structured interviews and field work among three generations of Flin Flon inhabitants Luxton was able to construct a concentrated case-study of the domestic labour spectrum spread over fifty years. Integrating her own observations with the views of her subjects, she described the sort of work shared by unpaid housewives in Manitoba and Western society in general. Her study analysed the work women performed as wives and mothers.[51]

The economic structure of the marital relationship was intrinsically interwoven with its emotional aspect. All adult women could recognize an economic inducement to be married, an impulse reinforced by non-existent or dismal alternative ways of obtaining financial support. Having accepted the notion of marriage as her meal ticket, a woman's domestic labour clearly reflected its economic imperatives. The wife's primary responsibility was to ensure her husband was able to work in order to earn the wages for her own, as well as his, survival. She furnished the domestic setting for recuperation after one day's work and his restoration before the next. She provided economic benefits of food, leisure, and rest as well as less tangible services such as tension management for hostility and bad temper. His timetable and his needs theoretically were paramount, taking precedence over other insistent demands, like children, within the household.

In Flin Flon, as elsewhere, there were clear generational differences in women's emotional relationships with husbands. Until after the Second World War, women's and men's leisure, as well as their work, was sexually segregated and a woman was more involved with the various manifestations of community, often church-centred, events than with personally entertaining her husband. The postwar development of household-centred leisure, usually based on watching television, meant wives and husbands became more dependent on each other for company and this in turn led to the prospect of more intimate friendship with a spouse and rising expectations of compatibility.[52]

Economic links within marriage were difficult to disentangle from the sexual ones. Why parents in Manitoba, as elsewhere, came to calculate that they should have fewer children was a decision rarely revealed in direct testimony.[53] Columns in the *Grain Growers' Guide* in the early part of this century show that its readers, who lived in the prairie provinces of western Canada, were urgently interested in birth control information.[54] In Saskatchewan, Violet McNaughton's writing in the *Western Producer* discreetly aired the topic, but in the 1920s contraception was generally considered an unfit subject for public discourse.[55] In 1923 when the Winnipeg Women's Canadian Club had the opportunity to hear a speaker on birth control, it was turned down as "not suitable for a Canadian Club audience."[56] After all, until 1967 it was an indictable offence to "offer to sell, advertise, publish an advertisement or have for sale or disposal any medicine, drug or article intended or represented as a means of preventing conception or causing abortion."[57] Considerable ingenuity was needed to circumvent official silence. In Winnipeg, the practical matter of supplying contraceptive advice and devices was a responsibility taken on in the 1930s by a low-profile, clandestine organization.

The Family Planning Association of Winnipeg was formed in February 1934 by Mary Speechly who continued to direct it for the next generation. She "was supported by a Board of Directors who in the main wished to remain anonymous."[58] Helped for the first four years with funds, staff, and supplies by A.R. Kaufman, a rubber manufacturer in Ontario known as the father of the Canadian birth control movement, the association operated on a voluntary basis for over twenty years. It employed "mature married women," usually retired registered nurses, to visit clients in their homes and remunerated them with small honoraria.[59] By the mid-1950s the association employed a home visitor. Describing the work in retrospect, one person wrote: "Every month or two Mrs Speechly received a case list averaging approximately twenty cases a month from a social worker at the Winnipeg General Hospital ... Most of the familes we visited live in the core area of the city and a large percentage of them were welfare recipients ... The pill came into cautious use in our association in the early sixties and was prescribed by a Winnipeg physician who was sympathetic to our 'cause,' as Mrs Speechly referred to it ... Our association paid the nominal fee charged by the doctor and supplied the pill free of charge if the client did not have the ability to pay."

Educated, economically secure women could usually find medical advice and attention regardless of the antiquated laws: "Physicians prescribed family planning to their own patients and did not appear to concern themselves beyond their own practice." In the days before medicare arrived in the 1960s, it was more difficult for poorer, or less educated, or rural women to have access to appropriate services. "Our work was quietly done and with discretion, so as not to rock any boats

Mary Speechly. (Western Canadian Pictorial Index A1224–36655)

... we continued on a small scale, reaching almost exclusively the very needy." However, "among our cases were a handful of middle class British immigrant families. On arriving in Canada they immediately looked for the kind of health care and facilities they were accustomed to in Britain ... I signed them up."[60]

As women's decisions about bearing children changed over the century, so did their methods of rearing them. The one constant was an almost universal acceptance that a mother, having borne her children, would then take primary responsibility for raising them. This task alone demanded a vigilance which eased as children become physically stronger but which did not entirely cease until they moved out of the parental home (or even later). A woman's training for this work – caring, nurturing, and socializing the children – usually came from memories of her own upbringing combined with current advice from relatives and friends.

In many groups, including traditional First Nations, there was a wider sharing of responsibility for child rearing, with grandparents active in raising their grandchildren.[61] Mary Redhead, a Cree living near York Factory on Hudson Bay, participated in an oral history project describing First Nations life in transition. She remembered that elders stayed home and looked after children while women were working outside, or away hunting.[62]

One difficulty mothers experienced as the twentieth century unfolded arose from "intruders in the nursery," the child care professionals who, introduced scientific theories of child-rearing in the interwar period.[63] A child's socialization was now shared with other agencies besides the immediate family and neighbours. Schools, children's peer groups, and, after the Second World War, ubiquitous television immensely influenced the way a child was brought up. As mothers had fewer children, they were expected to have a more intense emotional and instructional relationship with them. Beginning in the 1930s child development theory emphasized that the first five years of a child's life were uniquely crucial to its later development, stability, and welfare. This view provided an ideological reinforcement for emotional ties binding a mother with her children but could introduce conflict in a woman between her role as a wife and her responsibilities as a mother.[64]

The demand for labour during World War II brought difficulties for mothers who were recruited into the labour force despite their parenting responsibilities. In Toronto and Montreal the Canadian government established funded day-care centres for children of mothers working in war-related industries, and in 1942 considered extending such a service to Winnipeg.[65] The federal government, through social agencies in Winnipeg, organized a preliminary survey of children whose mothers were already in the paid labour force.[66] In the event, it was decided not to introduce day care to Winnipeg, but the survey brought to light information on the extent of maternal employment and on the varieties of child care used at a particular time of history.

The survey was administered through all elementary schools in the city of Winnipeg proper. Of a total enrolment in these schools of nearly 17,000 in 1942, 2,370 were identified by their home room teacher as having working mothers.[67] This translates to approximately 14 per cent of schoolchildren with working mothers, but the real incidence of maternal employment may well have been under-reported. The value of the survey lies in its indication that child care was unavoidably makeshift and could not be reliable. The key to child care of school-age children was what happened at the noon meal. What arrangements did the working mother make for her child to have lunch? Many children were on their own. About the same number of children went home and either got their own meal alone or were looked after by a relative. Together, these two arrangements accounted for almost 40 per cent of the children. As well, just under 10 per cent reported that the mother returned home for the meal; in almost 5 per cent of cases the father came home. Almost 6 per cent of the children were looked after by paid help, and about 4 per cent of them were cared for by a neighbour. Despite these lunch-time difficulties, the agencies concluded that "the employment situation in the city of Winnipeg [did] not warrant the setting up of additional day nurseries."[68] What the survey did show was the fragile and piecemeal arrangements parents were obliged to resort to in order to find any parental substitute for child care – a situation which had scarcely changed by 1970.

Housework as well as child care was a constant demand of the housewife's daily round. Cleaning and cooking maintained the material conditions of family life. The husband recovered his strength and the mother nurtured the next growing generation of workers within the family environment. The household reproduced both the short- and the long-term labouring power for the family and for society. Luxton's Flin Flon study dramatically highlighted the changes introduced by technology over time.

In the early days of its settlement, Flin Flon housewives in many ways conducted their work to the rhythms of a pre-industrial society. Like rural women elsewhere in the province, they gathered berries, grew vegetables in a garden, and cooked the game which the men had hunted and trapped. Few women in the twentieth century were still making their own yarn, but many continued to sew much of the family's clothing. Their weekly routine tended to be rigidly arranged. Monday was wash day, Tuesday was for ironing, Wednesday for baking and sewing, Thursday for shopping and other jobs. Wash day involved the most demanding physical labour, vividly described by a woman born in 1896:

Imagine ... one of those blistery hot summer days ... But it's Monday ... So I get up at 4.30 a.m. to start the fire in the stove – a fire and when it's already hot enough to fry eggs on the rocks! When the fire's going I fill the copper boiler with water and carry it from the tank to the stove and then lift it onto the stove – heavy work that and already the sweat is pouring down my back ... Then I go get the washing. Baskets of dirty things – clothes, bed sheets, towels and his dirty work clothes and I carry them into the kitchen and sort them into piles and then by 6.30 I'm ready to start scrubbing. Each thing to wash you wet in the warm water and then throw it in the boiler to boil awhile. The steam rises everywhere till the whole house is like one of them Finnish saunas. Then you take a wooden spoon and start fishin'. One at a time you pull the steamy things out of the boiler and you hold them there heavy and steaming that they are ... Then when they cool enough to touch you start scrubbing, rubbing the thing against the scrub board and rubbing with soap and a scrub brush. Oh and I forgot the soap, which you couldn't forget because you had to get it ready the day before by taking a bar of soap and grating it into flakes so it would dissolve easier. So then you scrub each thing and there were hundreds and the steam is boiling and the clothes are hot and heavy and when you've scrubbed it you throws it into a pail of warm water for rinsing then you squeeze it out, and you have to squeeze so hard and your arms already tired and it's so hot. Then you rinse again and wring and then pile all the stuff into the basket and carry it outside and one by one hang each piece on the line to dry and you have to hang them just right or you'll never iron the wrinkles out and that takes till 6.30 or 7.00 of an evening when he wants his supper and you go to sleep like the dead, hot and weary and worn to the bone ... All the while you had to keep stoking up the stove to keep it hot enough to keep the water boiling ... and all the water splashed on the floor so when I finished I had to scrub the kitchen floor too. And we didn't have no plastic clothes line, only linen so it had to be strung up before clothes could be hung. And of course you were forever slipping in the water and losing your balance and hitting that fiery stove and of course the kids wanted looking after all day at the same time. Well that was Blue Monday all right.[69]

Winter wash day brought its own hardship too, with clothes frozen heavy on the line.

Technological innovations connected with laundry transformed wash day in terms of physical labour and time. Mass-produced washing machines were available in the 1930s (although households hit by the Depression could not purchase them) and continuing innovations made washing an automatic procedure for many by the 1950s: dirty clothes were put in the machine, and clean wrung clothes came out, with no manual interruption of the process. By the 1960s dryers too were widespread.

Other household cleaning processes were also modified by new tools. The twentieth century brought a shift away from the traditional home harbouring greasy smoke from wood stoves and oil lamps, the smell of urine from chamber pots, and the mess from fuel and water spilled in transit from their storage places. Electricity and centralized sewage and heating systems reduced the amount of dirt and untidiness. This process came relatively late to Manitoba: rural electrification was not completed until the early 1950s.

With electricity all sorts of useful tools were introduced into the household: irons, refrigerators, and vacuum cleaners became widespread. Dishwashers were not as universally acquired, but Luxton found them appreciated. Another technical development which aided cleaning was the move towards standardization of materials for fixtures and tools. More construction materials and tools were made out of plastics and stainless steel rather than a diversity of copper, brass, and wood. These materials required less and less frequent cleaning as well as fewer varieties of cleaners. Nevertheless Luxton discovered that in 1976 an average of over eight hours per week was still spent on cleaning. It was frustrating for domestic workers to spend this time in eliminating dirt and in bringing order to the household, when both these achievements could be, and often were, so easily jeopardized by other household members.[70]

Many housewives preferred to spend time in food preparation and cooking. This single category absorbed more time than any other household job – an average of more than three hours per day. Sometimes a husband and children would help with preparation, and meals were important social occasions, so it was less isolated work than cleaning. Again, technology changed this work. Tools, gadgets, and differently powered and designed stoves reduced the requirements for muscle power. Prepared convenience food, ranging from purchased canned goods at the beginning of the twentieth century to frozen foods after World War II and to pre-mixed items by the 1960s, reduced both the time and the skill needed in meal production. The women Luxton interviewed had a realistic appraisal of the social and economic dimensions of their work connected with food. "I think my food keeps this family together," said one. And referring to her husband's need for a daily packed lunch, another said: "I always pack him a real good lunch with lots in it, even the day before payday ... If he don't have a good big lunch, he just can't work." Flin Flon housewives knew that other people appreciated their cooking and meals.[71]

Shopping and the procuring of supplies was a further component of housework. In Flin Flon the first people to settle there benefited from the natural abundance of game, fish, and berries. At later periods, too, when a more sedentary existence deterred people from spending time in "hunter-gatherer" activities, there were occasions when a deer or a moose would be most appealing. This was particularly true during the Depression, and when individual families fell on rough times.[72] Exclusive dependence on wild food, or even on cultivated vegetables, became rare in recent times. Instead, people bought food and other goods. Housewives prided themselves on comparing prices and learning, often on a weekly basis, where the best bargains were. Luxton's housewives spent up to two hours per week on grocery shopping, frequently with their husband's help.[73]

Spending money was not always enjoyable. Budget management was the last major responsibility of the housewife. During the twentieth century there were changes in who controlled the family's finances. Luxton's study compared information from three generations of residents: the first were those who settled in Flin Flon before 1929; the second, between 1940 and 1959; and the third, between 1960 and 1976. In the first generation, most households (80 per cent) conformed to a pattern where the man turned over most of his wages to his wife who gave him a personal allowance, paid bills, and managed the money generally. Of the second generation, only 57 per cent followed that pattern. Eighteen per cent had the man keep the money, pay the bills, and give a housekeeping allowance to his wife. She would then ask him for money for personal expenses. A quarter of this group shared management of the family finances. In the third generation, a third followed the pattern of woman as manager, 44 per cent followed the pattern where the husband held the purse strings, and 23 per cent shared management. So although there was considerable variety, one model, where the housewife managed the budget, predominated.[74]

The financial control implied by this analysis, however, was often elusive. Flin Flon women often said they felt powerless. The money was earned by someone else and the wives appeared to feel they were not free to decide how to spend it. They frequently experienced frustration in attempts to satisfy individual preferences in their families. Further frustration ensued when their disposable income did not even meet the demands of household expenses. Two basic options were open when debt loomed, besides cutting back on consumption.

One way of adding to the family income was to complement domestic labour: the housewife, usually on a temporary basis, could take in work. She catered for boarders or provided informal day care by supervising the children of mothers working in the paid labour force. She worked for others, for instance by doing laundry, baking, dressmaking, and knitting. As the century progressed, other avenues opened up. The housewife could provide personal services, such as hairdressing, or give craft lessons, such as how to do macramé work. She might sell items such as Tupperware, a business structured around sales representatives working out of their own premises. All of these devices permitted a housewife to apply some of her time to wage-remunerated labour while remaining physically in the home.[75]

In 1908 J.S. Woodsworth showed how widespread this practice was. He visited the homes in his parish and wrote an article describing how his parishioners lived. Boarders and "roomers" were taken for granted even when the family had only three, or fewer, rooms in which to live. Five years later, Woodsworth wrote a series of articles on "A Workman's Budget" for the *Christian Guardian*, official organ of the Methodist Church. In one he referred to the wife's dressmaking yielding an average of $2 a week, in the context of an annual family budget of $900. In addition, she kept lodgers. Without her financial contribution, the household economy would have been even more impoverished.[76]

During the Depression, many women took in roomers to make ends meet. The Winnipeg writer, Adele Wiseman, describes this experience:

There was one winter when the three-bedroom house had roomers in at least two and sometimes all three ... bedrooms. To sleep, we were moved around in the living room and in the dining room, just wherever we could sort out places. My dad was in Vancouver looking for work, and a down-and-outer came to the door. He was either Ukrainian or Polish – to my mother all people in trouble were the same – and he had been turned away from one of the shelters because he didn't have the necessary two bits. Mom told him that if he looked after the furnace he could sleep downstairs. He put up some boards on four logs, Mom gave him bedding and he slept down there for the whole winter. Mom fed him and he looked after the furnace.[77]

A second way of adding to household income was for the housewife to enter the formal labour market outside the home. By taking the housewife away from the place of her domestic labour this option contradicted a widespread expectation that her time would be totally absorbed by housewifery. However, the contrast between taking work in, and putting herself out, in order to earn wages was more apparent than real. In both instances, time and energy were diverted into work which was exchanged for cash and in both instances the housewife almost invariably retained exclusive responsibility for domestic labour. Often the work she performed outside her own home was domestic labour in someone else's. The result was a double load. The housewife continued to care for husband, children, and house and at the same time reduced her capacity to do so by sharing with her husband the breadwinning function. Making ends meet meant stretching herself very thin. Studies of domestic labour in households where both spouses were in the paid labour force demonstrated that domestic labour was rarely shared. The wife performed what work was done, decreasing both her own leisure time and her standards of cleanliness and comfort at home.[78]

Full-time homemaking as a way of life for women was under review by 1970. Betty Friedan's book, *The Feminine Mystique*, excoriated modern housekeeping as boring, demeaning, and alienating. However, many of the homemakers living in the new postwar suburbs appreciated opportunities for family and community living within a safe and comfortable environment: women were "both victims and beneficiaries of a nation's experiment with residential enclaves that celebrated the gendered division of labour."[79] By 1970 some critics seriously started to question the marketplace economics creating the conditions of women's work in the home and began to interrogate the value of consumer goods bought for the family.

There was a long history behind consumerism. In the eighteenth century Adam Smith recognized the potential of women as household consumers.[80] During World War I women began to behave more self-consciously as careful buyers. Margaret McWilliams, in 1916 a six-year resident of Winnipeg, addressed the University Women's Club that year on "the present situation in Winnipeg with regard to the prices of various foods, and gave some of the facts regarding apparently very great profits made by some firms supplying food."[81] Price monitoring of food like bread and milk was at this time a minority concern of a few civic-minded women. Later, similar concerns were voiced by Labour women. In 1930 the Winnipeg Independent Labour Party organized a mass meeting of women during the civic election campaign. The single Independent Labour Party woman candidate advocated a socialist solution to the high price of food. She wished to see the municipal ownership and distribution of necessities like bread and milk. She condemned "the outrage of the milling companies gambling in grain and making large profits, resulting in high bread prices though wheat costs were low."[82]

These women shared a suspicion of the price-setting powers of big business. They registered protests against them and also advocated an alternative economy. Labour women preferred a socialist solution, and while McWilliams shied away from complete state control, she nevertheless advocated centralized state planning in *If I Were King of Canada*, a book she wrote with her husband in 1931.[83] Farm women, too, had long criticized the discrepancy between the low prices paid to food producers and the high prices charged for food in the stores.[84] Before World War II in Manitoba, women in organizations like the United Farm Women of Manitoba, the Local Council of Women, and the Independent Labour Party gave leadership to a growing activism among women as consumers. These women still accepted the traditional duties of housewife and mother, but by no means passively. Many submitted those responsibilities to critical appraisal.

Activism increased after the Second World War when the Canadian Association of Consumers (CAC) was founded as an indirect extension to the Wartime Prices Board. In November 1947 a Manitoba chapter was founded when Margaret McWilliams "called together the provincial representatives" of the groups which had established the national association, a list which read like a roll call of the organizations which had nurtured liberal feminism in the interwar years. In Manitoba the new officers were "of the highest calibre – well-educated women, consumer-minded, trusted by all sections of the community, with long experience in women's organizations ... top-notch people ... willing to work incredibly hard to set up the new organization."[85]

Margaret Stansfield, daughter of Mary Speechly, when looking back over the early years of the Manitoba chapter, spelled out the difficulty any consumers' organization had in remaining independent of established interest groups:

We found that some intelligent consumers were hobbled by divided interests. One bright gal, the wife of an electrical contractor cancelled her membership in CAC because of our stand on Retail Price Maintenance. Another who had done valuable work in war-time rationing, withdrew from the provincial board because we worked for the legalizing of margarine – her husband owned a large dairy herd. Labour women, enthusiastic at the start, parted company with CAC because we held that if prices were controlled there must also be a ceiling on wages. And there is no doubt that masses of unthinking women found it easier to pressure their husbands to get higher wages, rather than to use their existing pay cheques more wisely.[86]

By 1970 the association was claiming credit for achievements such as standards for sausage and ground beef, standards for the sizing and quality of children's garments, vitaminized apple juice, coloured margarine, accurate labelling of foodstuffs, and the maintenance of milk prices. The provincial, as well as the national, association presented regular briefs to government committees and sent representatives to marketing boards. Since 1947, its membership had tripled.[87] This organizational involvement often led to wider fields of action. Many members of the Manitoba association joined in the demand for a royal commission on the status of women. Their formation as feminists was nourished in consumerism.[88] The tasks embraced in homemaking could nurture a critical concern for the way women were treated not only by big business but by other sections of the community.

ℱARM WORK

For most of the century 1870–1970 in Manitoba, most people lived in rural areas, and most of them lived and worked on farms.[1] But women's work on farms suffered the same fate as women's work in the household. Transparently obvious, it was invisible to official recorders who fell "victim to male bias" in their indifference to depicting women's work in agriculture.[2]

The agricultural work of First Nations women suffered from another sort of bias in the accounts of historians recording their society before 1870. Observers noted that First Nations women in southern areas of Canada, such as the Ojibwa (or Saulteaux), processed meat and hides from large hunted animals, trapped smaller animals, did much of the planting, hoeing, and harvesting of crops, and collected and processed prairie turnips, wild rice, and maple sugar.[3] Because so much of their work required hard physical labour the common interpretation of the white, male, middle-class recorders, many of them missionaries, was that the women were unfeminine drudges, suffering as a result of their men's pagan and barbaric attitudes towards women and clearly not conforming to the dominant Victorian ideas of womanhood prevalent in North America and Europe.[4] Only in the last twenty years have historians begun to reassess women's contributions to the First Nations economy. After aboriginal peoples in Manitoba were regulated by the Indian Act women continued to perform much of their traditional work on the reserves and their adaptabaility was crucial for the cultural and physical survival of their communities: "It was the more traditional work of women in diversifying the economic base of the community that saw the people through these lean years."[5] However, the transition to reservation life meant that few First Nations peoples were permitted to farm in the same way as their white neighbours.[6]

Work on the farm for many generations was mainly performed by immigrants from other areas of North America and the world.

Farm work in all the prairie provinces was infused with the myths of pioneering. Free land offered the opportunity to cultivate a "site for utopia." As Gerald Friesen wrote, the prairie west "could re-create the individual just as it improved upon the social order."[7] Rural life was celebrated by the homesteaders whose initiative, independence, ingenuity, and perseverance brought rewards. Successful pioneers shared the romantic stuff of dreams that were already part of a cultural landscape formed by previous generations of farm pioneers in the United States.[8] Women could partake of the pioneer mythology too but not as independent contractors: few women qualified to be homesteaders in their own right. Women were to be the helpmeet partners of the male farmer. Even in the rosy hues painted in the pictures of immigrant literature, their hard work was acknowledged.[9] Over the century working conditions changed, along with farm technology, size, and productivity. This chapter examines women's actual work on the farm rather than the images of myth.

Until recently, accounts of farming in Manitoba recognized farm women's economic role, if at all, only in their work as housewives in the farmhouse. Descriptions of farming routines focused on farm commodity production and identified male activity only. This approach served to obscure women's participation in the production of farm commodities. Further, gender-specific work performed only by women was largely ignored. Descriptions of farm technology were confined to tools handled by men. Even in the acknowledgement of women's role as homemaker, women's work was characterized as lacking "normal or typical routines" in comparison with the steady, reliable, and predictable work of men, despite the evidence to the contrary provided in an autobiography of a farm woman's work in Alberta.[10] A 1988 study analysing women's farm work more carefully restored "a man's and woman's *mutual* efforts" to their joint responsibility for success or failure on the farm.[11]

The farm wife's position in law was at first very vulnerable. She had little protection. Land ownership was the basic form of security. Yet the common law denied any claim of married women to own property. In the absence of a specific settlement at the time of marriage, which could establish a trust for the wife managed by designated male persons, a wife had no say in the disposition of land or other property connected with a farm or any other family resource. The common law itself had recognized this problem and made some attempt to provide a remedy through the concept of dower: the right of a widow to an interest for her life in one-third of the real property owned by her husband at any time during the marriage. Not only did this provide some security for a woman at the death of her husband, it also meant that any land sold during the marriage would be subject to her dower right. Her consent was necessary if property was sold, mortgaged, or given away.[12] In 1885 dower was abolished in Manitoba in order to eliminate encumbrances on land and to allow for a more efficient land registration system for the thousands of immigrants wishing to settle on homesteads. The position of women was even more vulnerable.

Organizations like the Woman's Christian Temperance Union, the Local Council of Women, and the University Women's Club all advocated a return to the security represented by dower, and in 1912 Manitoba introduced a very limited form of security for widows in An Act for the Relief of Widows and Children. Not until 1918 did widows gain a right to a life interest in the estates of their dead husbands. This gave no equal right to family property, however, and was only a modest curtailment of "patriarchy preserved on the prairies."[13]

Until the First World War, then, the majority of married women who lived in Manitoba, on a farm or anywhere else, had no security beyond what their husband in person could provide during his life. Nor could a married woman own the farm in her own name. The 1872 Dominion Lands Act allowed "every person who is the sole head of a family" to apply as well as any male aged eighteen years or older. Among women, only widows, divorcees, or separated wives, if they had dependent children under eighteen, were eligible. The tiny number of women who did come to own farms in their own names in the decades before World War I generally did so not through the Lands Act, but by purchase.[14]

Frontier conditions created fundamentally different demands on farmers than those of the more developed parts of the province. During the first ten years of homesteading, pioneer farmers could call on no economic substructure. There were few towns or country stores. A family had to produce as much as possible of its own food.[15] Before a farmer could even contemplate growing a cash crop, land for a vegetable garden was cleared. Few families were well acquainted with local soil and climatic conditions. Farming methods followed in the Red River settlement were the model: ploughs and carts pulled by oxen, crops harvested by scythes and raked by hand, grain sheaves bound and stooked by hand.[16] Hard physical labour, especially when the land was bush, or wooded, or stony, was required. The muscle power of men and women as well as that of oxen or horses was needed. A farm couple would construct the house together. Generally, "settlements were too sparse for neighbouring men to organize land-breaking and construction bees."[17] Adults, both men and women, expected to work together until the homestead was established.

Only immigrants who possessed considerable assets could do without women's labour. In 1888 A.J. Cotton arrived at Treherne, to the west of Portage la Prairie, with livestock, horses, a rail car of goods, and his own hired man as well as capital in cash and in Ontario. That first year, the Cotton family was able to camp out "in the abandoned shell of a neighbouring farm."[18] Their experience was untypical. In their first few years, most families needed all the help they could get, including women's, merely to construct a dwelling. "Women cleared, dug and built, despite their ongoing, gender-specific reponsibilities for food preservation, sewing, child care and numerous domestic work processes." Few women could afford to take much time away from this routine work, even when a new child was born.[19] "Families deprived of adult women due to illness and death were seriously debilitated" because men and children rarely knew how to orchestrate the gender-specific tasks performed by the women in addition to the work they shared with their husbands. The progress of bachelor farmers was generally expected to be slow.[20] The high failure rate of bachelor homesteaders and the tendency of widowers to remarry emphasized the importance of a woman's labour on the farm, especially in the early years when a strong back and versatile skills were at a premium.[21]

Such frontier pioneer conditions continued to be the norm in newly opened territory over the next two generations, but in the areas already settled, primarily in southern and southwestern Manitoba, economic conditions changed rapidly with the coming of the railway in the 1880s. Towns grew and were maintained as local service centres: it was no longer imperative for a family to accord absolute priority to subsistence agriculture. Railways gave access to the international markets for grain and research developed new strains of wheat better able to withstand the rigours of the prairie climate. Manual technology gave way to assembly-line commercial production. Heavy investment in monumental binding, threshing, and harvesting machines focused the attention not only of farmers, but also of subsequent historians, on the outward manifestations of these dramatic developments of industrialization applied to agriculture.[22]

With these changes women's work shifted as well, but it remained directly related to the family's capital assets. Those without the means to acquire the new machinery retained more of the former task-shared way of work. Others, like Nellie McClung's family, experienced a more rigid division of labour. Her father "was sixty-nine at this time, but he was strong and well, and worked as long hours as the boys" with the huge harvest binder while the job of the teenaged girls was to carry the lunches out to the fields.[23]

Women withdrew from field work because their labour was needed for other tasks. Fewer tasks were shared with men, but the time thus released went not into leisure but into different jobs equally important for the prosperity of the farm. Women were both pulled and pushed away from shared labour and this resulted in a more complete sexual segregation of the agricultural work force than was the case in a subsistence economy.[24] Anthropologist Carolina Van de Vorst identified the major factors pulling women's labour away from field work: women increased their work load in subsistence activities (at the same time that men *decreased* theirs), women continued to care for livestock, and higher standards of housekeeping demanded more domestic commitment on the part of the female farmer. There was also a powerful push factor: a new predominance of men in field work reduced the demand for women there.

As machines made their way onto the field, mechanics were needed for maintenance duties. A thresher, for instance, was powered by a steam engine attached by a large rubber belt. The crew included an engineer, a tank-man, and a fireman. As more men operated the various machines, men drove and led the teams of horses which pulled the machines and then the harvested grain to the granaries. A threshing crew could easily contain over twenty men. Many of the lesser skilled of this labour force were now recruited from the harvest excursion trains operated after 1890. Thousands of single men were transported from eastern Canada to provide casual labour at harvest time. Another source of labour was found among the men from the newer pioneer areas of the province who took the opportunity to earn cash to support their own family's requirements. Finally, the labour force was augmented by the single adult sons of earlier settlers. The need for brute strength and skilled mechanics, reinforced by stereotyped expectations of masculinity, served to push women from field work. Oral history interviews with women showed that they worked in the fields only when men were unavailable or unaffordable – during the Depression, or the wars, for example.[25]

The other side of this coin was an increase in women's domestic work because they had to cook for the increased numbers of field workers in the crews and for permanent hired men. Harvest time was the peak of the year for all workers and was vividly inscribed in the memory. Jane Aberson came to Canada from Holland in 1925 to live with her husband who had arrived the previous year. Their farm near Swan River was not very prosperous and she turned to journalism to augment their income, sending a bimonthly column, "From the Canadian Prairies," to her home town newspaper between 1929 and

Women Haying, 1916. (Provincial Archives of Manitoba, Jessop Collection)

1966.[26] Her 1931 analysis of women's work at threshing time, quoted in the appendix to this chapter, revealed the stress of this work and the continuing pressure from simultaneous child-care responsibilities.

Although harvest time was the "crown on a whole year's work" for the farm family, the farm wife had plenty of other food-related tasks over the year. She raised chickens. She supervised the garden. Canning had to be done when the vegetables and fruit were ripe. Some food could be purchased rather than made: a contributor to the *Grain Growers' Guide* in 1923 wrote that "anyone who has tried buying their bread ... will never again attempt baking during the threshing season."[27] During the poverty of the Depression, farm women became highly adept at subsistence production. In 1930, the government's Canadian Pioneer Problems Committee found that farm families had to purchase only about half of their household needs – the rest they produced themselves.[28] In the early 1940s, E. Cora Hind, agricultural correspondent of the *Winnipeg Free Press*, considered it was "quite possible for a family to live in Western Canada and produce practically everything absolutely essential for a comfortable living."[29]

Men's involvement in subsistence work declined from the little they did in pioneer days because of their service work, over the winter, in other tasks: hauling grain to the elevator, cutting and hauling wood for construction and fuel, and cutting ice. One woman who lived near

Portage la Prairie described the men "hauling home huge blocks of ice, cut from deep water, usually from Crescent Lake ... hauled home on a wide flat platform, fastened to bobsleds, pulled by horses. The ice was packed in sawdust (clean every year) and put into an ice house. This ice house was a low building or frame, over a fairly deep cellar place. Ours was made of logs, plastered and whitewashed, and had a regular roof. The ice 'kept' all summer. We had an 'ice' refrigerator and the top part, where modern refrigerators keep frozen foods, was filled with a block of ice, every four or five days. As it melted, water ran down a tube into a pan under the refrigerator. This pan had to be drawn out and emptied every day."[30]

As farms became more prosperous, the male labour force became larger and more food was needed to sustain the men. Women took on responsibility for livestock: "You had to look after everything that was living." Chickens, cattle, and pigs were kept. Surplus produce, and young animals, were sold for profit. Poultry, from setting the eggs through to the slaughter of the birds, was women's responsibility. So were the pigs kept for household consumption. While men usually cared for horses, women looked after the cows. This care included watering and pasturing as well as milking and then processing the milk into butter and cheese or transporting it to a local creamery. Animal care was "twenty-four hours a day, 365 days of the year."[31]

The countryside, like the towns, was affected by the industrialization of housekeeping. Paradoxically this reduced much of the drudgery of housework while transforming the work by the demand for higher standards. Mechanization introduced newer tasks and greater variety into the repertoire of all homemakers, but there was a difference between urban and rural homes: "Anyone who gives the matter a thought knows how much easier housekeeping is in town than it is on the farm," according to the *Grain Growers' Guide* in 1915.[32] The farm wife's experience tended to be different from that of urban women at least before the advent of running water and rural electrification in the 1950s: she had fewer "labour savers." For at least a generation longer than women in towns, she worked without a power refrigerator, washing machine, or vacuum cleaner, and consequently had to spend more resources of time and energy on daily routine.

Barry Broadfoot included a tribute to the coming of the hydro in his *Next-Year Country*:

When you read these historical books ... there's one thing that never seems to get mentioned. It was the most important thing of all, I think, and that was when the farms and villages and little towns got the hydro. Before that, farming was a real chore ... It is still hard work, but think what it was like with no

Beet Harvesters. (Provincial Archives of Manitoba, Martha Knapp Collection 99)

electricity. The hydro ... made the farmer's wife's job at least twice as easy. She could turn on the electric stove in the morning ... before that, you'd have to put the twisted paper in the box and then a bit of kindling and sprinkle coal on the top and light it and you'd wait and wait ... Wood. Ever see those wood-piles in the yards in the fall? Yea tall and this wide, like an old straw sack. And that was just one winter's wood.[33]

It is misleading to assume that farm women's absence from the fields gave them only an auxiliary role in the agricultural economy. Women's subsistence work enhanced the resources which could be devoted to commodity production. Additionally, right from the beginning women also generated cash income. Some hired out their labour in domestic service or as casual agricutural help, particularly in harvesting vegetables. Many marketed poultry and dairy products. Some developed cottage industries, often based on needlework.[34] Some women, especially in the poorer areas, sold cordwood or wild food like berries or seneca roots that were used as a remedy against snakebite. In southeastern Manitoba during the First World War, "it was hard to make a living on a stony farm and it was necessary to do something else to earn a little money":

We found that it was still possible to dig seneca roots south of the Boundary Line. In Canada, the root areas were all pretty well dug up. About eight of us women decided to go root digging. My husband drove us southeast into the States where we found a vacant house ... That was where we slept ... each night we would return to "our house" with a couple of sacks of green roots. We made

Potato Pickers, 1927. By Marie Guest. (Courtesy of Hessie Guest)

our meals out of the supplies we brought with us and would retire early: we were tired after working long hours each day ... After a few day of digging, we began to search for a better ridge ... the Indians noticed us in the clearing and the men got on their ponies and started to chase us ... When we sold our Minnesota-picked seneca roots, we earned more than we ever expected, but it was a horrible ordeal.[35]

Often seneca roots or other wild foods were bartered for flour and groceries. Another woman in the Gardenton area near Tolstoi joined with two companions on a seneca-gathering expedition, then "took the roots to the store and was able to get two bags of flour, some sugar, salt and soap in trade. This lasted us for about two weeks and I had to go back again to get more roots."[36] Mary Thomson, who was living on a farm near Portage la Prairie in 1907, recorded a reverse transaction in her diary: "August 14. Indians came along and I traded a loaf of bread, butter, cookies for some saskatoons."[37]

A survey completed halfway through the century 1870–1970 affords a snapshot of women's work on the farm, obviously typical for certain farms in 1922, but also relevant before and after. "You just did what had to be done," said farm wives working in Saskatchewan during the 1940s, confirming the general picture arising from the 1922 Manitoba

survey.[38] This survey was organized by the United Farm Women of
Manitoba, which had a membership of 2,151 in 1922. The organization employed a full-time secretary in Winnipeg and had representation
on several federal and provincial boards concerned with farm women's
interests. Its board asked for co-operation on a survey "so that we,
as farm women, can work for the things most needed" in farm homes.
They wanted to document the conditions in which their members
worked. Over 350 questionnaires were eventually returned.[39]

The respondents enjoyed greater prosperity than the rural population
as a whole: a higher proportion owned their farms and more owned
larger farms; they tended to live in larger houses; and they resided in
the more settled parts of the province. Nevertheless, less than half had a
hired man (and often only from time to time) and only 14 per cent said
they had domestic help. Most people lived within two or three miles of
school and church but had to travel seven or eight miles for shopping.
A high proportion of respondents, 70 per cent, had a telephone, but
fewer could overcome their relative isolation with the ability to drive a
car or truck: only 22 per cent of the women said they could drive themselves. They were the most favoured of Manitoba farm women, yet
their work in 1922 was unrelenting. The vast majority did some sort of
outside work, interpreted to mean work in the farmyard rather than in
the fields. In the house, few had piped water and only a quarter had an
indoor toilet. They had to fetch water daily from an outside source.
Less than half had "machine power," which would usually be provided,
if at all, from a generator, and those who had it used it for the cream
separator rather than for domestic appliances like a washing machine.[40]
"With a little thought and a minimum of expense," wrote Mrs James
Elliott, who prepared the report, could those farms with power "not
extend it a little further and do a few more of the woman-killing
chores?" Drawing a female conclusion about the purchase of prestige-
related farm machinery, she noted: "If a woman were allowed the sale
price of the half-worn, discarded, and need-never-have-been-bought
machinery on the ordinary farm, she would be able to install a conve-
nient water system in the home, which would tend to preserve her
strength and the health of not only herself, but the whole family."[41]

Only a quarter of the survey's respondents declared that they took a
vacation of any sort during the year. However, most took newspapers
and magazines, and only 14 per cent had no musical instrument
for leisure time.[42] If this hard work was typical of the more privileged
of Manitoba farm women, we can imagine how much more difficult
life was for the newer immigrants and poorer families. Through a
remarkable essay competition organized by the *Grain Growers' Guide*
– also in 1922 – we can glimpse in their own words the attitudes of
farm women towards their work.

The *Guide* asked the question, "If you had a daughter of marriage-able age, would you, in the light of your experience as a farm woman, want her to marry a farmer and make her future life on the farm?" Over 80 per cent who responded said yes, but there was a stoic acknowledgement of the overwork, monotony, loneliness, and financial pressure. Some were more critical. There was "not much encourage-ment for the growth of any of the virtues except it be patience." Sanita-tion was "hit or miss." There was a deplorable lack of facilities for women in childbirth. Schooling was "oftimes in the hands of a young, inexperienced and inefficient teacher." Some proud feminist claims were nevertheless made for the farm woman. A farm wife and her hus-band were "real partners." The opportunities for the farm woman to contribute cash to the family income allowed her to earn money "with-out losing social position." The average farmer "does not mind getting ready a meal occasionally, will lend a hand with the washer or anything that threatens to be a stress" in genuine "team work."[43]

After the Second World War mixed farming gave way to specialized commercial farming. Between 1941 and 1971, the number of farms in Manitoba declined from 58,024 to 34,981.[44] "In 1971 there was one car per family, two trucks, two tractors and nearly one combine."[45] Women no longer had to raise poultry, cattle, and pigs to feed the labour force. Instead, the women drove the machines and assumed many of the managerial responsibilities of the farm. If domestic help had not been plentiful in the past, it became almost non-existent by 1970. Moreover, farm women were sometimes employed off the farm as well.[46]

"I do not believe that farmers' wives are a down-trodden class of women ... They have their troubles, but there are compensations," wrote Nellie McClung in 1915. Certainly, many farm wives believed they were equal partners with their husbands.[47] "We may be the freest and happiest women on the earth in some respects," wrote a corre-spondent to the *Grain Growers' Guide* in 1925, and "we are certainly the busiest. No other class of women on earth are such close partners in their husband's business."[48] However, their "inequitable" work load reduced their ability to serve as advocates in their own cause. Veronica Strong-Boag argues: "Here was a major explanation for women's failure to seize the promise of the vote. They were already too hard pressed, as McClung lamented, as 'the unpaid servants of men,'" and as their farm work was unpaid, it attracted no formal recognition.[49]

Farm wives were in law as vulnerable as other dependents, despite their economic contributions. In 1968 this vulnerability was docu-mented by the Manitoba Committee on the Status of Women: "Many married couples own their farms or small businesses in 'joint tenancy'. But this does not seem to be recognized as a true partnership ... The non-wage earning wife is not considered to be in true partnership with her husband, nor is she considered as an economic asset by her country."[50] Farm work, like housework, still awaited its just deserts.

APPENDIX: HARVEST TIME 1931

... We copy the Canadian way, and at threshing time, of course, we need to follow Canadian customs.

Instead of making threshing meals simple but good they are regular feasts. As a newcomer I do not have the nerve to do it differently. For the men who are threshing the food is the highlight of the day. There are tales galore about threshing gangs that threatened to strike because they were not satisfied with the food.

The first few years I dreaded these days. Sometimes I could get help from a very young girl, but more often I had to handle it alone. Bread, cakes, cookies, tarts, etc., must all be homemade. You can buy these in a bakery in town, of course, but the homemade baked goods are far better ...

On threshing days our alarm clock rings at half past three. This is quite unusual for us because normally we get up at five o'clock in the summer and an hour later in the winter. So we are pretty drowsy when we start to light the coal oil lamps. Outside in the caboose there is no sign of life where the men are still sleeping. It does not take them more than half an hour to feed and harness their horses.

The house looks strange as we walk around in it. All unnecessary furniture has been carried outside. The table covers practically the whole length of the room, and boards on both sides of it serve as seats. Each person has a dinner plate and a porridge bowl. Next to each plate is a fruit dish, knife, fork and spoon. My head starts to reel already. As soon as the water boils I need to cook the rolled oats in it, and while this is boiling I must slice the cold potatoes left over from last night. I will need two frying pans because the workers like lots of potatoes. When the potatoes are done I empty them into a few bowls because now I need the frying pans for bacon and eggs. I run back and forth between table and stove because I need to slice the bread. I hope four loaves will be enough. And now the cake – two platters of cake need to be served for breakfast. Who ever heard of cake for breakfast? Two quart jars with canned fruit need to be opened and put into bowls. Did I forget anything now? Oh, sure enough! They have to have pickles. Without pickles it would not be a Canadian meal. Canadians serve pickles even with tea.

Right on the dot of five o'clock the whole caravan comes shuffling in. Some of the men are quite jovial and wish me a good morning, but others don't say anything. I don't notice that anyway – I only see that long table with the confusion of plates and bowls and platters full of food. Moreover I have my hands full filling all the teacups and handing filled porridge bowls to the men.

"More tea, please?" one jiggles his teacup. "More potatoes, missus" says another one. Quickly I fill the bowls again. "Is everybody here?" I ask. Two more men are coming, I am told, and the fireman is to have his breakfast at the threshing machine. While they are finishing their meal I pack the fireman's breakfast in a little box. With a sigh of relief I see them get up and leave the house.

Outside in the field the sun has risen and they are busy getting the engine of the threshing machine started. Exactly at six o'clock the whistle blows. They have started, and after a minute I see the dust from the threshing fly up again.

Relief until eleven o'clock! Then they will come in for their dinner. First I must wash all those dirty dishes, and then wake up the children. Better make the school lunch before I wake them. Afterwards, while the stack of dirty dishes slowly goes down and the stack of clean ones grows, I look out over the field again and see it bathed in brilliant sunshine. What a privileged country with so much sunshine! The men are making good headway in the field. Most of the wheat stooks have already disappeared.

These are wonderful days, really, the crown on a whole year's work, even if there is a bit too much work to do. A grain wagon comes into the barnyard again. I wave my dish towel and Bob waves back. We have had good crops the last few years, and that always makes these days exhilarating. The black spook of very low prices is pushed aside for the moment. That disenchantment will come back later.

When all the dishes are cleaned and piled up at the end of the table, I put down three smaller plates. Now I have the joy to top all joys – to sit on those wooden benches myself and eat from that immense table.

"Mammie, can we eat the same things the threshers have had? Please, please?" Bobby is a bit put out that he has to go to school while his little brothers will have all the fun today. There are so many cakes and cookies around, you can be sure they will have their share of them, not to forget the fun of riding with Daddy on the grain wagon. A few extras in Bobby's lunchbox will cheer him up a bit.

It is now eight o'clock, nice and early. I am sure I will be ready in plenty of time. Better start peeling that big pail of potatoes, then get a bunch of vegetables from the garden and wash them. Soon it will be time to put the meat in the oven. Later I will need the oven again to bake the pies. I better start setting the table again, put more sugar in the bowls and fill the salt and pepper shakers. Will there be enough bread for today? They eat bread here at every meal, which is why it disappears so fast. I am sure I can manage today, but tomorrow I will need to bake a new batch. I had better set the yeast at four o'clock. I write that on the blackboard, otherwise I am sure to forget it.

Now it is half past nine already. I better start making the pies. Pie is practically the only dessert served here. Pudding will be served the odd time, but pie is definitely the favourite. It is pie on Sunday and pie during the week. Pull out a piece of dough, line an enamel plate with it, fill it up with some kind of fruit, and then put another slab of dough on top. Make a nice design on it with a knife point so the air can escape while it bakes. After half an hour I have six pies standing in a row. The pies go in the oven at ten o'clock to be ready by eleven. While all this is cooking I quickly whip up a cake. That will need to be ready for the lunch in the afternoon.

Now the men come in for dinner and the breakfast story is repeated. The men come in, eat and leave me with a big mess. I need to watch the clock. Lunch must be served in the field at four o'clock, and that is a lot of work. Dishwashing will take more than an hour with all those greasy pots and pans. I have to rush, rush. Put Dickey in bed first for his nap, otherwise he will be trouble later on. He is a bit unwilling to leave the woodpile. Obviously the boys have had a great time there. By two o'clock the table is all cleared and the clean dishes neatly stacked at the end again.

Better make a batch of biscuits. I will need about thirty, but they do not take much time to make. When they are in the oven I can start making sandwiches. Making up four loaves of bread into sandwiches is a lot of work. I must not forget to ice the cake I baked this morning. If only my mother could see what a housekeeper I've turned into!

It is quarter after three already and soon time to boil the tea water. Start packing the lunch. This time I put the cups in a separate box, because I broke too many last time. The ride to the workers is over a rough stubble field. At quarter to four all is ready and I carry the box of goodies to the car. In front, on the floor next to my feet, is the scalding hot tea in a big kettle with a potato pricked on the spout so the tea will not splash on my feet as I cross the stubble field.

Distribution of the lunch takes place fom the running board of the car. The men come in little groups and squat around us. Sometimes they stop the threshing machine for a short while, but quite often they keep right on threshing with the men taking turns running it. In the beginning I used to send the lunch to the field and stayed home myself. But soon I heard complaints that some men did not have enough because some gluttons ate double portions. Now a watchful eye keeps them in line. I find this half hour in the fresh air very pleasant and relaxing.

Now the bustle for supper starts. It is the same as before. This meal does not differ at all from the noon meal except that pie will be substituted for cake and fruit. Meat, potatoes, vegetables, pickles, bread, etc. Around seven o'clock I put the two little ones to bed. Bobby can stay up for another hour to watch the proceedings and eat with all these men at the big table.

The first of the men start to come in for supper at about eight o'clock. I have set the table already, and wish they would hurry a bit. I am very tired now and I still have a lot of work ahead. But in the evening the men are not in a hurry. For them the only work remaining is feeding and bedding the horses, and then to bed for them. If only they would hurry a bit. All those dishes to wash yet, and to think that I need to get up again at 3.30 tomorrow morning. It makes me shudder.

The grain shovellers are tired, too. I can see it in their faces. Bob gets up from the table because he still needs to feed his animals and milk his cows. Slowly the others start to leave. Like a machine I keep on working, tired from head to toe. Not until eleven o'clock am I finished, with the table set for the next morning.

And so it goes. Every fall these days are repeated. Then the day comes that the threshing outfit departs, leaving in its wake the empty fields and an untidy house ... I am just as glad to see them go as I was to see them come.[51]

$\mathcal{P}$AID LABOUR

Most women who worked for pay in Manitoba before 1970 did so as maids, saleswomen, office workers, factory workers, teachers, or nurses. Over time, women's options increased, even though many features of the early twentieth-century labour force remained familiar.

In 1968, in Canada, Sylvia Ostry noted that "the adult male is expected to work throughout most of his adult life ... Few women, however, work throughout their lives ... The working life of most women is characterized by discontinuity: they may enter and leave the labour force several times over the course of their lives."[1] Such discontinuity was characteristic of women in the labour force by 1970. A century earlier, the model was simpler. When women worked for pay at all, the vast majority did so when they were young and single and they retired permanently when they married.

One change over time therefore was women's likelihood of re-entering the labour force after a temporary retirement for child rearing. A second, related, change was the increase in the overall participation rate of women in the labour force, and a third was in the nature and level of occupations women were likely to follow. These three major developments were general in the Western industrialized world.[2] Other characteristics of the Canadian female labour force similarly echoed international developments. For example, both women's earnings and their hours of paid work were less than men's, and women tended to cluster in certain occupations and in lower-paying jobs than men.[3]

Legislation regulating women in the labour force took note of the intimate relationship between women's labour inside and outside the family and framed the context in which women worked for pay.

LEGISLATION:
PROTECTION OR RESTRAINT?

Laws about women in the work place in Manitoba were strongly influenced by American practice. At the end of the nineteenth century the dominant trends were found in the settlement movement and the maternalism of its leaders like Jane Addams of Hull House in Chicago. Maternalism exalted women's capacity to mother beyond the bounds of the family: motherhood bestowed an authority on women to apply the skills of family nurturing to the wider problems of society. This belief fuelled the commitment of Addams to social work and inspired the vision of thousands of single women who saw it as a paid vocation and of many more thousands of married middle-class women whose economic circumstances gave them time to do good in their community. They took a particular interest in the welfare of women and children less fortunate than themselves and enjoyed a generation of remarkable political and social power at the turn of the century. The most obvious manifestations of maternalism were contained in the laws regarding mothers' allowances or pensions, which by 1920 operated in over forty states, and in two forms of protective legislation applicable to women in the labour force: maximum hour laws and minimum wage laws.[4]

Legislation regulating women's work in Manitoba in the province's early years was motivated by humanitarian as well as maternalist considerations. Throughout Canada there was a growing consensus that the state must attempt to vitiate the exploitation of employee by employer by insisting on certain standards of safety and decency. Added to this was the gender-imbued conviction that female employees must be subject to special protection and restriction.[5] This protection was required because these women were the nation's future wives and mothers. Their chastity must be protected for their future husbands and their physical health must not be allowed to deteriorate and interfere with their future fertility.[6] Their restriction to certain hours and places of employment had the effect of reducing the competition for jobs – in effect, male workers were protected in mining work and in night employment. Women's "protection" did not go so far as to interfere with conditions of work in the area where most women were employed – domestic service, which incidentally also contributed most to men's personal comfort.

In the United States and in England protective legislation was the subject of impassioned debate among feminists. Maternalists thought that state protection was the best way to improve working conditions for women workers; egalitarian feminists resented the implication that

women were in need of protection and advocated work-place regulation which would apply to all workers regardless of gender. In the
United States the maternalists held powerful positions in the bureaucracies of state and federal governments, most notably in the Women's
Bureau, a federal agency which provided leadership for social and economic policy regarding women. They were powerful enough to ensure
the defeat of the equal rights amendment during the interwar years,
persuading enough voters that such an amendment would jeopardize
the constitutionality of protective legislation targeted at women.[7] In
England the egalitarians held more influence than in the United States,
but there was still a strong lobby in favour of protective legislation.
The issue led to an organizational split within the major feminist organization, the National Union of Societies for Equal Citizenship, after
1927. A new organization, the Open Door Council, was set up to promote equal rights, and only equal rights, for women.[8]

In Canada there were echoes of this international debate. Most
policy-makers, provincial or federal civil servants, believed they were in
the forefront of progressive thinking by favouring protective legislation
in the years before the Second World War. Afterwards, they became
more receptive to egalitarian arguments. Manitoba feminists were able
to accommodate both protective legislation and equal rights in their
approach to social policy.

Before World War I in Manitoba, Shops, Mines and Factory Acts
(1888, 1897, and 1900) stipulated safety and sanitation conditions,
restrictions on the times of women's labour, and maximum hours for
women. The legislation was a form of "legal recognition of the value of
women's reproductive role, since it protected women, as active or
potential reproducers, from being totally consumed in the productive
process."[9] The majority of women workers were unaffected by the legislation: only work places employing twenty persons or more were covered. In the interwar period the Minimum Wage Act of 1918 extended
state protection to a much larger population. Domestic servants were
still excluded but the Manitoba Minimum Wage Board set minimum
wages, hours of employment, and conditions of labour for female employees in all "mail order houses, shops and factories."[10] Offices were
excluded but retail outlets were covered.

The purpose of the act was "to defuse labour tensions at a critical
juncture" by providing a "living wage" sufficient for a single woman.[11]
An article in the *Labour Gazette*, the publication of the federal Department of Labour, elaborated on this justification. As we saw in an earlier
chapter, men were assumed to need a wage sufficient to support a family and were expected to work to improve their working conditions
by collective bargaining through trade unions. Women were assumed

to be young, single, probably living at home, without dependents, and not to be organized in a trade union. "Owing to lack of organisation they are less able than men to secure adequate wages by agreement." Women therefore needed state intervention on their behalf to improve "unduly low" wages. This in turn was supposed to reduce "unfair competition" from employers who kept their costs down at the expense of ill-paid workers.[12]

The identification of women as different from men, and in need of different work-place legislation, was a view attacked by some British feminists in 1926, as reported in the *Labour Gazette*. Challenging the maternalist supremacy within the International Labour Office, an agency of the new League of Nations in Geneva, they condemned the policy which treated women "as a class apart, without the same personal rights as men ... women should keep constant watch on this insidious tendency to restrict under the guise of protecting."[13] Debating the protection of women workers from the lethal effects of lead paint, a woman minister in Britain's Labour government defended the policy on pragmatic grounds: "If we have to wait some time longer for men to get rid of this evil, then we will not wait so long before women will get rid of it."[14] As a British working women's organization put it: "We prefer to take what regulation we can get rather than to delay it ... women are less fitted than men for certain dangers and specially heavy muscular work ... Some forms of protection are necessary for women because of their function as mothers." Not only was there no level playing field in terms of equal capacity, women were also handicapped by their work at home: "If women could be relieved of domestic duties, it may be that their resistance to industrial fatigue would approximate more nearly to that of men, but legislation has to deal with things as they are."[15] Margaret Rhondda, founder of the Open Door Council, naturally disagreed with this strategy: "The only adequate protection of women lies in giving them equal conditions of work and equal pay."[16]

During the Second World War the idea that people should be paid on the basis of their job rather than their gender became more acceptable. Although trade unions still advocated a family wage, there were other voices. In the postwar period the move away from protective legislation for women found its expression in the Manitoba Equal Pay Act of 1956 and the Employment Standards Act of 1957 which applied to both men and women. However, since few women worked in precisely the same jobs, or under exactly the same conditions, as men, women's pay remained on average substantially lower than men's. Rhondda's "equal conditions and equal pay" could not be achieved merely by legislation.

Nor by trade union bargaining. Union membership was not popular among women. "Labour lagged behind government and other organizations in its recognition of the growing role and importance of women in the work place."[17] While some women were organized and like men participated in strikes, notably the telephone operators in 1918 and those involved in the Winnipeg General Strike of 1919, women unionists in Manitoba were mainly to be found in the garment trade, although some were unionized bakers, candy makers, and bookbinders.[18] During the Depression, unions were unable to make gains for their members and even during the greater prosperity of wartime, union leadership made little effort to serve the women who were actually a majority of their workers. "Women had not been well served by their unions," concluded Mochoruk and Webber in a 1987 study.[19]

The end of the Second World War brought increased business for the garment industry, and Winnipeg factory workers benefited from a switch to the Amalgamated Clothing Workers of America and an increasing number of women served as union officials: "We were happy the much-needed union came in to protect us ... Someone stood up for us workers."[20] Still, a 1959 report of the federal Women's Bureau noted that collective agreements generally failed to insist on the implementation of equal pay even after this had been legislated, both federally and provincially.[21] Not until the 1960s did women join unions in any great numbers and these new recruits were primarily employees of government.[22] For most of the twentieth century, trade unions kept a distinct distance from women workers.

Extreme examples of this attitude were voiced in Quebec, through the trade union organization, the Catholic Workers of Canada. In wartime, when women's labour was mobilized in the service of the state for the duration of a particular emergency, the Catholic Workers Confederation urged "that women be employed only when all available male labour was exhausted."[23] At the end of the war the Canadian Catholic Confederation of Labour said it was "impossible to reconcile the presence of women in industry and commerce with the natural order of things."[24] Even in the more moderate anglophone unions, the interests of women workers were not a priority. At the first constitutional convention of the Canadian Labour Congress in 1956, "restriction of the employment of working mothers was proposed as one possible way to curb juvenile delinquency." Another traditional prejudice was voiced by a delegate who suggested that "equal pay for equal work would soon stop the hiring of women because the reason women are working is because employers hire them for less money."[25] In Ontario, women were treated little better by unions. Until the 1930s in Peterborough, "women remained largely excluded from the local unions."[26] In Toronto in the early twentieth century, wage-earning women "could not count on their class allies to shield them from the exploitive practices of employers."[27] If women met negative attitudes from the labour movement, it was hardly surprising that they looked away from collective bargaining and towards state paternalism, or maternalism, for improved working conditions.

PARTICIPATION IN THE LABOUR FORCE

Participation in the formal labour force in Manitoba changed between 1891 and 1971 with respect both to the total numbers of women involved and in comparison with men.[28] In 1891 only 9 per cent of the female population of working age, at that time defined as those aged 10 years and over, was in the labour force. This small fraction of working women was in contrast to the proportion of males in the same age group who were in the labour force: 80 per cent.

The low female figure almost doubled after World War I, with the 1921 census reporting 15 per cent of the working age female population, now defined as those aged 14 and over, in the labour force. In 1931 the female participation rate was 17 per cent, in 1941 it was 18 per cent, and in 1951, 24 per cent. In 1961 it was 31 per cent and the single largest increase took place next, to 42 per cent in 1971. Meanwhile, the male labour force remained fairly steady. In 1961, 78 per cent of men of working age were in the labour force; in 1971 the proportion was 77 per cent.

When age is taken into account, it is possible to identify which women particularly changed work habits in the twentieth century, either by not retiring at marriage or by returning to paid work after an absence. In the age category 25–44, female participation more than tripled, to 46 per cent in 1971. A more dramatic increase was in the older category, ages 45–54, where the female participation rate went from 11 per cent in 1921 to over four times that in 1971, at 50 per cent. While all female age categories showed increases, the greater increase came in the older categories. The participation rate for men of all ages remained above that for women. In 1971 the gender gap was smallest for teenagers and then grew through each age category.

In an examination of the kinds of paid work people did, the Manitoba situation mirrored general trends in Canada but also exhibited qualities peculiar to an economy which initially was overwhelmingly agricultural. Because farm wives were not counted as workers in the census, the great change over the century between a society dependent on agriculture to a more diversifed economy was not even reflected in the formal statistics. In Canada over the period 1891–1921 women were employed mainly in ten occupational groups. In 1921, in order of size, these were servants, teachers, saleswomen, dressmakers, in agricultural occupations, laundresses, wholesale and retail managers, in cotton mills, in art, music, and drama, and as milliners. This list was already different from that of 1891 in which dressmakers were higher on the list and saleswomen were not mentioned.[29]

When the occupations listed for 1921 are compared with those for 1941, 1951, and 1961, certain trends become clear. Although "domestic servant" almost disappeared in the sense of a personal household maid, many women continued to work as babysitters or related service workers. Clerical work became the largest single occupational category for women. The jobs of sales clerks, schoolteachers, dressmakers, waitresses, nurses, and telephone operators also attracted much female labour. However, by 1961 the female labour force was not concentrated in these occupations as much as it had been in 1941: diversification was becoming more apparent (52 per cent compared with 62 per cent in 1941).[30]

Female employment statistics for Manitoba and Winnipeg for the middle of the period 1870–1970 show that women were concentrated in trade, clerical, and service (both professional and personal) occupations.[31] Trade included saleswomen. Clerical meant non-managerial, non-supervisory office workers. Professional service was composed primarily of nurses and teachers. Personal service included domestic servants, hairdressers, and laundry employees.

These figures bear testimony, first to the rise of office work for women, primarily in government and banking as well as in other areas of the economy. Secondly, they reflect the assumption that some areas of work were particularly appropriate for women. The retail trade, nursing and health-related work, teaching, and the hospitality industries all retained their 1911 pre-eminence as employers of women. In Manitoba, as elsewhere, work in the newly expanding numbers of offices and retail stores, where there was no large existing male work force to offer organized resistance, absorbed a high proportion of female labour. Other heavy demands for female labour arose in areas which now provided through the market services previously performed privately by women. These "de-privatized" caring jobs were in the provision of food, drink, clothing, education, and child rearing.

Although the participation rate of women in the paid labour force increased phenomenally, there was little integration. On the whole, men and women performed their work in separate spheres. Women were concentrated not exclusively, but nevertheless overwhelmingly, in new areas of the economy and were paid for work which was not performed in a formal market economy before the twentieth century. Indeed, in earlier times, much of this work had not been paid at all. In Western society before the 1870s much of the population was poor and lacked the surplus income to buy meals and clothing manufactured outside the home. The resources needed to help infants and sick people survive did not exist. Families tended to replace dead bodies with new babies. Now, many of the familiar features of modern society were provided by the newly mobilized paid labour of women in conjunction with new technology. This trend became increasingly clear throughout the twentieth century, but it was already in place in 1911. It is a mistake to assume that the two world wars had a revolutionary impact on the labour force behaviour of women. On the contrary, trends were already in place before war drew public attention to women in the work place.[32]

When women entered the paid labour force they brought elements of their traditional domestic role into the public domain. They also brought their traditional formal gender subordination to men. In the areas where women predominated in terms of numbers, many of the executive, management, and supervisory functions were performed by men. This was dramatically evident in the health and welfare occupations. In 1971 this sector employed over four times as many women as men, yet the professionals and managers in the field were mainly men.[33] It was also a visible feature in education. Since 1885 women had outnumbered men in the teaching profession in Manitoba. In 1910 there were over three times as many women; in 1960 twice as many; and in 1971 – the gap was decreasing – there was still a preponderance: 6,945 women and 4,786 men.[34] Yet school principals and inspectors were overwhelmingly male and most of the highly trained teachers were men.[35] Just as the sort of work women mainly did was a reflection of their historical concern with nurturing and hospitality, the level at which they performed was also a reflection of their historically subordinate role within the family. The higher paying jobs were held by men, even in fields in which women were numerically dominant or formed a high proportion.

Indeed, women's subordination was most clearly displayed in earnings. In 1911 the ratio of women's average earnings to men's was $398: $706, or 56 per cent. In 1931 it was $559:$929 (60 per cent); 1951, $1,159:$2,080 (57 per cent); and in 1971, $3,020:$6,110 (49 per cent).[36] These figures must be read with caution. They do not, for example, differentiate between full-time and part-time work. In 1961, whereas approximately 90 per cent of men worked 35 or more hours per week, only some 75 per cent of women did: that is, a quarter of the female labour force worked less than a full-time work week.[37] In Canada as a whole, the great flow of women into the labour force during the 1950s and 1960s was composed disproportionately of part-time workers.[38] The fact remained that the women in the labour force earned only a little more than half of what men were paid. The explanation was that women worked in jobs, in areas, and at levels with lower rates of pay. Moreover they were paid less than men in the same positions – substantially less.[39]

Asta Oddson tabulated this discrepancy in Manitoba for 1921 and 1931, using certain specific occupations in which both men and women were employed and in which strict comparisons could in fact be made: cooks, sales clerks, schoolteachers, telegraph operators, and waiters/waitresses. Women schoolteachers earned 70 per cent of what men earned in 1921, and 75 per cent in 1931. In the other categories women earned between 50 per cent and 60 per cent of what the men earned. Most women, however, did not work in occupations where their pay could be compared directly with that of male co-workers. Oddson's work stated the average weekly earnings for all industries in Manitoba in 1936. For women, the average was $7.85, and for men, $14.73. Overall, women earned 53 per cent of what men earned.[40]

Basic labour force trends for women in Manitoba during the twentieth century tended to support one major observation. Women came out of the home to do in the public sphere what they formerly did in the private sphere. As teachers and nurses they cared for children and the sick. They manufactured and sold consumer goods which were substitutes for the clothes, food, and tools previously produced in the household. In the new bureaucracies of government and business, women staffed the subordinate jobs. In the vast majority of cases women worked under the supervision of men. Women worked for lower rates of pay and on the whole worked fewer hours than men. For the century 1870–1970 these observations applied to most of the women in the labour force in Manitoba, in Canada, and in Western industrialized society.

Throughout the Western world the single occupation which employed most women before World War II was domestic service. Beginning in the twentieth century, sales and office work both started to employ women. Manufacturing, which in Manitoba never absorbed as much of the labour force as in eastern Canada, continued to provide work for many women, especially those without the English-language skills needed in clerical work and retailing. Other new jobs in professional work were available to more educated women – teaching and nursing in particular – but a few went into the established professions of medicine and law and the emergent ones of librarianship, for example, and social work.

DOMESTIC SERVICE

In Manitoba before World War II more of the women working for wages were in domestic service than in any other job. They performed cleaning, shopping, food preparation, and child-rearing work delegated by their employer. Generally isolated from domestic servants in other households, they worked in intimacy with their own employer. The high number employed in this work was due more to a lack of alternatives than to any inherent appeal of the job. As soon as other waged opportunities became available for women, domestic servants rapidly declined as the most numerous occupational group and became instead shadows inhabiting the informal labour market of irregular work, unreported cash payments, unprotected employment, and non-existent or at most informal fringe benefits.

Housekeeping and child care as work to be done did not however evaporate along with the classification of domestic service, nor did the work cease to be performed by women. Labour in the household retained its primacy as the foremost responsibility of women and served as key to an understanding of women's status, power, and privilege, or lack thereof, in modern society. Domestic labour became the domain of unpaid workers, and few women were without experience in the field. This commonality tended to emphasize women's solidarity, but it also diverted attention away from the real economic and cultural differences dividing women. Nevertheless, acquaintance with the drudgery as well as the acknowledged satisfactions of domestic work in the home was one of the many underlying continuities between women at the beginning of the nineteenth and at the end of the twentieth centuries.

The nature of domestic service was symbolized in the domestic architecture of bourgeois homes built during the early years of Manitoban prosperity. Dalnavert was a house built in 1895 for Sir Hugh John Macdonald, son of Sir John A. Macdonald. The historian Sarah Carter compared Dalnavert's domestic setting with the residence of Louis Riel, rebel leader in the 1860s and 1880s. The single most noteworthy distinction concerned the internal division of space. In the Riel home, visitors "entered immediately into the main room, which for the winter months was the only common room for the family, serving as kitchen, dining room, sitting room, and a sleeping room at night." During their waking hours, "family members were seldom separated from one another." In the Macdonald residence, by contrast, space was rigorously divided between a family zone and a servants' area. Within the family space, privacy for each member was ensured. This was suggested by the architecture and then reinforced through new technology: heat, light, and water were spread throughout Dalnavert but in the Riel house were concentrated in the one main room.[41]

At the turn of the twentieth century, most of the population of Manitoba was rural: about three-quarters lived in the countryside in 1901. Urbanization during the first decade was rapid, and by 1911 43 per cent of the population lived in urban settlements of which the largest was Winnipeg. There was a high turnover of domestic servants: a maid generally left the work as soon as she saw an alternative. First Nations women were not recruited on a large scale. Despite the policy of the Department of Indian Affairs, whereby young aboriginal women "should be encouraged to devote themselves to domestic service among the settlers," "the practice does not appear to have become a widespread phenomenon."[42] Acting in the interest of the employers of domestic servants, middle-class women's organizations, often in concert with similar groups across Canada, made deliberate attempts to increase the supply of domestics by encouraging the immigration of single women. Their strategies included supervised immigration, reception homes, and passenger fares advanced on credit.

Boarding houses for servants known as Homes of Welcome were purpose-built in Winnipeg. One of their superintendents, Mrs. Sanford, procured servants through promotional tours in Ireland and Scotland as well as in England with her expenses paid by the federal immigration ministry. Altogether, as Marilyn Barber noted, Sanford brought two thousand domestics to Winnipeg in the first fifteen years of this century. Each domestic had to refund her fare, usually equivalent to six months' wages. This indenture was recognized as such a problem, both for the employer who had to advance the lump sum and for the maid who had no other way of repaying it besides her wages, that the practice was outlawed after the First World War. It then became harder for middle-class women to find servants, for there was little incentive for single women to immigrate until 1926 when the British government's Empire Settlement Act reduced fares and provided government loans to immigrant women who agreed to be domestic servants for one year. During the next five years, 900 British women went to Manitoba under this scheme.[43]

In addition, a larger number of unskilled workers was recruited after 1923 through an agreement reached by the federal government with the Canadian Pacific Railway and the Canadian National Railway. The railways were to be permitted to "take orders" for groups of workers from would-be employers, initially for farm placement but subsequently also for city work. Each domestic had to provide her own fare. By 1931 60 per cent of immigrant domestics were of non-British origin. A large group included in the CPR-sponsored immigration was of Russian Mennonites. They had to repay the railway company, who had advanced the fare as a loan, and all family members made what contribution they could.

Servants' wages in Winnipeg were higher than in the countryside and this drew young women (both immigrants and those in rural areas) to the city. Young Mennonite women often sought work as domestics as their lack of education, especially in English, reduced their eligibility for other jobs. Their families considered work in a domestic environment safer than in a factory, and they had received extensive training in housework in their own households. To protect young women in the city, the Mennonite community, like other ethnic-centred groups, established two Homes of Welcome in Winnipeg in 1926.[44] Each had space for about a dozen young women who used the home as short-term accommodation while searching for employment as a live-in domestic. The homes also served as social centres where workers could spend free time. On Thursday afternoon, "which was 'maids' day off in Winnipeg ... after cleaning up the lunch dishes, the domestics would walk or travel by streetcar downtown where they might do some shopping ... the Eaton's store 'under the clock' was a popular meeting place. They would then head for the girls' Home."[45]

Wages for domestics were low, and varied considerably: a 14-year-old girl might earn as little as $5 a month. One woman earned $20 a month as a live-in maid with a German family. She had evenings, Thursday afternoons, and Sundays off, but the family tried to convert her to a pentecostal-style religion so after two months she left.[46] Most of the Mennonite women kept very little of their salary but sent it home to the family. Their work in the city was often quite different from what they had been used to. Electricity and running water, and appliances like a gas or electric stove, an electric iron, a vacuum cleaner, even a telephone, could be new. Mennonite women were valued as servants because they were honest and reliable, they followed a strict moral code, they valued persistence and endurance, and they "wouldn't talk back and they did what they were told." Some were undoubtedly exploited. There were cases of sexual abuse and unsatisfactory food. When conditions became intolerable, servants left. As they became more fluent in English and more familar with the working environment, Mennonite women, like others, in domestic service, deserted to other jobs.[47]

The servant problem from the point of view of the maids received an airing before World War I from journalists with a compassionate conscience. In a 1902 issue of *Freyja*, Margret Benedictsson printed the "rules" of "A Society of Working Women Formed in Chicago." "Working women" were exclusively identified as domestic servants.

The rules were primarily concerned with hours of work and personal freedom.

1. Work should not begin before 6 a.m. and it should end when the dishes are washed after the evening meal. The domestic should have 2 hours off every afternoon and 2 evenings a week.

2. The householder should have no right to hinder the social life of the domestics. They should be allowed visitors in their time off (if they do not inconvenience the householder) and be free to serve them food, providing they pay for that themselves.

3. Male visitors: Friends and relations should be allowed to visit the domestic in the kitchen and sit with them by the kitchen door. The householder should not listen to, or hinder the conversation in any way.

4. Domestics should be given time off on Mondays, so that they can take advantage of the bargains offered on that day, just the same as their mistresses.

5. All complaints should be referred to the executive of the society. The wages should be fixed when the domestic is hired and no reduction in price should be allowed.[48]

Freyja's circulation was confined to Icelandic readers. However, a wider audience could read the many news items and comments written by Lillian Beynon in the *Manitoba Free Press*, by her sister Francis Marion Beynon in the *Grain Growers' Guide*, by Pearl Richmond Hamilton and Cora Hind in the *Western Home Monthly*, and by May Clendennan in the *Farmer's Advocate*. These journalists related the abuses as well as the regular hardships built into the job. In 1912 Hamilton visited domestics at work to obtain the servants' point of view.

Inadequate accommodation which sometimes was shared with children was a problem as was dilatory payment of wages. Overwork almost inevitably followed in the wake of long and indefinite hours and no freedom: the employer hired the girl, not just her labour. There was a great sense of isolation and loneliness, especially for newly arrived non–English-speaking immigrants.[49] Compared with the work offered by the newly expanding offices in government and business, domestic service quickly lost what appeal it had.

Moreover, amongst the employer ranks there was a growing professionalization of housework, through the University of Manitoba's home economics degrees. Married women were urged to take advantage of appliances and electricity which could modernize the household, reduce drudgery, and increase the status of a servant-less housewife. Still, in the interwar years government-sponsored enquiries made recommendations to make domestic service more attractive. Most of these attempted to raise the job "to the status of a profession" by instituting training schemes and standardizing expectations. The ideas of Charlotte Perkins Gilman for socialized housework, with child care, cooking, and laundry performed in co-operation by groups of neighbourhood women, were rejected. As one committee set up by the Ministry of Immigration noted: "On the home rests this huge structure we call civilized society, and its continued maintenance largely depends on the intelligent and competent administration of the home. We shall otherwise drift to a communistic form of living (advocated by extreme socialists), but abhorrent to many people."[50]

Despite the evidence there remained a widespread expectation – or at least a hope – in some quarters that after the war domestic service would continue to employ a large number of women. The 1943 federal government report examining the postwar problems of women did, however, recognize the need to raise the status of domestic workers in a practical way. It suggested that working conditions should be standardized and reflected in individual written contracts of employment. In the event that a national labour code were developed, it should include household workers, and at the very least provincial minimum wage acts should cover household work as should new social insurance schemes of unemployment legislation, and worker's compensation should apply. Also, there should be a government-sponsored training plan to promote "a craft pride comparable to that obtaining in other skilled trades."[51]

Whatever the public exhortations, when there was alternative employment to domestic service, women took it. "The remarkable decline in the number of women working as paid domestics" was an outstanding feature of the post–Second World War labour market.[52]

SALES WORK

If domestic service dwindled as a prime occupation for women, sales work retained much of the attraction it had had since its early days as an important employer of women in the first decade of this century in Canada. In 1911 sales work gave jobs to eleven times as many women as in 1901.[53] As in the United States, most of this new work was in department stores. All over Canada, Eaton's and the Hudson's Bay Company were building impressive new stores that attracted customers, and workers, who were predominantly female. Susan Porter Benson describes their appeal:

The woman enticed by advertisements to visit a store found an unprecedented level of beauty and comfort. Windows were dressed with an artistic eye, as managers renounced the traditional practice of cramming windows with vast quantities of unrelated merchandise and instead presented smaller lots of related items in a pleasing and aesthetic way. For the bored or idle, window-shopping became a welcome diversion. Parading up and down the streets, women examined the goods displayed as well as their own reflections in the plate glass windows and the mirrors cannily placed to pander to their vanity. They stopped to discuss the merchandise and the quality of the display with their friends, their loitering in public space legitimized by its association with consumption.[54]

Customers were served by sales clerks who, like them, were women. Workers were offered "a place in the tantalizing giant emporium, spiced by a few dazzling possibilities for advancement, yet it also subjected them to low wages, overwork and persistent class-based conflict with customers."[55] This situation was brought to public attention in Winnipeg by a study undertaken by the University Women's Club in 1914. The report of this investigation was sent to the "employers and employees concerned, to the city council, city clergy, and those throughout the Province and Dominion interested in economic questions." A review of the report appeared in the *Labour Gazette* and was sent on request to various government and academic organizations in the United States and England. Members of the Manitoba establishment could not claim ignorance of its contents, and it undoubtedly helped to create the climate of opinion that lead to the appointment of women factory inspectors and the enactment in 1918 of a minimum wage law.[56]

The Work of Women and Girls in the Department Stores of Winnipeg summarized the working conditions of female sales clerks. The 21-page booklet also revealed the concerns, attitudes, and methods of the women who considered this subject needed investigation. The model was explicitly American: a 1912 book by Elizabeth Beardsley Butler, *Saleswomen in Mercantile Stores*, a study of the larger stores of Baltimore. Thus, findings were classified in three sections: one related to physical conditions, including store construction and arrangements for comfort of employees; a second described the organization of the work force, its hours and remuneration; and a third section explicitly detailed "hardships" of the occupation.

Four stores were investigated in the Winnipeg study. All had been recently enlarged and were experiencing the problems of a physical plant which had not been specifically designed for its current purpose. Ventilation was poor and heating arrangements were unsatisfactory. Many employees had to take unpaid time off because of contracting severe colds. The committee also faulted the stores for not conforming to provincial legislation in the matter of seats for sales women. The committee thought more should be done to provide a rest room containing a couch. Sales women were treated reasonably well with respect to their use of toilet facilties, but this was not the case for cashiers. Cash registers could not be left unattended, so if a cashier wished to relieve herself, she had first to send a messenger to the office and "naturally this amounts almost to a prohibition." The committee approved the stores' practice of giving a full hour off at noon and promoted the idea of a "well-regulated lunch-room, where nourishing meals could be procured at cost."

The committee examined the stores' "welfare work": their policies on sickness, pensions, and social organizations for employees. It praised the store which employed nurses to visit the homes of employees who were off sick and another store "where the old time paternal relation still exists." It reported, without editorial comment, the one store with a pension scheme: "This pension ranges from 4 dollars to 8 d. weekly, and will be paid for life, so long as the pensioner does not marry, does not enter any employment similar to that which the company gives, and leads a moral life." The committee strongly approved the promotion of athletic and social clubs which, it thought, contributed to the happiness of the employees.[57]

The report's second major section concerned the labour force's structure, hours of work, and remuneration. The committee found no fault with the hours of work: generally ten and a half hours per day, six days per week, with occasional half-days off during the summer. Overall, it commented: "the hours in force compare favourably with those in force in any city on the continent." Somewhat ambiguously, it reported that wages were considerably better than "they are popularly believed to be." There was general uniformity of wage levels among all stores and the committee discovered some sales women earning "at least 9 dollars a week."[58] This was relatively high. J.S. Woodsworth had noted in 1913 that only 20 per cent of working women in Winnipeg received over $7 a week and more than 10 per cent received less than $3. Carrie Derick of McGill University examined statistics for wage-earning women throughout Canada in 1913 and concluded that "for every woman who earns $8.50 a week there are twelve who get only $5.00 a week."[59] In 1917 the secretary of the Manitoba Bureau of Labour made a survey to discover "the accurate facts with reference to wages paid to females in the Province." The average weekly wage in the largest occupation category, women garment workers, was $10.47 a week. His observation was that, overall, wages were "hardly enough for subsistence"; but in 1914 the University Women's Club committee came to no such dramatic conclusion.[60]

The committee went to considerable trouble to understand the structure of the work force and its employment opportunities. In three of the stores an incentive system for wages was in place. With respect to managerial staff, "one of the stores has a rigid rule that no woman can be a manager," and another store "has no woman manager." The manager was responsible to the general management and supervised his or her own department and the associated work room. The heads of work rooms, where some merchandise was made and alterations were carried out, were women. Beneath these managerial staff were sales personnel, and below them were messenger girls, wrappers, stock girls, and cashiers. Altogether in February 1914, a month identified as the slackest in sales, the female labour force of the four department stores was 2,432.[61]

The report's third section – "hardships" – only cursorily mentioned the two most important issues – hours and wages – because neither had been considered by the committee to be unfair. The members of the University Women's Club did show their awareness of the concept of a practical minimum wage when they wrote that an adequate minimum wage should provide for "food, proper lodging, car fare, clothes, recreation and possible sickness." They quoted "social workers" in Winnipeg who put this figure at "eight to nine dollars" per week, and the committee reiterated that "the efficient adult saleswomen in Winnipeg" earned that minimum. The various categories of messenger, wrapper, cashier, and work room job frequently did not carry this wage but the committee vaguely justified this situation through the notion that "there must be an apprentice stage" and that the lower paid workers "constitute only a fair and legitimate percentage of the whole," even though the committee itself had no statistical information on the number earning each wage.[62]

The committee considered that the provincial legislation governing working conditions – concerning the provision of seats – was "excellent" and merely remained to be enforced. Ventilation was singled out as a hardship, and so was nervous tension. This was ascribed to the pressure of working under an incentive system and to the multiplicity of sales slips and forms which had to be filled in. A social problem which was not directly the employers' responsibility was the provision of housing. Appalling stories were current regarding the difficulty of finding accommodation. One of the committee's two major recommendations was that "some body of women interested in community service" should provide an accommodation referral service for "business women." Their other recommendation was that "the school board" provide training for women going to work in stores.[63]

This report by the University Women's Club throws light on life in Winnipeg department stores just before World War I and, by extension, on life as a sales clerk elsewhere. It also puts on show the university women themselves. The report is eloquent in its silences as well as in its observations. The committee made no mention of unions or of extended protective legislation (except in the matter of seats) and made no recommendations for fewer hours or greater pay. There was sympathy for women who had to stand up all day, in draughts and sometimes evil-smelling air, who had to dry their hands on unclean linen, who had to write a myriad of sales slips and receipts, who had to search for cheap living accommodation, and who were concerned about their moral reputation. These were practical and palpable concerns, aggravations the club women could readily understand. The committee's agenda did not extend to critical analysis of the labour force within which the sales clerks worked.

Department stores dominated but could never monopolize the sales labour market in Winnipeg. One woman whose education led her to hope for professional work found in 1934 that she needed to earn money at any kind of job. Through family contacts she was employed as a "soda jerk" at a drug store beside a theatre. Helen Peterson was paid $11 a week and was grateful that any shortfall in receipts at the end of the day was not deducted from her pay. Peterson was one of many working women who kept her marriage secret: "there was no work for married women." At the drug store a uniform was supplied, and her employer was kind. There were no financial fringe benefits.[64]

The large department stores drew sales clerks like a magnet. The Bay was a "high class store" in 1929 where the floor walkers wore tails and "only 'classy' people came to shop." The Bay employed Jews; Eaton's would not. Clara Charach, born in Winnipeg of Russian Jewish parents, worked in Eaton's mail order department, "the only department in which Jews were allowed to be employed at the time ... You would never see a Jewish saleslady."[65] Woolworth's hired "mainly Franco-Manitobans, Ukrainians, Anglo-Saxons."[66] Sales clerks conformed to a dress code. At Woolworth's they wore a smock and Eaton's "wanted them to wear black." In Eaton's baby shop, Charlotte Lepp had to wear a nurse's uniform. After the Second World War the dress code at Eaton's was not quite as severe: "you could wear only navy blue or brown ... arms had to be covered ... no slacks, no see through blouses."[67] No store employed married women before World War II. Sheila Mayhew married in 1938 but kept it secret and so kept her Woolworth's job. Margaret McTavish "had to quit when she got married" in 1952 but was hired again later.[68] Eaton's resisted unions, as did some employees. Noreen Rooke "had no use for unions. She felt those who wanted a union wanted to slough off [sic]. There was not enough dissatisfaction to organize a union."[69]

At the beginning of 1936 Winnipeg sales women had average weekly earnings of $11.36. Over the year, the average fell to $8.15, for they did not all enjoy full employment. Office workers made more. Average weekly earnings of stenograpers and typists were $15.50; over the year, that figure also fell, but only to $13.15: they were paid at a higher rate than sales women, and their employment was steadier.[70]

Office workers generally considered their work superior to jobs in factories and sales.[71] By 1930 a structural organization for the office was in place after the rapid expansion of the first two decades and it remained relatively unchanged until the introduction of word processors after 1970.

The historian Graham Lowe has analysed office mechanization through the spread of the typewriter, calculating machines, and Hollerith machines. By 1905 the typewriter was said to be a necessity for modern business. Calculating machines were in place in the 1920s, and Hollerith machines, which introduced basic key punch computerization into large offices, were also widespread in the 1920s.[72] This technology, allied with the expansion of corporate business and government bureaucracy, created the demand for a new labour market which was readily satisfied by women. In 1911 women made up 85 per cent of all stenographers and typists in Canada, and by 1971 that proportion had risen to 96 per cent.[73] In Manitoba and Winnipeg in 1931, and again in 1936, the occupations of stenographer and typist were second only to domestic service in the numbers of women employed. If those numbers are added to the category known as "other clerical," the number of office workers in Winnipeg actually exceeded the number of domestic servants.[74]

The new technology was introduced quickly into the new and expanding business scene of Winnipeg. Even the large and expensive Hollerith machines, manufactured and distributed by IBM, were used by Winnipeg Hydro in 1916 and Great-West Life in 1922.[75] The first typewriters coincided with the arrival in Winnipeg in 1892 of a woman who was later to become renowned for agricultural journalism, Cora Hind. A man held a typewriter agency as a business sideline and Hind rented one for a month. When she returned it the agent said he had just sold a machine to a law firm which had no one to operate it. Hind saw her opportunity and offered her labour at $6 per week to the owner of Dalnavert, Sir Hugh John Macdonald. In 1893 Hind set up her own business as "the first public stenographer, as she had been the first typist, west of the Great Lakes," until in 1901 she attained her ambition of working as a newspaperwoman on the staff of the *Manitoba Free Press*.[76]

Not all offices were organized according to efficient cost-accounting practices which took full advantage of machines. One worker at the Bay in the 1930s noted there were no adding machines or typewriters in the office and workers were not free to talk to each other. She preferred sales work where she could mingle with people.[77] Women who had already received some sort of business training at school or private business college (Success Business College) were in position to earn a higher starting wage. When jobs were scarce in the 1930s, however, people took what they could get.

Ruth Pauls, aged nineteen in 1936, took a job for $7 per week but in addition she was given carfare and lunch was paid for. She "would sneak out for smoking breaks in washrooms" and took books from the Eaton's lending library to read at work in a law firm as she had so little to do. Later that year she got another job and doubled her pay to $15 per week, so she "started saving to buy a fur coat and have orthodonture [sic] done." Two years later she met the marriage bar: "when the boss saw her engagement ring he asked her when she was getting married so he could start looking for a replacement – it was expected that if you were getting married you quit work."[78]

Pauls observed that in the 1930s, "jobs were really all temporary," and many women moved a lot. Like Pauls, Ruth Melman had her first job at age eighteen. She had taken university courses and would have liked to continue but instead took the minimum course at a business college. She rarely stayed longer than a year or two as the law firms who employed her could not afford to keep all their employees. Their technology was "just typewriters, adding machines, nothing fancy," but at a heavy equipment firm Melman took dictaphone dictation during the day and in evenings calculated the interest on overdue payments. A meat-packing firm was the "most horrible place you could ever work at." Not only was there prejudice against Jews, but "during the winter the company decided to save electricity by turning off the lights at 8.30 a.m. – this meant it was too dark to see." Melman noted that "people kept the fact that they were Jewish a secret if they could in order to find work." A union achieved improved working conditions in the firm and she eventually stayed for thirty-three years, but she "was never paid what a man would have been paid." She thought married women were "undesirable" as co-workers as they "did not have the same need to work as single women – they only work for luxuries – they did not have to push for a raise because it was not as important to them as to single women – women are their own worst enemy because they won't stick together."[79]

The prejudice against employing married women loosened but did not go away during the Second World War. In 1950 one married woman with many years of office experience was job hunting and "the woman at Manpower told her employers did not like married women … she looked at the list of jobs and some specifically said they did not want married women" but she found a job anyway. In the 1950s "there were quite a few women looking for work because they had been working during the war and liked the idea of working ... most clericals were women, both unmarried and married."[80]

Ethnic prejudice as well as marital status had a strong if sometimes unacknowledged impact on employment prospects. As noted, this was an issue for the large Jewish community in Winnipeg. But it affected others as well: one francophone "kept trying to get a job at CPR [Canadian Pacific Railway] or CNR [Canadian National Railway] because of the security but at first was not hired because she kept putting down French as her first language." This same woman was aware of gender prejudice. In 1942 she went to work in the car licences department of the provincial government. She "complained when she found out that a retired RCMP (Royal Canadian Mounted Police) man in her office was being paid more than she was even though she had more responsibility but she was told that he was a man and therefore got more money." The office expanded as more people bought cars, but she "got tired of having men making more money than she even though she had more responsibility, so left." Then she came up against sexual harrassment in her next job with a broadcasting company. The personnel manager was " 'oversexed' – the other men flirted, but he groped ... those who slept with him got the best hours – she complained to the manager who said that the man had to be excused because he had been in the war and his wife was not living with him." This woman planned to marry in 1950 and "needed special permission from the head office to allow married women to work."[81]

Women office workers frequently mentioned boredom as a problem, and working with machines brought physical strain. Compared to other work readily accessible to women, however, office work enjoyed high prestige and, generally speaking, high levels of pay – even though men in similar jobs earned more. High status also translated into better marriage prospects: Lowe noted that female clerks in banks and the civil service were three to four times more likely to marry men in professional or managerial positions than in semi-skilled or unskilled manual jobs.[82]

MANUFACTURING

Pre-industrial methods of manufacturing were common in the early years of Manitoba. Items of clothing and art continued to be produced by women's painstaking handwork throughout the century. First Nations women made goods used by men and women, such as caribou and deer clothing, beaded, quilled, and embroidered moccasins and pouches used for storing household items. They made sewing bags which would be used by women and they made firebags and dog-blanket sets for men's use.[83] Into the twentieth century, ornate items became goods produced, still by hand, for a tourist trade.[84]

Most women who earned money by producing goods were considered less skilled and joined an assembly line in a factory. According to the census, manufacturing was the fourth most important occupation for wage-earning women. In Manitoba, there was little heavy engineering and what there was – in the railways – tended to be staffed by men. The numbers of women in this census category in Manitoba were only half the Canadian female average in the 1930s.[85] But there were factories related to light manufacturing, food production, and, above all, the needle trade. Women without the language or educational skills needed in sales and office work, and disinclined towards domestic service, gravitated towards these factories.

Census statistics on the Manitoba work force go back to 1911. There were fewer changes in the female manufacturing labour force than in the male one during the twentieth century. In 1911, 12 per cent of the female labour force was employed in manufacturing. The figure dipped to a low of 8 per cent in the Depression year of 1931 and rose to a high of 15 per cent in 1951 but otherwise hovered around 10 or 11 per cent. Over the same period the proportion of men in manufacturing doubled from the 1911 figure of 9 per cent.[86] There were changes, however, within this apparent continuity. Women were unevenly distributed among the manufacturing classifications, and there were several developments within these classifications.

In 1911, the manufacturing occupation with the most women in it was textiles and clothing, which then employed 72 per cent of all women in manufacturing. The proportion of women in this work, although always dominant, was never so high again: by 1971 it had dropped to 37 per cent. Other categories with relatively large numbers of women were wood, paper, and printing, with a fairly constant 18 per cent of the female manufacturing labour force after 1921, and food, beverages, and tobacco, which increased from 7 per cent in 1911 to 17 per cent in 1931 and then remained constant. Only in the textiles and clothing segment did women outnumber men, a superiority which was maintained at each census date: in 1911 women constituted 71 per cent of the needle trade's labour force and in 1971, 73 per cent.[87]

Other sectors of the economy were more densely populated by women, but manufacturing seemed to harbour the most offensive working conditions – offensive, that is, to humanitarian sensibilities of woman's proper sphere. This concern was nicely illustrated by Nellie McClung's story of how she and Edna Nash were moved "by the plight of women workers in small factories" to persuade Premier Rodmond Roblin to tour factories with them before the First World War. Shocked by the working conditions, he admitted to being "greatly disturbed" and promised to consider the appointment of a woman factory inspector.[88]

An impulse to improve conditions, at least to the level of a "living wage," united several groups in Manitoba to support the move towards minimum wage legislation. Linda Kealey has shown that the labour movement, including the socialist Women's Labour League, was in favour of the new Liberal government's proposal to introduce such a law in 1916 and that employers overcame their reluctance in the hope that this minimal protective legislation would defuse unionization initiatives.[89] As a preliminary to the drafting of legislation, the provincial Department of Labour hired a special investigator – at the high rate of $20 a week – to work in a variety of factories and report first hand on the actual conditions. Ed McGrath, secretary to the Labour Board, said that the total number of employees covered by this survey was 9,354.[90]

Departmental employees interviewed several hundred women and recorded their responses on a long schedule designed to ascertain not only their wages and certain demographic characteristics but also their personal living expenses: the idea was to demonstrate that the subsistence needs of these workers could not currently be met by their earnings. There were, however, other ideas shared by the various reforming groups themselves which tended to offset an insistence on a decent minimum for a single woman.

Most pervasive was the notion that girls under the age of eighteen were not, and should not be, independent. The general assumption was that they lived at home, that their wage contributed to family expenses, and that they did not face the full overhead costs of maintaining a separate household. Even women over eighteen years of age were considered transients in the formal labour force – working only so long as it took to acquire a husband and retire. Consequently different standards operated: the labour movement regarded a family wage as the desideratum for men whilst remaining satisfied with the notion of a wage satisfactory for single subsistence for women. Moreover, the labour movement considered that bargaining through trade unions was the more effective strategy for men, and state regulation through protective legislation was more appropriate for women.[91]

The departmental report was summarized in a sessional paper of February 1918.[92] Its first part was a classification of Winnipeg factories showing the number of employees working at various wage levels. The category "Wearing Apparel, Garments, etc" employed the most women: 908 altogether. The next largest classification was "Confectionery," with 313. This occupation employed a much higher percentage of girls under the age of eighteen; 48 per cent of the total as compared with 15 per cent in the needle trade. The only occupation which employed a majority of girls under eighteen was "Paper Box Factories." Of the total of 2,960 reported to be at work in the Winnipeg factories, 749, or 25.3 per cent, were under eighteen. Everywhere, those under eighteen were paid at lower rates. Overall average earnings in the needle trade were $10.47 per week; in confectionery, $8.04; in paper box factories, $7.92. In all the Winnipeg factories described, only 38 per cent of the women made $10, or more, per week; the majority made less.

Those figures were derived from data provided by employers. McGrath's private investigator, who was over twenty-one years of age, reported on six places of work where she was hired between June and October 1917. At three her wages were $6 a week; at two, $7; and at one, $5. However, there were discrepancies between the rate at which she was hired and what she received. In each case the pay she actually received turned out to be lower than promised. The investigator, Alice Blackburn, also reported on the number of hours required: 50 or 53 per week.

The survey also compared wages with expenses. The sessional paper offered only a sample of seven individual employee accounts; so it is impossible to know how typical they were. One woman, aged twenty-two, worked in a paper box factory. She earned $8 a week, just over the average for that category. She was of Russian Jewish extraction. She did not live at home or with relatives, but boarded. Her declared annual expenses, including $13 per month for meals and $5 per month for her room, amounted to $415.25. Her income, if she missed no working day, was $416. The survey's comment: "This girl has been working for 5 years, getting a rise of 50c per week every 6 months. Expects to be able to buy woollen underwear this winter for first time. Boards herself, and does so quite cheaply."

Two other paper box factory workers were included in the sample. Their wages and expenses were less. One girl, who was fifteen and a half, also Russian Jewish, earned $5.50 per week. She lived at home, "the oldest of 5 children ... mother sick." The girl had no gloves the previous winter. "Her greatest wish is to see a real drama, but has heard they are not really good for young girls." Her meals and room expenses were calculated as higher than the former example: $20 a month altogether. She spent $2.60 a year on "movies" for amusement. Her total expenses were noted as $288.74. A full year's wages would be $286. The third paper box worker, English Jewish, was seventeen, earning $6 a week and living at home. Her meals and room were estimated at $18 a month. Her carfare was high: 50 cents a week. Her total expenses were $329.39; a full year's wages for her would be $312.

Schedule number 83 described a candy factory worker, aged sixteen, Canadian nationality, living at home, earning $5 a week. The relatively low cost of her hats ($3.74, compared with a paper box worker's $10) was explained by a comment that she had taken millinery lessons the previous winter. Her total expenditures were $250.04; a full income for her would be $260. Another schedule described a chocolate factory worker, Russian Jewish. She was eighteen and living at home. Her wages were $6 a week, $312 in a year. Unlike the others in the sample, this young woman had vacation expenses: $1.50 covering two trips to the "beach" – Grand Beach or Winnipeg Beach. Again, a high proportion of her expenses – 6 per cent – went on carfare. Her annual expenses amounted to $385.55, $73.55 more than an annual income.

A twenty-four-year-old Canadian woman who worked as a button-machine operator for a clothing company boarded with relatives, at a cost of $20 per month. She gave 10 cents a week to her church and for amusement went to one show a year. Her expenses were $363.80. Her annual income, at $7.50 a week, would be $390. The last sample was of a twenty-year-old Polish woman who worked for a bedding manufacturer for $5.35 a week. She boarded with relatives for $22 a month. Her total expenses were $379.75, a hundred dollars more than her income of $278, and she was in debt for a doctor's bill of $35 and for two months' board.

These individual examples give us an impression of the human struggles underlying the bare statistics. McGrath thought "there can be only one conclusion arrived at, i.e. that no matter what the causes determining wages are, the earnings of women in industry, in a great many cases, are hardly enough for subsistence." He also noted, doubtless anticipating the observation that young girls living at home might not need to pay as much board or rent as an independent single woman on her own, "that the great majority of women employed in industrial plants are over the age of 18 years." "The question arises," he added: "should not something be done to change or improve these conditions?"

On the Minimum Wage Board there was a consensus that $500 a year was sufficient to support a single woman. Canvassed before the legislation, Helen Armstrong of the Women's Labour League had mentioned $10 a week as a fair minimum, although Gertrude Puttee, wife of the editor of The Voice thought $12 a moderate minimum. In 1919 this $12 figure was mainly adopted for adult women, but less was required for minors and beginners. The board also regulated working conditions concerning ventilation and light and hours worked (maximum 48 hours per week) and insisted that minors and learners could comprise no more than a quarter of an employer's labour force.[93]

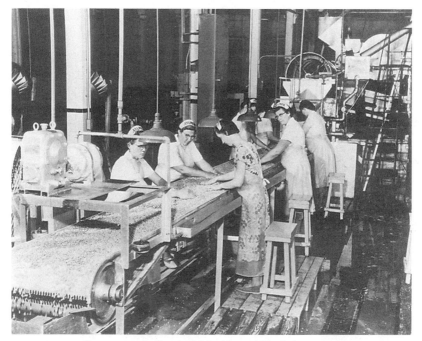

Canners, 1958. (Provincial Archives of Manitoba N9165)

Enforcement was a separate issue. By the time of the Depression, take-home pay in the needle trade had fallen in some instances to under $9 a week. These wages were further reduced by cuts during the 1930s as well as by seasonal layoffs and curtailed hours. Oddson, writing in 1939, referred cautiously to some "circumvention" of minimum wage legislation. Women interviewed in 1984 about their work experience in the 1930s frequently remembered weekly wages of $5 to $7.[94] Another, interviewed in 1986, started working in 1937 at the age of sixteen. "The most I ever made on piecework was $5 a week ... During the work day in the winter, it was so cold working at our sewing machines that we girls had to wear our boots and sometimes coats to work in ... as a body we would go to the boss for heat. He would call us all a bunch of Bolsheviks and tell us if we didn't return to our machines, we would all be fired."[95]

During World War II the industry was again solvent and prosperous because of war contracts. By this time much of the garment industry was organized into trade unions, largely under the idiosyncratic direction of Sam Herbst, organizer of the International Ladies' Garment Workers' Union.[96] The better performance of the firms brought increased security for the workers, and better deals from another union, the Amalgamated Clothing Workers of America.[97]

Meat Packers, 1958. (Provincial Archives of Manitoba N7129)

Wartime and postwar booms came to an end by 1953. During the 1950s, technological and organizational change started to transform the needle trade. The firms which survived were those able to find capital to invest in modern assembly line machinery. Decentralization, whereby rural branches of Winnipeg businesses were established in country communities, became a new trend. As Barbara Roberts has shown, the low pay, long hours, and tedious work experienced by workers before the First World War were repeated into the 1950s. Only the physical plant was sometimes, though not always, better ventilated, lit, and heated. Quoting from a 1957 provincial enquiry into the Winnipeg garment industry, she noted that wages were then still close to Depression levels. Sixty per cent of the workers were immigrants, many with little or no English. Most were women.[98]

In the garment industry, the working poor, mainly women, experienced a tough life. One dimension, perhaps magnified by nostalgia, disappeared over time: "Today's 'lifers' recall pride of craft, close friendships with fellow workers, and sometimes with bosses." Boosted by overt and covert government subsidies, the industry streamlined production methods and maintained low wage costs by recruiting immigrant labour, especially from the Philippines. Productivity increased, accompanied by deskilling and minute division of labour. "Good for the company, but not so good for the workers," remarked one worker, Juuka. Nevertheless, the lack of better alternatives for low-skilled individuals meant that this manufacturing sector continued to offer work to women who needed the money.[99]

PROFESSIONAL WORK

A "professional" occupation is one that possesses at least four characteristics: post-secondary education and training in a subject requiring specialized skill and knowledge; a certification test; a degree of self-regulation by practitioners; and the provision of a service to the public.[100] In the 1881 Manitoba census, the category of "professional service" included teachers (and differentiated them as male and female). By the time of the 1911 census, after training schools for graduate nurses had been established in the larger Manitoba hospitals, nurses also were included in this category. In 1881 professional occupations claimed 23 per cent of the total female labour force, if nuns, who were at that time mainly nurses and teachers, are included, and until the Depression years, women working in professional service continued to comprise about a fifth of the female labour force. After World War II, the numbers rose but as the economy expanded and more women entered the labour force, more jobs were available in other sectors, particularly in office work, and the actual proportion of women who were in professional service declined to about 10 per cent. Most of the women in this category were teachers or nurses. At every census year, teachers furnished the largest single group of women considered professional, and indeed provided about a half of the category. Graduate nurses comprised from about a fifth to almost a third of professional women.[101]

Teaching

Between 1891 and 1921 in Canada, "the most significant increase from the point of view of the economic and social status of women workers occurred in the teaching profession ... the number of women teachers almost doubled between 1891 and 1901, and continued to increase during the following twenty years."[102] This trend was paralleled in Manitoba. Women became a higher proportion of the number of teachers and the profession became "feminized."[103] By the 1930s, women teachers formed the third largest group of women workers in Manitoba, ranking after domestic servants and office workers. In Winnipeg they shared fourth place: there the third largest group was sales clerks, with female schoolteachers sharing fourth place with women in "textile goods and wearing apparel."[104]

The Second World War proved to be a watershed in teaching as a profession for women. Conditions changed in three important ways. First of all, more married women were teachers, and consequently the average age rose. Secondly, pay was increased in comparison to other work for women and with the increased pay and corresponding increase in status, more men entered the profession. Thirdly, pay schedules abandoned sexual differentiation. This last development did not necessarily mean equality within the profession. The qualifications of women teachers remained on the whole lower than men's, more women tended to teach in elementary grades, where the pay scale was lower than at the secondary level, and before 1970 very few women became secondary school principals or inspectors. Nevertheless, equal pay for equal work was achieved in the early 1950s.[105]

Until the Second World War, the one-room schoolhouse was a common experience for Manitoba schoolchildren and their teachers. In 1922 there were 1400 one-room schools, with an enrolment of 40,000 students, but an average attendance of only 56 per cent of the school-age population: large numbers of children still did not attend school regularly.[106] Such a school's internal organization was described by Francis Marion Beynon in 1916. The work "covers everything from the receiving class to grade eight – work that in a city school would probably be distributed among ten or twelve teachers. The intelligent teacher will see at once that to cover the work at all with any degree of thoroughness it will be necessary to confine herself, in all but the senior classes, to such essential subjects as reading, writing, arithmetic, composition, history, geography and drawing. Even so, it is almost like working out a Chinese puzzle to make out a timetable which includes all of these subjects for eight grades, since a lesson cannot very well last less than fifteen minutes and some must continue for at least half an hour."[107]

Outside the schoolroom the teacher had other problems related to community expectations of how a teacher should live. Accommodation was a major worry: "Nobody seems to want to take the teacher to board ... it may be necessary for the teacher to share her room with one of the girls of the home."[108] Boarding could be pleasant but was just as often "intolerable." Some teachers occupied a "teacherage" if such existed.[109] Social scrutiny could also be a trial. Mamie Pickering described the experience of a neighbouring teacher in 1896: "Edie Wadge is very nice ... She has a school of seventeen scholars now ... You know that they wouldn't have Mr Pinn back there because there are so many bachelors that they wanted a lady teacher. There are about twenty-five of them, and the first Sunday they all sat on one side of the church and stared at her until she felt like leaving the building."[110]

Rural schools had a rapid staff turnover: "The rural school ... has to accept the young, inexperienced teacher, and ... after she receives experience and more advanced training it is not able to keep her."[111] She might go to a place where she was paid better, or offered a longer contract, she might marry, or she might just be restless. In 1901, after Nellie Hislop had gone to the trouble of earning a university degree, she became frustrated at the limited opportunities for women in paid employment: "Few vocations other than teaching, nursing, and stenography were open to women in that day." Hislop eventually went to teach in British Columbia, married, then managed a hardware store.[112]

By the 1930s the rural teacher's routine had changed little:

They taught large classes in substandard buildings, with little or no resources, and even less recognition. Their living conditions were often incredibly bad. But they were strongly motivated, worked hard, far longer than the five and a half hour days prescribed by law. After hours and on Saturday mornings they tutored their grade eight students in preparation for the dreaded Entrance Examinations, on the results of which they as well as their students were judged. They spent hours making seatwork and preparing lessons to keep children at various levels gainfully employed while they, the teachers, were trying to teach the rest. They were responsible for coaching teams, organizing track meets and field days, Hallowe'en parties and Christmas concerts, Empire day programs and closing day services ... they often had to teach a 10 month program in fewer than eight months as children were kept out of school for seeding and harvesting, the girls as well as the boys. They were also expected to take part in community activities, of which teaching Sunday School was by no means the least.[113]

Sybil Shack's personal memory of teaching grades 9–12 in a consolidated rural school was distilled through her "sense of smell":

My nose registered a rich mixture of odours: the oil on the floor, the stove, wet wool, moccasins and felt boots, dirty bodies (in 1930 not many farm houses boasted bathtubs or even a pump in the kitchen), manure, the memory of many lunches eaten or half eaten, mice.

The outside of the building showed the remnants of peeling white paint. I don't think the inside had ever seen paint. Its wood had a dark, time- and smoke-stained finish. On the empty strip of floor at the back where the children hung their outer garments was a piece of worn linoleum. In the right hand corner was a rickety table or stand with a milk can on it, and a long-handled dipper hanging on a hook over it. That was the water supply. Everyone drank from the dipper. In the other corner was the stove, with a long pipe leading across the ceiling to the chimney and so distributing its uncertain heat. Beside it was the box of wood with the shovel for removing the ashes. I discovered that it was part of my job to use that shovel. There were 30 children in that school, in every grade but grade three.

The teacher, like most women teachers in those little schools, had done her best to relieve its ugliness. There were paper cut-outs pasted on the windows, and pictures of birds and flowers cut from magazines arranged above the blackboards. Displayed at the front – as in most classrooms throughout the province – were framed pictures of King George and Queen Mary in frames that must have previously enshrined Edward and Alexandra if not Victoria and Albert. There were a few tattered books in a broken bookcase, and the children's textbooks, having survived the ravages of older siblings, cousins or possibly even the children's parents, were at least as tattered. In those days textbooks were not supplied; parents had to buy them.[114]

In the city, where salaries were higher, positions were more secure, and there was more specialization in the subjects taught, the schoolteacher nevertheless had to do more than teach. After the rapid immigration just before the First World War, when children went to school with little English of their own, and their families were struggling to survive, the teacher would often have to be concerned about her students' welfare. If a child scratched her head, the teacher would call her to her desk:

The little girl would usually burst into tears before getting to her feet ... the teacher would appeal to one of the other children to explain to the little girl in her own language what was involved and what had to be done ... it always seemed to take two other little girls, both talking at once in Ukrainian, Polish, German, or Yiddish, to quiet the object of the teacher's attention and get her to co-operate.

What was involved was a hair-combing with a fine-toothed comb, in search of lice in the hair of the pupil ... At Machray school our teacher was Miss Horn, who kept a newspaper in a bottom drawer. This she spread out over the desk, and leaned the pupil's head over the centre of the sheet so that the lice that failed to adhere to the comb dropped onto the paper, to be squashed with an inkwell ... as the weeks passed the lice hunt eventually lost its zest and we ignored it and went on with whatever we were doing while the operation was being performed.[115]

For the majority of women teachers, paid work was considered a short bridge between education and marriage, and they felt obliged to put up with the double salary scale. Nevertheless, women teachers in Winnipeg were outraged when they suffered larger cuts in salary than

Sybil Shack. (Western Canadian Pictorial Index A1009-30274)

men in 1932 and 1933. Because of the difficulties generated by the Depression, the Winnipeg school board – like other school boards around the province and, indeed, the entire country – imposed salary cuts, but not uniformly. "Biggest Part of Burden to be on Women," announced the local newspaper.[116] The Winnipeg women teachers then formed their own organization and separated from the Winnipeg Teachers' Association, a unit of the Manitoba Teachers' Federation. From 1933 until the men teachers rejoined the women in 1966, the women worked to abolish, and the men strove to maintain, employment policies which were based on gender.[117]

"For thirteen years I paid the membership fee" of the federation, wrote teacher Vera Patrick in 1935, "believing the Federation was what its motto declared it to be, 'Quisque pro omnibus,' but during the past two years, to the disillusionment of many, it has been found to be, not each for all, but mostly for the male members."[118] The women teachers worked hard, with their own briefs presented to the school board, to bring about equal pay for equal work, equal retirement and pension policies, and greater access for women to administrative positions. After a brief hesitation they also supported, in 1946, the abolition of the requirement to retire on marriage. With support from women trustees, they were successful in instituting a single salary schedule in the early 1950s, and a single retirement and pension scheme in 1957.[119] But the reforms of the 1950s did not completely transform the working conditions for women.

By 1970 there was still a long way to go, as Sybil Shack, stalwart reformer, teacher, principal, and administrator, described: "The bargaining unit represents the interests of five or six hundred teachers of whom more than two thirds are women, but the committee that does the negotiating has not a single woman member. The teachers' organization has about twelve thousand members; its executive body, duly elected at the annual meeting, consists of nineteen people. Three are women. The school staff is made up of twenty-five women and three men; its representative on the governing body of the professional association for the past six years has been a man." Within the Manitoba Teachers' Society, men predominated; within the profession, men held most of the senior teaching, and administrative positions. Shack noted that women rarely had ambitions for promotion and she regretted "the sheer waste of human resources ... based on tradition rather than on necessity."[120]

As in nursing, the other professional occupation which attracted large numbers of women, success in achieving equity for women workers was a realistic prospect only by the end of the century.

Nursing

Nursing originated as a profession in Manitoba with the establishment of a training school in the Winnipeg General Hospital in 1887. After three years' training, a mixture of apprenticeship and theoretical work, the graduate nurse could be at the beck and call of three masters: a patient, a physician, and, within the hospital, an administrator. The concept of selfless service attracted recruits and, as well, public support. As Archbishop Matheson told the nurses graduating in 1904: "I am one of the conservative school who believe that the true place for a woman is in the home, but I say that if women are to follow professions then nursing is one of the truest and noblest callings for her."[121]

The quest for self-regulation, and for more authority commensurate with their responsibility within the health care profession, absorbed much of the discipline and attention of nurses within Manitoba, which provided early leaders for the profession not only in Canada but in the United States. Ethel Johns, editor of the *Canadian Nurse* who served frequently as a government consultant on nursing, was trained in the early years of the twentieth century at the Winnipeg General as was her friend and colleague, Isobel Stewart, who later instituted many reforms through her position at Columbia University in New York.[122] The structure of the profession in the interwar years gave opportunities for considerable independence: nurses on private duty and in public health both worked with little supervision from doctor or hospital administrator.[123] After the Second World War the private duty nurse virtually disappeared, and almost all nursing was carried out within hospital walls.

In wartime adventurous nurses sought work in war service. A 1909 graduate nurse, Alfreda Atrill, was the first Winnipeg nurse to go overseas in World War I. She served on the Salonika Front, and later in the French military hospital at Le Touquet. Frederica Wilson, formerly in charge of the school of nursing at the Winnipeg General Hospital, enlisted from the west coast and travelled as matron of the Fifth Overseas British Columbia Hospital Unit. She too served on the Salonika Front and at Le Tréport Canadian base hospital in France.[124] Agnes Baird graduated in the spring of 1914 and went overseas in 1915, working on a troop ship in the Gallipoli campaign. Along with Vera Brittain, who expressed so much of her generation's reaction to the war in her book *Testament of Youth*, Baird spent time in Malta, where she saw new technology in military aircraft and submarines. Later she served in France. Plunged into the labour troubles of postwar Winnipeg after her return, she thought it would be "more peaceful" to be near the front than in the midst of the 1919 Winnipeg General Strike.[125] Other nursing workers were under the command of Dr Ellen Douglass, one of the tiny number of women physicians in Winnipeg, who organized the Winnipeg Women's Volunteer Reserve. Douglass took some Volunteer Aid Division women to England and then served in France as a major in the Royal Army Medical Corps before returning to her Winnipeg practice in 1919.[126] During the war, the graduate nurse association was not happy with the recruitment of untrained enthusiasts and expressed concern that "some persons who are not graduate nurses are wearing our uniform."[127] It was necessary to continue to insist on the professionalism of graduate nurses.

Similar concerns recurred at the outset of the Second World War. This time, only registered nurses were permitted to enlist for military duty, and they were first trained in Canada for overseas service as commissioned officers. The second nurse to land after the Allied invasion of Sicily was Trenna Hunter of Winnipeg – part of a group described as "grimy, tin-hatted girls, perspiring in the terrific heat and burdened with cumbersome equipment."[128] Concern for the dilution of standards, this time in the hospitals at home, resurfaced. The superintendent of nurses at the Winnipeg General, Bertha Pullen, noted: "The tortuous path over which quality nursing service has climbed to its prewar heights fell into disrepute during the war. Why? Because those nurses, with their careful three years' scientific and technical grounding, were suddenly swept away from us to enter the military service, and it was necessary to substitute them with short course volunteer aides, who were enthusiastic, willing and sincere to be sure ... [but] their hours were limited to their personal convenience. We had no hold on their time. We were not free to demand the quality of service we would have required of our paid employees."[129]

Right from the beginning there were opportunities for nurses in the field of public health where nurses tended to work as much as social workers as health care professionals. Even before the spectacular wave of immigration in the first decade of the twentieth century, provincial and city authorities were involved with the preservation of health as well as the containment of disease. They were particularly concerned about maternal and infant mortality, schoolchildren's health, the prevalence of tuberculosis, and the general issue of urban sanitation.[130] Some improvements were brought about, partly through the development of medical technology and the provision of a clean and plentiful water supply, and nurses were on the front line in the provision of basic health care in remote rural outposts.

Nursing stations were under the shared jurisdiction of the provincial government and the Canadian Red Cross. Several of their staff had been trained in Britain and some, like Hilda St. Germain, had also served in the First World War.[131] After working in a Winnipeg hospital during the 1920s, with the summers spent as a nurse in charge of the Red Cross station at the resort town of Winnipeg Beach, St. Germain was appointed to the Red Cross station at East Braintree and remained there for twenty years. Forty miles east of Winnipeg, there were "no doctors, no roads, and very little means of transportation" except for a "jigger" on the railway line, a dirty, ill-ventilated, and unheated car propelled by a small engine. St. Germain would travel as near as she could to a patient's home on the railway, and "the relatives would meet you with a slow-going team of horses and a wooden sleigh" in winter. "Then followed a trip into the bush of anything up to ten or fifteen miles, over badly rutted roads ... the whole making a trip of close to fifty miles." St. Germain "had never acted without a doctor or been so far from help before ... [but] four years of war had equipped me for any kind of emergencies."

St. Germain was more than a medical health worker. She advised people about money and marriage. She organized a sewing circle for women. She taught Sunday School and was remembered by the wife of the minister who took services three or four times a year: "a small group of women gathered for a World Day of Prayer service arranged by her. At the close of the service, the Lord's Prayer was said, each woman repeating it in her own native tongue." When no clergyman could attend a funeral, St. Germain, "donning a clean uniform and pinning on her war medals and decorations ... taking her prayer book with her, she would head the procession to the graveyard under the pines, read the burial service and lead the prayers."[132]

Margaret Litton Hodgins worked at the Fisher Branch outpost, north of Winnipeg, from 1922. A major problem was language: "many of the older Ukrainian people did not speak English." In her memoir she described the hair-raising difficulty of treating a young man who appeared to have a ruptured appendix. The road to Winnipeg, 120 miles away, was blocked by snow, and Hodgins arranged for the patient to travel on the railway line by jigger. She kept him warm with a charcoal brick, blankets, and the body warmth of his mother, herself, and the driver. Other dramatic incidents were centred on childbirth. During one twenty-four-hour period in 1925, Hodgins travelled seventy miles and delivered five babies.[133]

Ruth Evans was among the last generation of Red Cross nurses. She was trained at the Winnipeg General Hospital and in 1951 was appointed to the station at Alonsa, 75 miles north of Portage la Prairie near Lake Manitoba. The post served a population of about 2000, mainly farming and fishing families. Although Evans, like other post-war health workers, had the benefit of penicillin and other technological advances, the problems of climate, transportation, and isolation remained. As with the nurses of the interwar years, Evans had only limited and infrequent access to a physician's help and advice and often had to take full responsibility for diagnosis, treatment, and preventive measures.

Her first action after moving to another outpost at Gillam, on the Hudson's Bay Company railway line in the north, was to make an inventory of the families in her cachement area, "immunizing the babies and young children as I went." Evans found that gastro-enteritis and chest problems were severe because of inadequate water supplies and poverty, and there were always accidents. She remembered "a man who had cut his foot badly with an axe, in the bush. He had walked back to his cabin, a distance of two or three miles, to get help." Evans was able to suture the cut successfully. "In the fall, there were always nits, impetigo and scabies to treat." Evans noted that conditions changed substantially in the 1960s. After the provincial government assumed full responsibility for health, "improved living conditions, emergency plane service, radio communication and back-up medical advice" altered the nature of the work performed by nurses in the north.[134]

Elizabeth Russell was director of the public health nurses employed by the province in the 1940s. She vividly described one Christmas Day in her 1943 report. The nurse was called to help a woman in labour at a home which "rivalled the stable of Nazareth for poverty and lack of comfort," a two-room shack which housed two families. There were no curtains, no radio, no pictures, no newspapers, and no toilet, inside or out. Snow was melted for water, and there was a cow which only gave a quart of milk per day. There were two beds for eight people, each with a straw mattress in a flour sack cover, and one quilt. The children "curled up like so many puppies fully clothed and unwashed" on a bed with the other woman. The two fathers stretched out on the floor, using their overcoats as pillows. The nurse was able to sit down on the single chair, homemade and uncomfortable, and "an animated battle with wild life began which drove out any thought of sleep as any bare spot of human flesh became a target for fleas and bugs." Christmas dinner was salt pork and macaroni. There was no mention of Christmas and no toys for the children. Finally, at three in the afternoon, a son was born. Russell's report ended: "Five more calls waited at the nursing station. Quite a busy Christmas."[135]

In 1930, 60 per cent of nurses were employed in private duty nursing, where a nurse would attend a patient in his or her own home. The patient was responsible for paying the nurse's wages, a charge which might or might not be covered by private insurance: the private duty nurse could not always be sure of getting paid. One private duty nurse recollected that during the 1930s, "you were lucky to get work. There were so many nurses out of work during the Depression."[136] After the war, apart from some public health jobs, the largest number of nursing positions was in hospitals, where student nurses provided apprentice labour: "We had a really tough time, obeying all rules, attending prayers before breakfast, having our rooms inspected daily. No overnights out, finally getting our first late-leave – 11 pm! which we'd lose if we were late for prayers or signing in; our uniforms inspected suddenly during class to see that we had two straight pins attaching our collars to our dress, no safety pins in place of buttons, etc., hairnets to keep our hair off our collars, our shoes polished; plus lectures if we'd gone on an elevator before a senior student; lights out at 10.30 pm; no radios and no smoking ... You had to want to be a nurse!"[137]

The ferocious discipline, reinforced by strong peer pressure generated in the residences, was maintained until the 1970s, when nurse training was transferred away from hospitals to the universities. Graduate nurses did experience change within their profession after the Second World War, most notably with respect to opportunities for married nurses. Before the war, married nurses would not be employed by hospitals. Afterwards, more married nurses continued to work and the hospitals accommodated their nurses' family responsibilities by offering more shift or part-time work. Nursing was one of the few occupations which deliberately tried to offer the sort of flexibility which allowed a mother to combine paid work with family responsibilities.

Seeds of more change, which would grow apace during the 1980s and 1990s, were also planted before 1970. One welcome development, to nurses, was the displacing of the doctor from his pedestal; another was the increased formal recognition of nurses as professional workers with important responsibilities within the health care system. In 1970, however, a view of the nurse as a quintessential feminine carer, passive and obedient, contained elements of truth. "Back in the 60s one just followed orders and never questioned why," said one nurse.[138]

Other professions

There were women doctors in Manitoba from 1882, women teaching at the university level since 1890, and women lawyers practising since 1915. The overall numbers and male/female proportions in these three occupations were always low: in 1971, for instance, only 2 per cent of Manitoba's lawyers were women.[139] In the twenty years from 1971 to 1991, conditions changed for both lawyers and doctors, and by 1993 over half of the first-year students in the University of Manitoba Faculty of Medicine were female. Women participated in most other professions before 1970 but the numbers were small. A few professional occupations were so inhospitable that few or no women entered: there were hardly any women engineers, for example. Others specifically excluded women – some religious denominations excluded women from ordination as ministers or priests, and the armed services restricted the entry of women.

The history of women's experience in professional work is salutary, because although a few specific occupations were female-dominated, most were male-dominated. Even in nursing and teaching, men exercised authority within the profession and in teaching men monopolized its higher ranks. Some women, particularly teachers in Winnipeg during the 1930s, organized to confront institutionalized inequality head on. Most women were resigned to it, however, and reacted with a combination of bitterness, fatalism, and humour.[140] At the end of the twentieth century, women had not acquired equality with their male colleagues in occupations where they did the same work. And in jobs where women performed different tasks from men, it was still the women who largely populated the positions of lesser responsibility and skill. Equality remained an elusive objective.

$\mathcal{P}$UBLIC SERVICE WORK

"Opportunities for Women in Public Service" was the title of a speech given at Banff in 1938 by Margaret McWilliams. The only woman alderman on Winnipeg City Council, she had been invited to address the nineteenth annual convention of the Quota Club International, a women's organization committed to community service and international peace. While paying tribute to the traditional strength of women in voluntary associations, she identified increasing employment opportunities for women in "all work which is done directly for human persons" and also exhorted women to be bolder in entering "the elected services." Public service was the touchstone of a new confused and confusing role for women: woman as citizen.

To McWilliams, public service was both useful and noble. It "raised the standard of the community" by allowing those involved, both as workers and clients, to become more civilized. It was particularly suited to women: "When we women get out into this work ... then, indeed, I think the business of living will begin to improve and civilization will move onward."[1] McWilliams, like so many of her generation, was influenced by the civic idealism of the British philosopher, T.H. Green, who believed that public service was itself a form of divine service: serving the public was synonymous with serving God. His voice was just one of the more modern manifestations of a civic republican tradition stemming from Aristotle's Athens and Rousseau's Geneva. Faith in Christianity, coupled with confidence in the potential of women, was a dominant current in Canadian progressive social reform of the time. Now, thought liberal feminists, women would travel from exclusion to inclusion in the ideal of citizenship.[2]

Women like Margaret McWilliams were to be found in all those countries where female suffrage, the badge of citizenship, was acquired early in the twentieth century – or, in the case of New Zealand, earlier. Historians have traditionally seen suffrage as the end of one story rather than as the beginning of a new one. However, contemporary historians like the Australian Marilyn Lake position the vote at the start of the interwar generation's exploration of the significance of citizenship for women.[3] The vote's opportunities were welcomed with optimism. It was thought to be a precondition for the improvement of women's position both politically and economically and in the widest sense of those terms. Measures leading to individual personal rights, economic independence, and bodily self-possession were on the agenda. As energetic and enthusiastic women, generally working within existing women's organizations, pursued these ambitious aims it gradually became clear how very fundamental was the challenge to the status quo mounted by the feminists. As time went on, individual women, and groups, had to select priorities: not everyone could simultaneously combat all the various manifestations of patriarchy. It became clear that the vote, although necessary, was not by itself a sufficient tool to ensure full citizenship status for all women. In the early days of enfranchisement, however, limits were less obvious than opportunities. The world, it appeared, was now open to women.

Or rather, in Canada, to non-aboriginal women. If citizenship includes the legal right to participate in the formation of policy which affects the community, then by virtue of customary practice before 1870, many First Nations women traditionally exercised considerable power in their society. Before the establishment of the province of Manitoba, women in some Ojibwa bands had served as chiefs, medicine women, shamans, and military advisers, although work by historian Laura Peers cautions that the data supporting this conclusion are not definitive. In Cree culture, men were more likely to monopolize positions of authority. Traditional teachings, according to Marilyn Fontaine of the Manitoba Aboriginal Women's Unity Coalition, observed that "the lodge [was] divided equally between women and men ... and provide[d] a model for the exercise of self-government."[4] The situation became both more certain and more uniform with the Indian Act legislation. "The women in our communities are suffering from dictatorship government that has been imposed on us by the Indian Act," said Joyce Courchene of the Manitoba Indigenous Women's Collective in 1993.[5] The Indian Act of 1869, which was extended to Manitoba in 1874, gave no individual identity to aboriginal women and clearly discriminated between male and female persons: a woman could only be identified as Indian, for legal purposes, if she were married to a male person of Indian blood belonging to a particular band. She had no rights by virtue of her own existence. First Nations women were, in Kathleen

Jamieson's phrase, "citizens minus" according to Canadian law until after 1970.[6] For the years 1870 to 1970 First Nations women were legally excluded from much of the public service work which was considered so important by the first generations of enfranchised women.

McWilliams's all-encompassing optimism was expressed when she welcomed the incipient shift towards professionalization in social welfare work. The horizon was wide, the limits were far away. Both women and men would be paid to do "all those new things which are arising for the improvement of health; better nutrition; better housing; ... better preventive medicine; better lighting; better sanitation; better air conditioning; protection of children; protection of young women ... adult education." In 1931 she was an advocate of the welfare state, when she promoted state-funded health, education, and child-care systems in her blueprint for social reform, *If I Were King of Canada*. In 1943 she welcomed the Beveridge Report in Britain and its Canadian counterpart, drafted by Leonard Marsh, noting its particular appeal for women in her own subcommittee report for the federal government's enquiry on postwar reconstruction.[7]

McWilliams's did not see a contradiction between her endorsement of the state planning and delivery of services and her support for the continuation of volunteer social welfare activity. For several generations such work had been socially acceptable for women, and it would remain so for at least a further thirty years after the Second World War.[8] Volunteer work was not merely a self-indulgence, an idle pastime: she thought women should educate themselves in the responsibilites of citizenship and consider public service as a serious vocation. McWilliams did her share to familiarize women with current events. She frequently gave talks on politics in the University of Manitoba's extension lecture series, often travelling to small rural communities. For over thirty years she conducted annual series of current events classes for women, which attracted enrolments of hundreds. Her lecture notes indicate the extraordinarily high quality of her talks which offered analysis of events behind the week's news.[9]

This chapter samples women's organized voluntary welfare work, particularly in the early twentieth century, and then examines some political activism in the years preceding and immediately following the acquisition of the vote. Finally, there is a survey of women's participation in "the elected services" in Manitoba's largest city, Winnipeg.

SOCIAL WELFARE WORK

A wide-ranging, although incomplete, description of women's voluntary social welfare work in the early twentieth century, the heyday of

Winnipeg's expansion and confidence, appeared in a city newspaper in
1907. On 8 May the *Winnipeg Telegram* published a supplement, the
"Women's Paper," whose aim was to record the volunteer work of
Winnipeg women since the onset of organized activity in the 1880s.
The supplement reflected the importance given by wives of the wealthy
to "doing good" and identified appropriate outlets for their attention.
Pride of place was given in fourteen columns to "The Wide, Wide,
World," namely, missionary support work. Churches raised funds to
sponsor women missionaries abroad as well as nurses, physicians, and
teachers, and they supported institutions such as schools, orphanages,
and kindergartens both at home and overseas. Women helped build
and furnish ministers' houses and supported denominational newslet-
ters and publications.

Drawing on women's traditional deeds of charity and the more
recent example of settlement work epitomized by Jane Addams in Chicago were the groups which cared for the poor, the sick, and the needy.
The Paper described only organizations which were Christian and
Protestant. Some were funded completely by private agencies; others
also received government funding. One which enjoyed income from
both public and private sources was the Margaret Scott Nursing Mission, named after "the city's missionary to our poor." The mission
provided trained nurses to visit home patients. Its purpose was "to
minister spiritually and physically to the sick poor in our midst," especially to those unable to have a prolonged hospital stay through poverty, responsibility for dependents, or because their illness demanded
constant attention.[10] The Margaret Scott Mission was unique to Winnipeg, founded by one determined woman with the administrative
capacity to mobilize financial and human resources for a specific
purpose.[11] The mission and some other local organizations required
more direct involvement in welfare work. The activities of other organizations were devoted to raising awareness and funds for particular
causes.

Many of these organizations drew on the experience of national
societies, and the Paper listed several local chapters of dominion-wide
societies: the Red Cross, the groups which became the Victorian Order
of Nurses, the Girls' Friendly Society, the Aberdeen Society, and
the Local Council of Women. Officers of these societies were drawn
repeatedly from the wives of Winnipeg's business and governing élite.
Wives of lieutenant-governors served as honorary and active presi-
dents, and the same names appeared on boards over and over again.[12]
The primary activity of these societies before 1907 was fund-raising
but that in turn raised the awareness of women and the general public
on behalf of their causes. The Council of Women, founded in 1893 by

Lady Aberdeen, wife of the governor-general, was an umbrella society, with an international branch to elevate members to a high level of unity, whose object was to apply the "Golden Rule to society, custom and law."[13] The agreed conventions of these organizations were expressed in the Paper's account of the Children's Aid Society: "Wayward children are not necessarily children of vicious tendencies ... Their surroundings do not afford sufficient outlet, and they make this outlet for themselves in wrong-doing. The evident remedy is to change the character of the surroundings."[14] This was one of the beliefs which sustained the preachers and believers in the Social Gospel in Canada and the idealism of women who worked for the benefit of the poor and needy.

The women in these organizations worked primarily through committees and became skilled in techniques modelled on parliamentary procedure. They determined the policy and objectives of their boards and also set about fund-raising. They solicited large donations from the businessmen of their acquaintance and raised money themselves. Referring to the Children's Aid, the Paper wrote: "Young girls have held flower shows for [children's] benefit; boys have had acrobatic performances in the barn, and donated the proceeds; artists and musicians have given their services freely to the cause; busy women have taken time from their many home duties to plan and work for them, and have gone back to their own little flocks with more thankful hearts."[15]

Women maintained this sort of social welfare work during the post–World War I generation with strength and assurance. There was less emphasis on foreign missions and more on community work at home as the teachings of the Social Gospel came to be widely accepted.[16] Voluntary organizations worked with a new developing cadre of professionals in pursuit of McWilliams's civilized society. In this partnership, some women perceived actual and potential tensions. Charlotte Whitton, the most famous of Canadian social workers, was commissioned by a voluntary organization, the Winnipeg Junior League, to study child welfare in the city. In her report she expressed severe misgivings about the capacity of volunteers to work alongside professionals in the social welfare field.[17] Nevertheless, in the interwar years women's organizations were able to raise money and equipment related to welfare work through groups like the Margaret Scott Mission. Increasingly, these organizations turned their energies away from the actual delivery of services towards canvassing governments at the federal, provincial, and municipal levels for changes in policy and services.

An increased emphasis on lobbying can be seen in the activities of the Local Council of Women. By the time of its seventy-fifth anniversary in 1969, the council was able to list its past endorsement for about fifty projects, pieces of legislation, and campaigns. These included the appointment of policewomen, the establishment of a school for the deaf, the colouring of margarine, protests against water pollution, the appointment of women as jurors and as members of government boards and commissions, and support for consumer vigilance.[18]

Neither the interwar Local Council of Women nor the 1907 "Women's Paper" acknowledged three areas of women's volunteer work which were extensive and important for the women concerned and for their communities. These three areas were weekly parish activities, activities centred in non-anglophone ethnic groups, and the work performed for politically oriented associations. Few churches, whatever the denominiation, were without women's groups. In Roman Catholic communities in particular, women's volunteer work tended to be centred on parish activities.[19] They not only helped maintain the material and social cohesiveness of the congregation but also performed work of benefit to the larger community. Parish records bear witness to the significance of women's work inside religious life. St. Stephen's Presbyterian Church on Broadway organized local Bible study, a Sunday School, and social meetings for quilting. As well, it paid the salary of a missionary in India and sponsored a settlement in Winnipeg's North End while operating its own building, Church House, "a throbbing centre of religious, social and athletic activity."[20]

Groups organized around ethnic cultures benefited from women's volunteer work and often religious and ethnic bonds were intertwined. In the early Icelandic settlement at Gimli, the membership of the ladies' aid societies of the Lutheran churches overlapped with that of parish women's societies. Both helped new immigrants and the poor of their own communities. Their interests were cultural as well as material. The Icelandic emphasis on education bore fruit in money raised for bursaries to allow children to study music.[21]

POLITICAL ACTIVISM

Political work occasionally grew from a foundation of ethnic or religious interests. The Interlake Icelandic community was a case in point. Under the leadership of Margret Benedictsson, the publisher of *Freyja*, devoted to woman's political, economic and social rights, the ladies' aid societies in the Icelandic parishes after 1905 incorporated women's suffrage into their aims. By 1908 an Icelandic women's organization devoted excusively to women's suffrage was founded in the small rural community of Argyle, and others followed. They petitioned the Manitoba legislature and were instrumental in helping to create the climate of public opinion which finally permitted the solicitor-general,

T.H. Johnson, son of an Icelandic suffragist, to introduce women's suffrage in the Manitoba legislature in January 1916.[22]

This was a successful end to the story of suffragist activity in Manitoba, the first province in Canada to gain female suffrage. The story is one of the few tales of women's work of any sort to be told at all in history books. Catherine Cleverdon provided an analytical account in her 1950 book, *The Woman Suffrage Movement in Canada*, and Nellie McClung added a vivid recreation of the movement in the second volume of her autobiography, *The Stream Runs Fast*, published in 1945. There she described the fun of the Political Equality League's suffrage campaign, with its dramatic highlight in January 1914 when the league filled the largest theatre in Winnipeg with an audience to watch a satirical cabaret of Conservative Premier Rodmond Roblin's condescending and dismissive attitude towards women's suffrage.[23]

The campaign was based on extensive organization. Members of the league were predominantly urban, of British or Ontario origin, and either Methodist or Presbyterian, at a time when over 56 per cent of the province's population was rural, over 40 per cent was neither British nor from Ontario, and more than 75 per cent was not affiliated with either the Methodists or the Presbyterians. The league was thus not a demographic reflection of the population at large, but it did reflect the more established families of Winnipeg and the long-time residents of the prosperous agricultural areas of southern Manitoba.[24] Its aims were supported by the largest farm journal, the *Grain Growers' Guide*, whose women's page editor, Francis Marion Beynon, was a league officer. Although one historian[25] has claimed there was a conflict of interest between farm and labour women over women's suffrage, the evidence suggests otherwise.

From the outset, the league actively canvassed in rural areas, using their agricultural journalistic connections to staff booths at agricultural shows. During the 1914 provincial election campaign, after the Liberal party had endorsed women's suffrage, several league members spoke on behalf of the Liberals in rural constituencies. They included McClung, Francis Beynon's sister Lillian, and two other journalist sisters, Lynn and Winona Flett.[26] Rural support was critical just before the bill was to be introduced in the Manitoba legislature. Lillian Beynon Thomas discovered that the bill as drafted did not permit women to become candidates for election. She "informed her sister, Francis Beynon, who was attending the Grain Growers' convention in Brandon. Miss Beynon's threat to bring the matter to the attention of the convention quickly brought results and the bill was changed."[27]

Among members of the league executive were staunch labour supporters like Winona Flett and her husband Fred Dixon, leader of the Direct Legislation League and after 1914 a Labour member of the

Political Equality League, 1915. *Top*: Lillian Beynon Thomas (left),
Winona Flett Dixon (right); *bottom*: Mary Crawford (left), Amelia Burrit (right).
(Provincial Archives of Manitoba, Events 173/3)

Manitoba legislature. Lillian Beynon Thomas and her journalist husband, A.V. Thomas, were labour supporters as was Gertrude Puttee,
wife of the printer and editor of the Winnipeg *Voice*, "the oldest labour
organ in the Dominion."[28] The *Voice* gave consistent coverage to the
league's activities, devoting a weekly column to them under a special
boxed heading. Some of these columns reported local activities, others
printed speeches given by prominent Canadian, American, and British
feminists. As early as 1907, five years before the league was founded,
a "Woman's Column" signed by Ada Muir, "written by a Woman for
Working Women," was a regular feature. Muir supported suffrage and
criticized the Local Council of Women for their reluctance to endorse
votes for women.[29]

After the league began to work, suffrage was specifically urged by
the Woman's Column. "As a socialist, I naturally favour universal
suffrage," wrote "Pessimist" who urged all women concerned with
science, economics, sweatshops, and "domestic women" to "concern
themselves to get the ballot."[30] In 1915, the *Voice* noted, on its front
page, that suffrage by itself would not bring a new political era, but
"we do not wish to be understood as trying to throw cold water on
the woman's movement ... On the contrary ... the extension of the
suffrage to women, being in strict conformity with the principles of
democracy, will do nothing but good."[31]

The league concentrated on votes for women, but its objectives were wider. Its president, Lillian Beynon Thomas, said its aim was "to explain ... what it meant to women and children who were in the power of weak, coarse, unfair, sick or brutal men."[32] The vote was a tool to be used in effecting remedial state action for injustice. The league wished to elect candidates interested in introducing social and economic legislation affecting women, including a minimum wage law, mothers' allowances, a dower act, women factory inspectors, and a law relating to the guardianship of children. The vote could also be used to bring about prohibition.[33]

An organization whose mandate was to promote the interests of working women was the Women's Labour League. Founded in 1909, it was no longer functioning two years later, but was revived in 1917. Both organizations had wide-ranging goals. The first worked for suffrage, for the reform of dower and property laws affecting women, and on behalf of a single moral standard. It did not campaign for equal pay, "nor did it devote a great deal of energy to advancing the cause of trade unionism among women."[34] The second league of 1917 had five objectives: to improve the lives of working women through unionization and protective legislation; to foster co-operation among working women; to educate the public about the labour movement; to provide assistance to wage-earners in industrial difficulties; and to do research for legislation governing the working conditions of women and children. Its president was Helen Armstrong, like her husband George an energetic radical, who actively pursued all the league's goals as well as associating it with other political causes, such as anti-conscription.[35] When a minimum wage board was established in Manitoba after the First World War, members of the league were appointed to it. However, the league did not challenge the cherished trade union norm of a family wage paid to a male breadwinner.[36]

An organization particularly dedicated to peace after the Great War was the Women's International League for Peace and Freedom (WILPF) which included Manitoba women among its members. Gertrude Richardson from Swan River, a friend and colleague of Helen Armstrong, was a member of WILPF who worked on behalf of conscientious objectors.[37] Other women's organizations, like the University Women's Club or the Women's Canadian Club, took a postwar interest in peace, even if they were not pacifist. During the 1930s women candidates for elected office at the municipal level, as aldermen or school board members, frequently noted their membership of peace groups.[38]

Just as the interests of labour attracted women who were to some extent personally involved as workingmen's wives, workers themselves, or intellectuals, so too did rural interests lead to the creation of two broad women's organizations which sought to promote the interests of farm and country women: the Women's Institutes, first established in the province in 1910, and the United Farm Women of Manitoba (UFWM), named in 1920 as the successor to the Women's Grain Growers' Association, originally founded in 1910. Neither organization was narrowly partisan political, but their goals and methods were structured in order to improve society.

The Women's Institutes, organized first at Morris and Dauphin in 1910, took a particular interest in the development of the new Department of Household Science at the University of Manitoba. Local activities emphasized good housekeeping, and during the First World War, along with many other women's organizations, the institutes turned their hands to sewing shirts for soldiers and making bandages and equipment for military hospitals. But they were not a truly conservative organization. Visiting speakers included many of the Winnipeg feminists: the agricultural correspondent E. Cora Hind, her friend and fellow journalist Kennethe Haig, labour activist Lillian Beynon Thomas, and Mary Speechly (the future advocate of family planning). Resolutions at their annual meetings showed that the institutes were concerned about community welfare. Not only did they campaign for, but they frequently also directly provided, supervision for children's playgrounds in holidays, hot lunches at schools, circulating libraries, war memorials, community halls, relief work for those unable to provide for themselves, and child welfare centres.[39]

Like members of the Women's Institutes, the United Farm Women of Manitoba took credit for several tangible achievements: "better medical facilities for rural districts," the establishment of free child welfare clinics, "the betterment of rural schools," rest rooms in towns for the benefit of rural women, travelling libraries, and well-appointed cemeteries.[40] On the same wavelength as Margaret McWilliams, the UFWM's objectives stressed "the finer things of life, the things that are more excellent" and translated this into practical efforts to reduce drudgery in the household and to enhance the social, cultural, and educational amenities of their local communities. During a year, a local chapter of the UFWM typically held nine monthly meetings, where "special UFWM topics" were discussed: public health, social service, young people, education, and the marketing of the byproducts of the farm.[41]

Lobbying governments and other organizations became an important part of the activities of these various women's organizations after the First World War. They were not content merely to let the Local Council of Women submit petitions to municipal, provincial, and federal governments but frequently sent resolutions demanding action directly. However, only a very small number of these women dared to brave the riskier opportunities of elected service offered by enfranchisement.

AN INCORRUPT ELECTORATE?

Unless they surrendered their status as Treaty Indians, aboriginal women could not vote until 1960, but other adult women gained the suffrage in Manitoba in 1916.[42] The immediate issue was whether provincial enfranchisement entitled women to vote federally. Prime Minister Borden, a Conservative, dispelled the doubt with his infamous legislation of 1917 which actually disfranchised some women in the province while confirming the vote for others.[43] His priority in 1917 was to bring about conscription, and he had formed a coalition union government with pro-conscription members of the Liberal party. He created an electorate favourable to the issue by two measures: the Military Voters Act, which enfranchised all members of the armed forces and their wives, mothers, and sisters, and the Wartime Elections Act, which disfranchised conscientious objectors and persons born in enemy countries who had become naturalized Canadian citizens after 1902, unless they had a son, grandson, or brother on active service. This second act served to disfranchise most Manitoba women who had emigrated from parts of the Austro-Hungarian empire after 1902 – a substantial proportion of the population.

Ironically, the suggestion of selective enfranchisement had actually been put forward in December 1916 by Nellie McClung. This contradicted her own published transcultural support of "the foreign women's vote," and Francis Marion Beynon was swift to point out the inconsistency. If democracy is good, wrote Beynon, "it is good when applied to the Icelandic women who worked so hard to get the vote, and to the Polish and Ruthenian and other women who took a keener interest in the suffrage petition than many of our British women."[44]

McClung was in the sorry position of wishing to support a wide suffrage while wanting to promote patriotic support for the war in which her own young son had volunteered. By January 1917 she considered "a partial franchise seems to me better than none" but, reeling from Beynon's attack, in the interests of unity "I will withdraw the suggestion of a partial franchise."[45] Borden however took over the plan. The Wartime Elections Act was described by Beynon, who by this time had left Manitoba for New York, as "that monstrous act of injustice." At the very least, women should stay free of the existing political parties and develop a position as an "incorrupt electorate."[46] The first opportunity women had to exercise their new right was therefore shrouded in what some considered to be the unclean aura of partisan politics from which many wished to keep their distance.

Nevertheless, in Manitoba some women were unconvinced of the virtues of non-partisan politics and participated in that 1917 election with gusto: some of the fault-lines within the women's movement were already being revealed.[47] Canvassers for the Union government courted the women's votes as did newspaper advertisements explicitly addressed to the "Next-of-Kin" or "Your Ballot is For Your Boy." "Stand Behind Your Boy and Not Too Far Behind ... There is not time for tea or referendums," referred to some pacifists who urged a referendum before conscription. Union organizers used women volunteers to ensure the registration of eligible women. The Canadian Red Cross sponsored a visit from Captain Julia Henshaw of Vancouver who exhorted the "women who work" to vote for the war effort. Tributes were made to the influence of women: "There seems to be a stampede from the ranks of labour to the support of a Union government ... the women are entitled to some credit for this change of opinion, as many of the most earnest workers among them are the wives of mechanics who have enlisted."[48]

In all areas of Winnipeg, headlines pronounced women to be "Solid for Union Government," and there were frequent accounts of meetings addressed by women speakers appealing specifically to women voters. At one mass rally, "arrangements for taking care of babies" were in place. Some speakers tried to respond to the concerns which Francis Marion Beynon had voiced. To one North End rally, Mrs Vere Brown announced: "At the beginning of this war, I, like many others, had the sentimental idea that voluntary enlistment would raise a better army than would conscription. I was wrong. We should have had conscription, not only of men, but of money, labour and wealth, right from the start."[49]

During the campaign one woman declared herself against the Union government: Helen Armstrong, president of the Women's Labour League. She supported an anti-Union candidate in a debate in Teulon, a town forty miles north of Winnipeg, while Margaret McWilliams supported the Union candidate. The unsympathetic reporter described Armstrong's address as "made up of violent attacks ... she classed the members of the Union government as brigands ... denounced conscription as an attempt on the part of capital to crush organized labour." McWilliams's speech, on the contrary, "was a splendid example of what may be expected from the right type of modern woman."[50]

Few of the prominent speakers in this first women's balloting had been actively involved with the Political Education League, successor to the Political Equality League. McWilliams had not been a member. The organization which actually furnished many speakers in 1917 was the Canadian Women's Press Club: journalists Anne Anderson Perry and Cora Hind had belonged to the league as well.[51] Another league officer, Genevieve Lipsett Skinner, made one of the more outspoken appeals of

Canadian Women's Press Club. (Provincial Archives of Manitoba N7677)

the campaign. At a meeting in suburban Winnipeg called by the Imperial Order of the Daughters of the Empire, she told "Elmwood women to vote against [the] Hun."[52] Harriet Walker, who had produced the 1914 women's parliament cabaret, wrote an election poem, "The Soldiers' Next-of-Kin," issued in December 1917 by the Union government's central publicity committee. Appealing to "lonely, loyal women, faithful, waiting wives, weeping widows, spartan mothers, and silent sisters," she put the responsibility for helping the soldiers firmly on the shoulders of the next-of-kin who must, she wrote, support the Union government.[53] Like Perry, Hind, and Skinner, Walker had served an active apprenticeship in the league, but most of the women involved in the 1917 election were the articulate wives of male Union government candidates and supporters.

Francis Marion Beynon wryly observed in the summer of 1917 that many members of the Local Council of Women who had previously been indifferent or even opposed to women's enfranchisement were now confidently anticipating the exercise of their vote.[54] Even on women's suffrage there was no ideological unity among women, and in subsequent elections, women would be found in the ranks of all political parties. No federal election campaign after 1917 made such a concerted and direct attempt to mobilize women's votes, but only a small handful of the suffragists were later candidates for election.[55]

ELECTORAL POLITICS

For the most part, women who became candidates were drawn from a new and different generation. They were few and far between. The work needed to create McClung's new society of "free men and free women" turned out to be monumentally difficult and daunting. Like newly enfranchised women elsewhere, Manitoban women encountered unacknowledged discrimination and were only occasionally able to

Margaret McWilliams. (*Saturday Night* 29 May 1920)

make inroads into the man's world of politics. What success they had was largely in municipal government.

There were five provincial elections between women's enfranchisement and the Second World War. One woman, Edith Rogers, a Liberal, was elected to the Legislative Assembly in 1920 and re-elected in 1922 and 1927 before retiring in 1932. A second woman, Salome Halldorson, a member of the Social Credit party, was elected in 1936. These were the only successful female candidacies out of a total of seventeen. Federally, only two women were attracted into electoral politics during the interwar period. Harriet Dick was a candidate in 1921 and Beatrice Brigden in 1930.[56] Neither was elected. Against this discouraging background, women in the generation after 1940 displayed considerable courage. In the nine provincial elections, 1941–1969, thirty-four women were nominated, representing a total of thirty-nine candidacies. Only three were successful.[57] Federally, it was not until 1963 that Manitoba sent its first woman to the House of Commons: this was Margaret Konantz, a daughter of Edith Rogers, the first woman member of the Legislative Assembly. Twelve women were candidates in the ten federal elections between 1940 and 1968, furnishing sixteen candidacies in all.

Edith Rogers. (Western Canadian Pictorial Index
A0862–25742)

All municipal politics in Winnipeg – and also much of the politics at
the provincial and federal levels – was structured by the events of the
1919 Winnipeg General Strike. For over six weeks in the summer of
1919 the city ground to a halt under the impact of a well-organized
strike – an event which many feared was the beginning of a North American Bolshevik Revolution. Eventually crushed by mounted police and
militia and its leaders put on trial for sedition, the strike left a powerful
legacy of bitterness and martyrdom. In 1919 a Citizens' Committee was
formed to counter Labour's supporters, and the committee survived,
under different names, for several generations.[58] Generally speaking, this
committee favoured the interests of business and property.[59] For most of
the post-1919 years the endorsement of the Citizens' Election Committee (later the Greater Winnipeg Election Committee) was clearly important in the election of women both as aldermen and trustees.

At the municipal level in the interwar period, two women were
successfully elected alderman, and ten women were elected as a school
trustee, three of them for more than one term.[60] After 1940 more
women served as alderman, but there were never more than two female

aldermen at the same time.[61] Women experienced the most success in gaining election as school trustees. While not a single woman was elected in 1950 or 1962, the system of electing half the trustees every other year meant that there were always some women on the Winnipeg school board. After the 1968 election, and again after 1969 election, women comprised a majority on the board.[62]

Seventy per cent of the 34 women aldermanic candidates between 1940 and 1970 were endorsed by the committee, and the only women who were elected alderman were among those supported by the committee. In the period after 1940 four of the women aldermanic candidates acknowledged a Labour designation and five candidacies were Independent.[63] At the trustee level, while most of the successful candidates after 1940 were still among those endorsed by the Citizens' Committee, some Labour women won election: six women for a total of eleven times.[64] Two of these women were on the far left: Margaret Chunn (elected in 1947) and Mary Kardash (1960, 1965, 1967) were members of the Labour Progressive or communist party and were among a group of long-lived Winnipeg communist municipal politicians,[65] who regularly, if not invariably, achieved election to the City Council or school board.

Over the entire period, women at all levels and of all affiliations shared one view: they all tended to claim that their concern for women's issues would be an advantage in civic politics. Women candidates invoked gender in three ways. They appealed to the right of women to participate fully in the political arena; they said that women's kind of service was distinct from men's and would benefit the entire community; and they concerned themselves especially with issues thought particularly to affect women and children.

The women emphasized a desire to be in partnership, not conflict, with men. They were conscious that they could contribute "as a housewife," "as a mother," "as a woman." Jessie Kirk, the first woman elected alderman in 1920, set the tone: "I am not here to do any antagonising whatever. I am here to stand on my merits as a woman." Helen Armstrong, an unsuccessful candidate for alderman in 1923, acknowledged women workers as her constituency: "I shall continue to work for more protection for our girls and women workers, also for the enforcement of all laws relative to wages, better conditions and our social welfare problems."[66]

Labour women differentiated themselves from Citizen women on two issues: the distribution of basic foodstuffs and peace education in the schools. In 1930 the Independent Labour Party organized a mass meeting of women during the civic election campaign. At this rally, the party's one woman candidate, Alice Hunt, advocated the municipal ownership and distribution of bread and milk and condemned "the outrage of the milling companies gambling in grain and making large profits, resulting in high bread prices though wheat costs were low." Another speaker, Jessie Maclennan, a member of the school board, promoted the idea of peace education, which "would be quite an undertaking unless some of the history books were changed." The meeting was addressed by other women on the public ownership of transportation, child welfare, the municipally operated central steam-heat utility, and unemployment. Several speakers appealed directly to gender, and Maclennan forthrightly noted that women were needed on City Council because she had not noticed "any signs of staggering intelligence among the men."[67]

Although Margaret McWilliams was elected with Citizen support, she also benefited from a draft from the Local Council of Women at her first election in 1933. She continually appealed to women's shared experience: "As a housewife, she had been interested in securing a dollar's worth for every 100 cents spent." Women could apply good housekeeping principles to City Hall. More women should enter public life: "Come on in, sister, the water's fine." Women had the best training: "All their days, in their own homes, they have been caring for people; men take care of *things*." She shared with Labour women a propensity for caring for "people rather than things."[68]

Whereas the pre-1939 women candidates almost invariably claimed common cause with other women, after the war they seemed to consider that plea irrelevant, or unhelpful. In one of the rare direct appeals to gender, Mary Kardash, an unsuccessful candidate for the school board in 1950, argued that "a mother's opinion on such matters as more kindergartens, more playgrounds, better health facilities and general improvement of the school system" was needed on the board.[69] Even the single female mayoralty candidate, Gloria Queen-Hughes in 1966, confined her official platform to issues of property development, provision of services, and a more open procedure for meetings.[70]

One characteristic shared by women in both ideological camps and in both time periods was their background as community activists. Only a few women candidates had been employed in the labour market. Before 1940, work-force experience was rarely emphasized as a qualification for public service. After the Second World War, women's work-force experience, which had often ended long before their candidacy, was mentioned, but the emphasis throughout was on work in community and women's organizations. The few women politicians appeared to consider this form of public service work, usually but not always politically non-partisan, as a necessary apprenticeship for electoral politics.[71]

Unlike the few female candidates for elected office, most of the women involved in these voluntary organizations considered their participation an end in itself: part of the normal daily routine of adult women. This expectation marks one of the distinctive features of the century 1870–1970 and to a large extent was peculiar to that period. Like Margaret McWilliams at the time of the First World War, Manitoba women activists in the 1960s passionately cared about their society and their participation in it. They unabashedly considered their involvement in women's organizations to be political, and the solicitation of testimony from over forty women's groups and from many individuals in the preparation of the brief to the Royal Commission on the Status of Women was a reflection of the political consciousness of those who contributed to the brief of the Manitoba Volunteer Committee on the Status of Women. These women wished to see more women in electoral politics, but at the same time they wished to have a formal recognition of the political nature of their own extra-electoral work. The social and economic as well as the political nature of their concern is evident in the brief.

The major concerns were framed on behalf of the married woman whose work was not remunerated by pay. Economically, she was highly vulnerable in the event her marriage failed. Recommendations were designed to protect such women primarily through state welfare legislation but also by a broadening of economic opportunities. Unlike McWilliams, women of the post–World War II generation were more attuned to the ways in which economic disadvantage could undermine formal political rights. The limits of citizenship were by now more apparent.

Involvement in community work attracted many women. Public service work of one sort or another allowed women to work for others – men, and children as well as other women. Women volunteers in a variety of organizations – rural and urban, church and school, educational and reform – were able to do much to bring about "the finer things of life," as the United Farm Women put it, and in the process developed their own skills beyond the family circle. No doubt cynics could condescend with "images of the busybody who keeps the neighbours in line, or does the work of welfare agencies for free."[72] The women themselves were convinced that work to help others was in itself civilized behaviour. As for electoral politics, by 1970, women were achieving parity at one level, on the school board. In political work generally, women had their gender in common, but were never united with respect to policy.

$\mathcal{L}$OOKING BACK

In 1870 everyone agreed that all women's work related, in one way or another, to motherhood. Motherhood was situated within a family. The most elementary division of labour was for the woman to do her mothering while the father fulfilled the patriarchal role of provider. Girls knew that when they grew up they would leave the parental family to marry and form a new household with a husband. This behaviour was learned and transmitted from one generation to the next in the family and in countless other institutions and ways of behaving.

It was understood that there would be times when neither people's opportunities nor their behaviour would conform to the normal process. A father might be unable to support his daughter before a spouse took over. A girl might choose to turn down a prospective mate. After marriage, a couple might turn out to be infertile. The husband might not earn sufficient income to support the family. For these instances there were remedies.

It was assumed that during adolescence a single girl would earn her keep and, in addition, that she might earn wages which could be saved towards the cost of establishing a separate household on marriage. The conditions surrounding her work had to be consistent with her future function as a mother: her respectability and health must be safeguarded so as not to jeopardize her marriage prospects or her future fertility. As a mother, her labour was to be concentrated on the domestic work of making a home for her husband and family of children and possibly other, often elderly, dependents. If her partner was unable to earn enough money, she might contribute to the family's resources but only by doing women's work which was distinct from, and not in competition with, the work of her husband or other men. If widowed, then her participation in the labour market was tolerated, even if she continued the work engaged in by her husband when living.

For the woman who defied the familial morality there was little consideration. An adult woman who did not marry was not readily admitted into the jobs populated by men. She was expected to work only in the jobs whose low pay and limited horizons were intended for girls waiting for marriage. Women who wished to enter the same occupations as men were treated with suspicion by professional associations and trade unions. A single woman with a child was in a real bind. Female jobs paid scarcely enough to support one individual, much less any dependents.

In the late nineteenth century these women, all in some way deviants, were the object of pity or condemnation. Protestants impelled by a Social Gospel to be their sisters' keepers and progressives inspired by visions of sexual equality joined forces to make life less severe for single women and unmarried mothers. Feminists advocated the entry of educated middle-class women into professional work. Voluntary welfare societies administered to poor and needy members of society. Increasingly, however, people looked to the state to regulate work and family. Legislation concerning the terms under which women worked both as employees and as wives and mothers refracted the dominant ideology of those in power. The state came to assume many of the responsibilities associated with the patriarchal husband.

Labour and welfare legislation over the century 1870–1970 reflected these commonplace attitudes about women. This was particularly evident for women with limited access to the basic resources for life. The state became "provider and patriarch" for women who had no alternative and especially for women with children or other dependents.[1] The growth of the welfare state during the twentieth century expanded these services way beyond those of an agency of last resort. Through taxation, public insurance, and the provision of services, as well as through legislation governing wages and working conditions, the state extended its domain to a position from which it eventually sought to retreat. By the late twentieth century a majority of taxpayers were no longer willing to fund the high cost of the services, in cash and in kind, delivered by various levels of government.

If there was one consistent thread throughout the shifting approaches of state policy as it attempted to balance the provision of goods, services, and people, it was the notion of women's dependency. If for various reasons a woman could not depend on a father or husband for material support, then she must be dependent on the state. As Stephen Leacock, the anti-feminist humorist, wrote: "Social policy should proceed from the fundamental truth that women are and must be dependent. If they cannot be looked after by an individual … they must be looked after by the State."[2] For a woman, the necessities of life were inextricably linked to the controlling authority of her provider.

The notion of a woman as an individual, morally and economically self-sufficient, challenged the pervasive concept of woman as dependent. Some nineteenth-century feminists began to develop the idea of an autonomous woman, a concept which grew in appeal during the twentieth century. Much feminist reform was directed towards replacing the dependent female with a new independent woman. The demands of motherhood, however, were difficult to reconcile with a traditional notion of independence, based as it was on the model of male citizens who had wives to look after their reproductive needs. Individual women always had to negotiate simultaneous demands of work, family, and self.

In this book I have presented examples of women individually negotiating the demands of production, in paid work, and of reproduction, within their families. When Manitoba entered Confederation, most women worked in the family and when they worked for pay at all it was when they were young and single. Rarely did married women, with their unpaid family responsibilities, work outside the home for pay, although it was not uncommon for them to provide, for a price, home-based services for others. A 1913 document setting out the legal conditions under which women performed their various sorts of responsibilities revealed attitudes towards the work of women not only on the part of the state but also in the understanding of feminists who wished to change society.[3] A second document published in 1968, the provincial brief prepared by feminists for the Royal Commission on the Status of Women, described how feminists reacted to the way women performed their responsibilities in the 1960s, when increasing numbers combined both family responsibilities and paid work in a double burden.[4] Both documents revealed the interests of certain feminists of the time and their attitudes towards the nature of the state and the work of women.

In 1913 feminists in Manitoba were caught in the throes of an exciting and popular campaign over votes for women. Members of the Manitoba Political Equality League fully recognized that the franchise was only one step towards full equality.[5] One of the league's publications, in the form of a cheap tract, was an account of the general status of women in Manitoba life as revealed in law. *Legal Status of Women in Manitoba*, compiled by Dr Mary Crawford, showed what Manitoba feminists of 1913 believed to be the major conditions governing women's legal status at the beginning of the twentieth century. Modelled on a 1908 publication of the National Council of Women of Canada, the pamphlet printed extracts from the laws in what might appear superficially to be a dry description of the way in which the state regulated women's lives.[6] However, the arrangement of material and Crawford's editorial comments reveal a polemic, with moral indignation permeating even the selection of extracts. The overriding vision was of woman as she ought to be: a self-possessed citizen, mistress of herself. This autonomy included control over her own body. At least for the unmarried woman, her body should be her own, inviolable to unwanted male trespass. At a distance of eighty years we cannot completely recover the mind-set of the people who compiled, or read, this pamphlet, but certain features of it reveal their special concerns.

Over a quarter of the 41-page pamphlet dealt with "domestic relations" – a reflection of the primacy of the family in women's lives. A woman's economic security was supposed to be furnished by lifelong marriage. The dissolution of marriage, upon application to the Senate of Canada, was "so costly a procedure that unless action is taken as a pauper, only the rich can avail themselves of this way of obtaining a divorce. The cost without legal fees is about five hundred dollars – with legal fees it amounts to about a thousand dollars." Divorce was rare, yet marriage could not always provide security, still less happiness, for women, and Crawford was indignant that the law did not make men more accountable for their responsibilities. Resentment permeated Crawford's statements: "An unmarried mother has the absolute control of her children. The rights of a married mother in her children during the life of the father and while she is living with him are not recognised by law"; and "The consent of the father only, to the exclusion of that of the mother, is necessary for the marriage of their minor children."[7] Mothers were not given equal rights of custody and guardianship until the passage of the Child Welfare Act in 1922. With respect to divorce, "it is hard to get a decree, and meanwhile the husband may have left the country and sold his property, unless the wife's lawyers have registered an attaching order against his real estate."[8] A widow's lack of security was also a concern for Crawford. In 1912 Manitoba had introduced a very limited form of security for widows in An Act for the Relief of Widows and Children, but they did not gain the right to an interest in their dead husbands' estates until 1918.[9] Crawford's attitude in 1913 was expressed typographically: she wrote, in capitals, "IN MANITOBA, THERE IS NO 'DOWER'."[10]

Crawford devoted five pages of her pamphlet to the subject of female employment. Noting that white women were prohibited from working (or residing) in any business owned or managed "by any Japanese, Chinaman, or other Oriental person," she offered no condemnation. Discrimination against orientals was common among early twentieth-century feminists who regarded them as bogeymen – white slave traders and drug traffickers preying on innocent white women.[11] Crawford noted extracts from the Manitoba Factory Act of 1900 which limited the hours of female workers in a factory and other work places. The law permitted, but did not require, the appointment of female factory inspectors – an objective achieved in 1914 with the appointment of Ida Bauslaugh, a nurse who had been a factory inspector in New Jersey.[12]

Extracts from the Criminal Code, a federal responsibility, took up over a third of Crawford's pamphlet, and she confined her selection to laws concerning the legality of marriage, rape, abortion, neglect in childbirth, seduction, abduction, and the support of children.[13] Much of this section was concerned with the protection of young women's chastity and reputation and this was dramatically illustrated in her list of "comparisons of punishments under the criminal code." Here she contrasted the stern punishments for theft of property or for counterfeiting currency (maximum sentence: imprisonment for life) with the much lighter punishments attendant on the "seduction of girls between 14 and 16 previously chaste ... indecent assault on female ... seduction of ward, or employee, by her guardian or employer, said ward or employee being under 21 years," all carrying a maximum sentence of only two years' imprisonment.[14] Crawford's indignation over the attitudes thereby demonstrated reflected contemporary maternalist concerns with violence against women and with wife and child abuse.

Crawford's final three pages demonstrated the close association between the advocates of political rights for women and those who wished to ensure professional status for nurses. She printed the new provincial act, the second in Canada, requiring the state registration of graduate nurses. Crawford saw this act as a measure of women's increased professional status and opportunities, for at the end she added: "In Manitoba women were admitted to the study and practice of law in 1912."[15]

Legal Status of Women in Manitoba revealed a desire to protect the respectability of young and single women in the labour force and to ensure the security of women who were widowed. There was less emphasis on women's role or status as wives. There was some indignation that they did not enjoy joint custody over their children, but overall Crawford silently accepted the prevailing notion that while married a woman was provided for by her husband and in less need of extra-familial assistance.

By 1968 when the provincial brief to the Royal Commission on the Status of Women was prepared, there had been a sweeping change in views. That brief revealed widespread misgivings about the economic status of married women as well as concerns about divorcées. There was much more emphasis on the environment in which women lived and on the responsibility of government for maintaining a person's economic sufficiency. More comprehensive in its sweep, the 1968 document took for granted an expanded notion of state involvement in the lives of women which in 1913 had been scarcely imagined. Underlying the later analyses and vision was an acceptance of an "assisted independence" for women. The writers had a view of a world where a benevolent, powerful, and prosperous state would provide basic necessities of income and certain public services such as education and health. The assistance should come in the form of welfare supplements, mainly to single mothers, "to help them acquire an acceptable standard of living" consistent with their "dignity or worth as individuals."[16]

The 1913 pamphlet was the work of one woman, endorsed by one reform organization, which reflected the dominant maternalism of progressive social thought of the time.[17] The 1968 brief was the work of a large volunteer committee formed from over forty women's organizations. If the earlier document displayed a concern for women as mothers past, present, or future, the 1968 report in addition paid considerable attention to single women: never-married adult women and divorcées. While not denying the economic responsibilities of husbands and fathers, the committee also saw women as independent agents who ought to possess improved opportunities to be self-supporting. The brief concerned itself with conditions for women (single, married, widowed, and divorced) who were responsible for dependents or who lived alone and in many of its comments clearly favoured the conception of woman as equal. A woman was entitled to equal pay for work of equal value and previously unpaid work in the home should be accorded economic recognition. Within the family, the spouses should have equal entitlement to allowances, pensions, and incomes provided by social security programmes.

June Menzies, the committee's research director, expressed dissatisfaction with what she described as anachronisms which arose when all women were considered dependents: "In our changing social structure and in our rapidly developing social legislation affecting the family, the concept of the wife and mother as a dependent has disappeared. Under legislation concerning the welfare of children the mother has become an equal partner with her husband, bearing with him the responsibility for the financial support and other care of the children ... Women no longer go from being dependents of their fathers to being dependents of their husbands." Pointing out that a third of the labour force was female, of whom over half were married, she urged that taxation laws be rendered consistent with new circumstances: "Equity will have to be achieved by dealing with the wife as an individual and taking into account the economic role she plays in the family and in society." This involved "the right of everyone to a recognition of his or her economic contribution to society whether the labour is paid in the labour market or unpaid in the home and community."[18]

June Menzies at the Legislature. (Western Canadian Pictorial Index A1197–35860)

June Menzies was an economist and a former president of the Local Council of Women with a wide-ranging and long-standing interest in women's concerns. Even before the Royal Commission was announced, she had done a lot of local research, inspired by the work of the 1961 Commission on the Status of Women in the United States. Menzies was a strong voice insisting on a new notion of woman's identity, a notion which was repeatedly echoed in the Royal Commission's report and found its way into subsequent legislation. Menzies identified the two principles which "became the cornerstone of the struggle for equitable family law in Manitoba: that marriage is a legal, social and economic partnership of equals and that work done in the home is of equal value in a marriage partnership to that done in the labour force."[19] These family law provisions were echoed in the Canadian Charter of Rights and Freedoms of 1982.[20] As Jane Ursel stated in 1992: "Changes in labour, criminal, constitutional and family law in the 1970s and 1980s ... repositioned the state from the role of benevolent patriarch in the 1950s to the self-professed champion of sexual equality in the 1980s."[21]

In 1970, Manitoba feminists were optimistic about their prospects in a new order. By the 1990s, however, the electorate's confidence in the ability of the state to deliver various forms of income support to large numbers of people became overshadowed by bleaker economic considerations.²² At the very end of the twentieth century there appears to be a reversion to an earlier period when the state needed to "minimize the number of dependents upon the public purse."²³ Politically, it has become increasingly apparent that the cost of social programmes is becoming too high for taxpayers to maintain. The prosperity of the post–Second World War generation has not been maintained for many in subsequent generations.

This story of women's work of all sorts in one prairie province shows that women participated in all fields where they could combine family obligations with other responsibilities. Where the combination was impractical, family life had priority, with women as well as with other members of society. True in 1870, the supremacy of family remained true for women in 1970. But there was an ideological shift. The dominant discourse of maternalism had always contained undercurrents of egalitarian feminism. By 1970 there was more mention of a woman as a person with individual human rights than of her authority as a mother.

Whilst women continued, as before, to work in the household without pay, an increasing number also worked for money as the twentieth century unfolded. This created a double burden. It cemented men's dependency on women for comfort, security, and self-esteem, for without the energy of women's domestic labour men would have been lost. Insofar as women were aware of a power relationship with men, however, their own position was rarely supreme. In law and in economics, adult women were supposed to be dependent on men. This was a matter of fact in the formal labour market where women earned less than men, even when they performed the same work. Mostly they were segregated along with other women into jobs requiring less skill and responsibility.

In 1870 most women in the labour force were young and single and retired at marriage. Although many married women continued to earn money, when they did so it was usually in their homes. One significant change over the century was in the migration of married women out of their homes and into the formal labour market. The location of work changed. The age of the female labour force rose. The nature of work also changed although many limitations remained. Women entered new occupations in offices and sales which had not existed in earlier times. However, much of the paid work that women in the twentieth century performed replicated the nurturing and supporting work they had hitherto done in the home: much cooking, clothing, and caring was, as it were, "de-privatized." Women provided services for male managers, and in the professions, female teachers and nurses were under the direction of male principals and physicians. Women still continued both to manage and to do most of the manual work in their households. A study published by the Organization for Economic Co-operation and Development in 1965 found that in developed Western societies "the average married woman with one child and a full-time job works about 38 and a half hours a week at home in addition to time spent on the job and travelling to and fro."[24]

These shifts in women's participation in the labour force were accompanied by conflicting interpretations of moralists. Feminists were divided over the practice of allocating a family wage to a male breadwinner; they both supported and opposed protective legislation, which restricted employers and employees; and in 1970 they were still divided over whether mothers should go out of the home to work. A further class-based division was sometimes evident. Women with high incomes and professional aspirations often had a different outlook from poorer women subject to exploitation from their bosses.

The trend towards greater participation by women in the labour force was unmistakable and unrelenting. Another trend, out of segregated work places and into occupations where men and women worked together, if not in partnership, was not as forceful but nevertheless clear. Both men and women gained more formal education, but in 1970 it was still evident in the universities that women were concentrated in arts, education, social work, and home economics – all components of a feminine economy.

This story of women working in Manitoba between 1870 and 1970 can be repeated in the rest of Canada and in other modern countries. The history chronicles women's work that has already been recorded in documents or oral archives. It is provisional and incomplete. When we know more, we can add more light and shade to the busy features of the labouring landscape. We may change some shapes in the picture when we have more information – for instance, on the work of First Nations women, or on the strategies of women on welfare. *A Female Economy* shows only slow progress on the road to the "full and complete development of a country, the welfare of the world, and the cause of peace," as the authors of the 1968 brief put it.[25]

The irony of Daisy Goodwill in Carol Shields's *The Stone Diaries* reminds us that we do not know all the answers:

The real troubles in this world tend to settle on the misalignment between men and women – that's my opinion, my humble opinion, as I long ago learned to say.

But how we do love to brush these injustices aside. Our wont is to put up with things, with the notion that men behave in one manner, and women in another. You might say it's a little sideshow we put on for ourselves, a way of squinting at human behavior, a form of complicity. Only think of how we go around grinning and winking and nodding resignedly or shrugging with frank wonderment! Oh well, we say with a knowing lilt in our voice, that's a man for you. Or, that's just the way women are. We accept, as a cosmic joke, the separate ways of men and women, their different levels of foolishness. At least we did back in the year 1936, the summer I turned thirty-one.

Men, it seemed to me in those days, were uniquely honored by the stories that erupted in their lives, whereas women were more likely to be smothered by theirs. Why? Why should this be?[26]

Forty years later Daisy Goodwill, the ordinary Manitoba woman, is more in control but not yet in command: she "enlarges on the available material, extends, shrinks, reshapes what's offered; this mixed potion is her life."[27]

$\mathcal{N}$OTES

ABBREVIATIONS

NA National Archives of Canada
PAM Provincial Archives of Manitoba

CHAPTER ONE

1 "He who would do good to another, must do it in Minute Particulars …
For Art and Science cannot exist but in minutely organized Particulars":
William Blake, *Jerusalem*, 108.
2 Sangster, *Earning Respect*, 5.
3 Clark, *Working Life of Women in the Seventeenth Century*; Pinchbeck,
Women Workers and the Industrial Revolution; Tilly and Scott, *Women,
Work and Family*. For references and reviews of some recent examinations
of women's work, see Amott and Matthaei, *Race, Gender and Work*;
Baron, ed., *Work Engendered*; Bradbury, *Working Families*; Boris, "Beyond
Dichotomy"; Brandt, "Postmodern Patchwork"; Errington, *Wives and
Mothers, Schoolmistresses and Scullery Maids*; Folbré, *Who Pays for the
Kids?*; Kobayashi, ed., *Women, Work, and Place*; Kuiper and Sap, eds., *Out
of the Margin*; Milkman, "New Research in Women's Labor History";
Walsh, "Women In or Out of American Economic History."
4 Shilliday, ed., *Manitoba 125*. Recent historical regional studies which pay
considerable attention to women, including women's work after 1870, are
Barman, *The West beyond the West: A History of British Columbia*;
Cavanaugh and Warne, eds., *Standing on New Ground: Women in Alberta*;
Creese and Strong-Boag, eds., *British Columbia Reconsidered: Essays on
Women*; De Brou and Moffatt, eds., *"Other" Voices: Historical Essays on
Saskatchewan Women*; Guildford and Morton, eds., *Separate Spheres:*

Women's Worlds in the 19th Century Maritimes; Kealey, ed., *Pursuing Equality: Historical Perspectives on Women in Newfoundland and Labrador*; Lévesque, *Making and Breaking the Rules: Women in Quebec, 1919–1939*; Sangster, *Earning Respect: The Lives of Working Women in Small-Town Ontario, 1920–1960*; Strange, *Toronto's Girl Problem: The Perils and Pleasures of the City 1880–1930*; Clio Collective, *Quebec Women: A History.*

5 Mill, "On the Definition of Political Economy." In Robson, ed., *Collected Works of John Stuart Mill*, 4: 313.

6 Mill, "On the Subjection of Women." In Robson, ed., *Collected Works of John Stuart Mill*, 21: 301, 298.

7 Ibid., 298; Caine, *Victorian Feminists*, 32–7.

8 Helmbold and Schofield, "Women's Labor History, 1790–1945," 503, 505.

9 McCloskey, *Rhetoric of Economics*; Nelson, *Feminism, Objectivity and Economics.*

10 Jennings, "Public or Private? Institutional Economics and Feminism," 126; Blank, "What Should Mainstream Economists Learn from Feminist Theory?" 134.

11 Waring, *If Women Counted*, 284.

12 Ibid., 26.

13 Parr, *Gender of Breadwinners*, 3.

14 Phillips, *Divided Loyalties*, 25–8.

15 See Armstrong and Armstrong, "Beyond Sexless Class and Classless Sex," 23–5.

16 Phillips, *Hidden Hands*, 74–92.

17 Peterson, "Ethnic and Class Politics in Manitoba," 87.

18 See Map 150, "Elisée Reclus' Map of French Canadian Settlements in Manitoba c1890," in Warkentin and Ruggles, eds., *Manitoba Historical Atlas*, 330–1.

19 Peterson, "Ethnic and Class Politics in Manitoba," 69, 74; Wiseman, "Pattern of Prairie Politics," 305.

20 Pentland, review of Bercuson, *Confrontation at Winnipeg*, 27.

21 Gutkin, *Worst of Times, Best of Times*, 24–7, 203–4.

22 Gray, *Winter Years*, 128.

23 Peterson, "Ethnic and Class Politics in Manitoba," 101, 102, 110, 113; Wiseman, "Pattern of Prairie Politics," 315.

24 Dickason, *Canada's First Nations*, 12–15, 419–20.

25 Offen, "Defining Feminism," 31.

26 Cott, *Grounding of Modern Feminism*, 4–5.

27 Offen, "Defining Feminism," 135, 147, 151–2; Cott, "Comment on Offen's 'Defining Feminism'," 203–5; DuBois, "Comment on Offen's 'Defining Feminism'," 195–7.

28 See Bumsted, *Winnipeg General Strike.*

29 Bumsted, "Developing a Canadian Disaster Relief Policy," 347, 365; Toronto *Globe and Mail*, 24 April 1998.

30 Horodyski, "Women and the Winnipeg General Strike," 28.

31 Angel, "Workers, Picketing and the Winnipeg General Strike," 51.

32 Bumsted, "Developing a Canadian Disaster Relief Policy," 361, 363.

33 Toronto *Globe and Mail*, 19 April 1995, 6.

CHAPTER TWO

1 Kerr, ed., *A Historical Atlas of Canada*, 56; Morton, *Manitoba*, 325.

2 *Census of Canada 1951*, 1, Table 13; *Census of Canada 1971*, 1, Part 1, Table 10; Artibise, *Winnipeg: A Social History*, 170.

3 Albers and Medicine, eds., *Hidden Half*; Peers, *Ojibwa of Western Canada*, 35–6, 54, 58–9, 80; Peers, "Subsistence, Secondary Literature, and Gender Bias"; Van Kirk, "Role of Native Women"; Van Kirk, *Many Tender Ties*; Brown, *Strangers in the Blood*. See also Chapter 5, "Homemaking," pp. 85–99.

4 Van Kirk, "Role of Native Women," 64.

5 Healy, *Women of Red River*; Lee, "Myth of Female Equality in Pioneer Society."

6 Spry, "The 'Private Adventurers' of Rupert's Land," 51, 54–5.

7 Van Kirk, "'The Reputation of a Lady'," 10; Van Kirk, "'What if Mama Is an Indian'," 126, 133.

8 Coates and McGuinness, *Manitoba*, 7–8.

9 Friesen, "'Justice Systems' and Manitoba's Aboriginal People: An Historical Survey," and Maps: "Indian Territories of the Prairie West ca 1820," and "The Numbered Treaties of Western Canada," both in Friesen, *Canadian Prairies*, at 66–8 and between 90 and 91; Peers, *Ojibwa of Western Canada*, ix.

10 Friesen, *Canadian Prairies*, 13–21; Tough, *'As Their Natural Resources Fail,'* 3–13.

11 Peers, *Ojibwa of Western Canada*, x–xi.

12 *Report of the Royal Commission on Aboriginal Peoples*, 1: 163.

13 Ibid., 161–71.

14 *Census of Canada 1911*, 11, Table 12; *Census of Canada 1921*, 1, Table 25; *Census of Canada 1931*, 1, Table 38; *Census of Canada 1941*, 11, Table 31; *Census of Canada 1951*, 1, Table 32; *Census of Canada 1961*, Catalogue 92–545, 1, Part 2, Table 35; *Census of Canada 1971*, Catalogue 92–723, 1, Part 3, Bulletin 1.3–2, Table 2.

15 Ward, "Population Growth in Western Canada," 174.

16 *Census of Canada 1946*, 1, Table 13; *Census of Canada 1951*, 1, Table 54; *Census of Canada 1961*, Catalogue 92–549, 1, Part 2, Table 64; *Census of Canada 1971*, Catalogue 92–725, 1, Part 3, Bulletin 1.3–4, Table 18.

17 Miller, *Shingwauk's Vision*, 199.

18 Hébert, "Les grandes gardiennes de la langue et de la foi," 343.

19 Ward, "Population Growth in Western Canada," 159.

20 Jackel, "Introduction," xxi.

21 Dawson and Yonge, *Pioneering in the Prairie Provinces*, 12.

22 For brief periods in the first decade of the twentieth century, men did outnumber women, and some historians believe this sexual imbalance accounts
for the prostitution of the time. Artibise, *Winnipeg: A Social History*, 147, 50.

23 *Census of Canada 1881*, II, Table 8; *Census of Canada 1891*, IV,
Table G; *Census of Canada 1901*, IV, Table I; *Census of Canada 1951*, I,
Table 19; *Census of Canada 1971*, Catalogue 92–715, Table 7.

24 Ward, "Population Growth in Western Canada," 160, 162; Gee, "Life
Course," 264.

25 Davidson, Grant, and Shefrin, *Population of Manitoba*, 13.

26 *Census of Canada 1941*, I, Table 18, Table 20; *Census of Canada 1981*,
Catalogue 92–901, Table 3.

27 Gee and Kimball, *Women and Aging*, 89.

28 For an explanation of these widespread trends, see Phillips, *Untying the
Knot*, 224–51.

29 *Census of Canada 1921*, I, Table 35; *Census of Canada 1931*, I, Table 43;
Census of Canada 1941, II, Table 36; *Census of Canada 1951*, I, Table 38;
Census of Canada 1961, Catalogue 92–546, I, Part 2, Table 42; *Census of
Canada 1971*, Catalogue 92–724, I, Part 3, Bulletin 1.3–3, Table 10.

30 See Map 306, "The Distribution of Resident Clergy in Manitoba in 1926,"
in Warkentin and Ruggles, eds., *Manitoba Historical Atlas*, 562–3.

31 Davidson, Grant, and Shefrin, *Population of Manitoba*, 33.

32 Kristjanson, *The Icelandic People in Manitoba*; Arnason, *New Icelanders*.

33 Luciuk and Kordan, *Creating a Landscape*, map 4.

34 Dawson, *Group Settlement*, 12.

35 Francis, *In Search of Utopia*; Swyripa, *Wedded to the Cause*.

36 Gee, "Female Marriage Patterns," 462.

37 *Census of Canada 1951*, I, Table 13; *Census of Canada 1961*, Catalogue
92–536, I, Part I, Table 12; *Census of Canada 1971*, Catalogue 92–709, I,
Part I, Bulletin 1.1–9, Table 10.

38 Gee, "Female Marriage Patterns," 464, 470.

39 Murphy, *Janey Canuck in the West*, 40, 42, 45, 47; Mander, *Emily Murphy*,
67–9.

40 Van Kirk, " 'The Reputation of a Lady'."

41 Roy, *Enchantment and Sorrow*, 5.

CHAPTER THREE

1 Taylor, "On Marriage." In Robson, ed., *Collected Works of John Stuart
Mill*, 21: 375.

2 Okin, *Women in Western Political Thought*, 229; Mill, "On the Subjection of
Women." In Robson, ed., *Collected Works of John Stuart Mill*, 21: 301, 298.

3 Pujol, *Feminism and Anti-Feminism in Early Economic Thought*, 1, 21.

4 Jackel, ed., *Flannel Shirt and Liberty*, 31–65.

5 Ibid., 37, 38, 42.

6 Ibid., 55.

7 Canadian Pacific Railway, *What Women Say about the Canadian North West*, 45, 50.

8 Canadian Pacific Railway, *Women's Work in Western Canada*, 34.

9 Proverbs 31: 10–31.

10 Hanawalt, ed., *Women and Work in Preindustrial Europe*, viii; Hanawalt, *Ties That Bound*, 107–23.

11 Power, *Medieval Women*; Clark, *Working Life of Women in the Seventeenth Century*; Pinchbeck, *Women Workers and the Industrial Revolution*.

12 See Fraser and Gordon, "Genealogy of Dependency," 318–19.

13 Allen, *Social Passion*, 3–4.

14 McClung, *In Times Like These*, 85.

15 *Maclean's Magazine*, 15 February 1928, 71.

16 Bodichon, "Women and Work," 1–15, 41, 61–3.

17 Gilman, *Women and Economics*, 5, 15, 18, 285–6, 299, 316.

18 Degler, "Introduction," vi.

19 Dyhouse, *Feminism and the Family in England*, 15; Brittain, *Testament of Youth*, 41.

20 Schreiner, *Woman and Labour*, 50, 54, 79, 205, 259, 274, 275.

21 *Le Manitoba* (Winnipeg), 2 February 1916.

22 Quoted in McClung, *The Stream Runs Fast*, 101–5.

23 Artibise, *Winnipeg: A Social History*, 192–3.

24 Woodsworth, *My Neighbour*, 96, 104.

25 Addams, *Democracy and Social Ethics*, 104; Addams, *Twenty Years at Hull-House*, 339–41; Addams, *Second Twenty Years at Hull-House*, 89.

26 Addams, *Second Twenty Years at Hull-House*, 196; Davis, *American Heroine*.

27 PAM, University Women's Club, *Work of Women and Girls*.

28 Kealey, "Women and Labour during World War I," 78.

29 Manitoba, Legislative Assembly, *Sessional Paper* 27, 7 February 1918, Helen Armstrong to Ed Mcgrath, 5 December 1917.

30 Kealey, "Women and Labour during World War I," 95; Oddson, *Employment of Women in Manitoba*, 31–4.

31 See Chapter 7, "Paid Labour," pp. 100–37.

32 Oddson, *Employment of Women in Manitoba*, 82–3.

33 Cott, *Grounding of Modern Feminism*, 121, 125, 127.

34 Wexler, *Emma Goldman*, 166; Martin Zeilig, "Emma Goldman in Winnipeg," 23–7.

35 Wexler, *Emma Goldman in America*, xv.

36 Kinnear, "Icelandic Connection."

37 Jackel, "First Days, Fighting Days," 66.
38 *Grain Growers' Guide*, 31 July 1912, 9.
39 Winnipeg *Voice*, 7 December 1917.
40 Kinnear, *Margaret McWilliams*, 65.
41 PAM, University Women's Club, Minutes, 28 October 1920.
42 MacInnis, *Woodsworth*, 70–2.
43 Cook, "F.M. Beynon and Christian Reformism," 188–9.
44 Strong-Boag, "'Wages for Housework'," 29.
45 See Ladd-Taylor, *Mother-Work*.
46 Dyhouse, *Feminism and the Family in England*, 93.
47 Rathbone, "Remuneration of Women," 120–1.
48 Stocks, *Eleanor Rathbone*, 76–7.
49 Pugh, *Women and the Women's Movement in Britain*, 236–44.
50 Harrison, *Prudent Revolutionaries*, 148; Lewis, "Eleanor Rathbone and the Family," 137; Brittain, "Women in Industry," 110.
51 Manitoba, *Report into the Administration of the Child Welfare Division*, 41, 44, 45.
52 Davidson, *Employment in Manitoba*, 27.
53 Goeres, "Disorder, Dependency and Fiscal Responsibility," 180.
54 Ibid.
55 Oddson, *Employment of Women of Manitoba*, Table 33.
56 University of Winnipeg, Winnipeg School Division, Scrapbooks, 1: 15.
57 For more information on this issue, see my article: "'Mostly for the Male Members'."
58 Oddson, *Employment of Women in Manitoba*, 23, 25, 46, 55, 60.
59 Ibid., 64, 65, 71, 77, 87, 89, 105.
60 Pierson, *'They're Still Women After All'*, 22–3, 216, 220.
61 Canada, Advisory Committee on Reconstruction, *Report of the Subcommittee on the Post-War Problems of Women*, 8, 9–10; Brandt, "'Pigeon-Holed and Forgotten'," 247, 259.
62 Manitoba, Advisory Committee on the Co-ordination of Post-War Planning, *Report of the Subcommittee on Women's Services*, 1, 2, 4–6, 7.
63 Duverger, *Political Role of Women*, 212.
64 Strong-Boag, "Home Dreams," 381.
65 Duverger, *Political Role of Women*, 212, 213–14.
66 Friedan, *Feminine Mystique*, 346; Friedan, *Second Stage*, 82–123, 233.
67 Canada, *Report on the Status of Women*, vii, 395–418.
68 Manitoba, *Report of the Manitoba Volunteer Committee on the Status of Women*. See also Chapter 9, "Looking Back," pp. 156–67.
69 Canada, *Report on the Status of Women*, xii, xi.
70 Armstrong and Armstrong, *Double Ghetto*, 41–6.
71 Canada, *Report on the Status of Women*, 66–77, 422.

72 Tilly and Scott, *Women, Work and Family.*

73 Fraser and Gordon, "Genealogy of Dependency," 318–19, 324; Kobayashi, Peake, Beneson, and Pickles, "Introduction: Placing Women and Work," in Kobayashi, ed., *Women, Work, and Place,* xiii.

CHAPTER FOUR

1 Gregor and Wilson, *History of Education in Manitoba,* 1: 45.

2 Woods, *Education in Manitoba,* 1: 15–18.

3 Osborne, "Introduction," 5; Henley, "School Question Continued."

4 Morton, "Manitoba Schools and Canadian Nationality," 12–13.

5 Dickason, *Canada's First Nations,* 273–9.

6 Barman, Hebert, and McCaskill, "Legacy of the Past," 1:6; Gray, "Methodist Indian Day Schools in Northern Manitoba," 2–3.

7 Dickason, *Canada's First Nations,* 335–7; Gray, "Methodist Indian Day Schools in Northern Manitoba," 5.

8 Barman, Hebert, and McCaskill, "Legacy of the Past," 1:6.

9 Titley, "Industrial Education for Manitoba Natives," 372.

10 Ibid., 382.

11 Miller, *Shingwauk's Vision,* 219–22.

12 Sealey, *Education of Native Peoples in Manitoba,* 33.

13 Beardy and Coutts, eds., *Voices from Hudson Bay,* 60.

14 Miller, *The Spirit Lives On,* B11–12.

15 Ibid., C–4.

16 Ibid., N–2.

17 Christie and Gauvreau, *A Full-Orbed Christianity,* 165–96; *Turtle Mountain Rural Survey,* June-July 1914, and *Swan River Rural Survey,* August-September 1914.

18 *Turtle Mountain Rural Survey,* 17.

19 *Swan River Rural Survey,* 19.

20 *Census of Canada 1911,* II, Table 12.

21 *Turtle Mountain Rural Survey ,* 34–5.

22 Ibid., 34; *Swan River Rural Survey,* 36.

23 *Swan River Rural Survey,* 38; *Turtle Mountain Rural Survey,* 43.

24 *Turtle Mountain Rural Survey,* 39–40; *Swan River Rural Survey,* 38.

25 Manitoba, Department of Education, *Annual Report,* 1886, and 1887, Table 5; Heriot, "School Inspectors in Manitoba," 2; *Census of Canada 1901,* VI, Table XI; *Census of Canada 1921,* I, Table 5.

26 Kristjanson, *The Icelandic People in Manitoba,* 38.

27 Toronto *Globe,* 4 October 1890.

28 Kristjanson, *The Icelandic People in Manitoba,* 37, 65.

29 Kinnear, "Icelandic Connection," 25.

30 Francis, *In Search of Utopia.*

31 Mennonite Heritage Centre, Evril Wiebe, "Early Days: An Interview with Mrs Agatha Wiedeman," 2 April 1977.

32 Woods, *Education in Manitoba*, 1:25. See also Enns, "Mennonites and Modernism."

33 Enns, *Gretna*, 64; Mennonite Heritage Centre, Helena (Penner) Hiebert, "Granny Stories," XII: 4–9; Kinnear, "Women and Post-Suffrage Prairie Politics," 43.

34 Hryniuk and McDonald, "Schooling Experience of Ukrainians," 292–4.

35 Ewanchuk, *Pioneer Profiles*, 49, 108, 116.

36 Ibid., 64, 174.

37 Ibid., 233.

38 Ibid., 69, 71, 170.

39 Hryniuk and McDonald, "Schooling Experience of Ukrainians," 297, 294.

40 Galloway, *I Lived in Paradise*, 193–5, 198.

41 *Turtle Mountain Rural Survey*, 37–8; *Swan River Rural Survey*, 37.

42 Woods, *Education in Manitoba*, 24; Shack, "Making of a Teacher 1917–1935," 442–9.

43 Thomson, "Diary," 9, 21, 37.

44 Ibid., 40, 42–66.

45 Shack, "Making of a Teacher, 1917–1935," 452.

46 Ibid., 454.

47 Bonin, "Grey Nuns and the Red River Settlement"; Johns and Fines, *Winnipeg General Hospital School of Nursing*, 5.

48 Johns and Fines, *Winnipeg General Hospital School of Nursing*, 12.

49 Street, *Watchfires on the Mountains*, 60.

50 Johns and Fines, *Winnipeg General Hospital School of Nursing*, 14.

51 Ibid., 16; Birtles, "Tribute to the Pioneer Nurses of Manitoba."

52 Johns and Fines, *Winnipeg General Hospital School of Nursing*, 44.

53 Fines, "History of the Manitoba Association of Registered Nurses," 11.

54 Johns and Fines, *Winnipeg General Hospital School of Nursing*, 46.

55 *Winnipeg General Hospital Nurses' Alumnae Journal*, 1979, 62.

56 Fines, "History of the Manitoba Association of Registered Nurses," 71; Kinnear, *In Subordination*, 98–122.

57 Morton, *One University*, 17–41; Fraser, *History of St John's College*, dates the admission of women to St. John's in 1892.

58 On women and medicine, see Hacker, *Indomitable Lady Doctors*, and Kinnear, *In Subordination*, 53–77. On women in law, see Harvey, "Women in Law in Canada," and Kinnear, "That There Woman Lawyer." Oddson, *Employment of Women in Manitoba*, 79; Manitoba Museum of Man and Nature, Oral History Tape 597, Margaret Gow.

59 NA, Canadian Federation of University Women, Early Women Graduates, Lillian Ponton Saul to Edith McColl, 22 March 1937.

60 Ibid., Jessie (Holmes) Munro to Edith McColl, 23 March 1937; Alice Maud (Williams) Young to Edith McColl, 19 March 1937.

61 Ibid., Edith (Sutherland) Clark to Edith McColl, September 1937.

62 Ibid., List, "First Ten Women to Graduate from the University of Manitoba," June 1937.

63 Nuffield, *With the West in Her Eyes*, 100–1.

64 Ibid., 105, 109, 117, 133, 134.

65 Sheehan, "National Issues and Curricula Issues," 233–40.

66 Yuzyk, *Ukrainians in Manitoba*, 147; Turek, *Poles in Manitoba*, 22–3.

67 Hébert, "Les grandes gardiennes de la langue et de la foi," 271.

68 Roy, *Enchantment and Sorrow*, 52.

69 Ibid., 52–3.

70 *Western School Journal*, 1919–20, 179.

71 Wilson, *History of Home Economics Education in Manitoba*.

72 Oddson, *Employment of Women in Manitoba*, 80.

73 Strong-Boag, *Parliament of Women*, 33.

74 Davis, "Mary Speechly," 38.

75 Strong-Boag, *New Day Recalled*, 126–7, 151.

76 Sheehan, "National Issues and Curricula Issues," 233.

77 Woods, *Education in Manitoba*, 1: 74.

78 Manitoba, Department of Education, Programme of Studies, 1919.

79 Jewish Historical Society, Oral History Tapes, tape 337, Clara (Taylor) Shames.

80 University of Manitoba, Office of Institutional Analysis, "Numbers of Women Graduates by Faculty, 1880–1942, 1942–89," July 1991.

81 Ferns, *Reading from Left to Right*, 35, 37.

82 Pierson, '*They're Still Women After All*', 91.

83 University of Manitoba, Office of Institutional Analysis, "Numbers of Women Graduates by Faculty, 1880–1942, 1942–89," July 1991.

84 McCracken, *Memories Are Made of This*, 102–3.

CHAPTER FIVE

1 Mill, "On the Definition of Political Economy." In Robson, ed., *Collected Works of John Stuart Mill*, 4: 313.

2 *Winnipeg Tribune*, 8 September 1934.

3 Waring, *If Women Counted*, 284.

4 Longino, "Economics for Whom?" 161–3.

5 William Blackstone, *Commentaries on the Laws of England*, quoted in Perkin, *Women and Marriage in Nineteenth Century England*, 1.

6 Table A2.3, Disposition of Marital Property, in Ursel, *Private Lives, Public Policy*, 327.

7 Crawford, *Legal Status of Women in Manitoba*, 5.

8 Canada, *Report on the Status of Women*, 254–60; Phillips, *Untying the Knot*, 216.

9 Manitoba, *Report of the Manitoba Volunteer Committee on the Status of Women*, 42.

10 *Labour Gazette*, April 1915, 1183.

11 Strong-Boag, "'Wages for Housework'."

12 *Labour Gazette*, June 1919, 714–15; August 1924, 663; February 1929, 179.

13 Hurl, "Politics of Child Welfare in Manitoba, 1922–3." For an overview of contemporaneous policies in the United States, see Gordon, *Pitied but not Envied*, 37–64.

14 See White, "Restructuring the Domestic Sphere," for a detailed analysis of this policy.

15 Buffalohead, "Farmers, Warriors, Traders," 241; De Mallie, "Male and Female in Traditional Lakota Culture," 238.

16 Peers, "Subsistence, Secondary Literature, and Gender Bias," 44–7.

17 Carter, "First Nations Women of Prairie Canada in the Early Years," 68–9.

18 White, "Restructuring the Domestic Sphere," 4.

19 Ibid., 134, 138.

20 Carter, "First Nations Women of Prairie Canada in the Early Years," 56, 57–8, 59–61.

21 White, "Restructuring the Domestic Sphere," 134–7.

22 Ibid., 224.

23 Ibid., 227–33; Carter, "First Nations Women of Prairie Canada in the Early Years," 66.

24 Beardy and Coutts, eds., *Voices from Hudson Bay*, 47.

25 Carter, "First Nations Women of Prairie Canada in the Early Years," 71.

26 "Mother-work" is the term used by Molly Ladd-Taylor.

27 Strong-Boag, *New Day Recalled*, 113–77.

28 Strong-Boag, "Keeping House in God's Country," 127.

29 Wilson, *History of Home Economics Education in Manitoba*, 37–9.

30 Ibid., 174.

31 Knox, *Girl of the New Day*. This book was a guide to careers suitable for women. The title of the chapter on motherhood was "The Queen of Them All."

32 Statistics Canada, *Vital Statistics*, volume 1, *Births and Deaths 1977–1980*. CS 84–204.

33 Prentice et al., *Canadian Women*, 471: Table A.4, Size of Completed Families.

34 Ewanchuk, *Pioneer Profiles*, 25.

35 Nuffield, *With the West in Her Eyes*, 41, 45, 49.

36 *Swan River Rural Survey*, 21.

37 *Turtle Mountain Rural Survey*, 23.

38 Kinnear, "'Do You Want Your Daughter to Marry a Farmer?'" 143.

39 *Swan River Rural Survey*, 20.

40 Nuffield, *With the West in Her Eyes*, 85.

41 Artibise, *Winnipeg: A Social History*, 158, 165.

42 Woodsworth, *Strangers within Our Gates*, 335–6.

43 McColl, *Vignettes of Early Winnipeg*, 2, 24–5.

44 Woodsworth, "Report on Living Standards 1913," in Artibise, *Winnipeg: A Social History*, 311, 315.

45 McColl, *Vignettes of Early Winnipeg*, 3.

46 Kinnear, "'Do You Want Your Daughter to Marry a Farmer?'" 145. See also Chapter 6, "Farm Work," pp. 85–99.

47 Artibise, *Winnipeg: A Social History*, 235.

48 Kinnear, "'Do You Want Your Daughter to Marry a Farmer?'" 146.

49 Broadfoot, *Ten Lost Years*, 106–8.

50 Canadian Welfare Council, *Rural Need in Canada*, 23.

51 Luxton, *More Than a Labour of Love*, 24.

52 Ibid., 43–79.

53 McLaren and McLaren, *The Bedroom and the State*, 10; Silverman, *Last Best West*, 59–71.

54 *Grain Growers' Guide*, 22 November 1911, 29 November 1911, 20 March 1912, 15 May 1912, 24 July 1912, 18 September 1912, 25 September 1912, 6 November 1912, 4 March 1914. See also Kelcey and Davis, eds., *A Great Movement Underway*, 66–8.

55 Strong-Boag, *New Day Recalled*, 88.

56 PAM, Women's Canadian Club, Executive Minutes, 16 May 1923.

57 McLaren and McLaren, *The Bedroom and the State*, 9.

58 University of Manitoba Archives, Mary Speechly Papers, Eileen Mestery to M.F. Bishop, 6 February 1980.

59 Ibid., Family Planning Association of Winnipeg to Hugh A. Benham, 8 January 1958; McLaren and McLaren, *The Bedroom and the State*, 71.

60 University of Manitoba Archives, Mary Speechly Papers, Eileen Mestery to M.F. Bishop, 6 February 1980.

61 Buffalohead, "Farmers, Warriors, Traders," 241.

62 Beardy and Coutts, eds., *Voices from Hudson Bay*, 90.

63 Strong-Boag, "Intruders in the Nursery"; see also Prentice et al., *Canadian Women*, 240–62.

64 Luxton, *More Than a Labour of Love*, 81–115.

65 NA, Department of Labour, "Employment of Women and Day Care of Children," RG 27, Vol. 609, 6–52–1.

66 PAM, Council of Social Agencies, Working Mothers' Survey, 1942–3.

67 PAM, Department of Education, Half Yearly Attendance Reports, Winnipeg, 1942–3. I thank Cathy Chatterley and Daphne Gilbert for their research assistance in the tabulation and analysis of the surveys.

68 PAM, Council of Social Agencies, Annual General Meeting 1943, Mrs Robert McQueen.
69 Luxton, *More Than a Labour of Love*, 152–3.
70 Ibid., 145, 150, 117–59.
71 Ibid., 143, 144.
72 Gray, *Winter Years*, 180.
73 Luxton, *More Than a Labour of Love*, 127.
74 Ibid., 164–5.
75 Ibid., 173–6.
76 Artibise, *Winnipeg: A Social History*, 308–19; MacInnis, *Woodsworth*, 62–5.
77 Gutkin, *Worst of Times, Best of Times*, 199.
78 Luxton, *More Than a Labour of Love*, 177–89.
79 Strong-Boag, "Home Dreams," 393.
80 Smith, *Wealth of Nations*, I, I, viii, 51; I, x, 50–1; II, 4, viii, 4.
81 PAM, University Women's Club, Minutes, 8 December 1916.
82 *Manitoba Free Press*, 21 November 1930.
83 Stowell, *If I Were King of Canada*, 34–44.
84 Friesen, *Canadian Prairies*, 329, 370; Kinnear, " 'Do You Want Your Daughter to Marry a Farmer?' " 149.
85 University of Manitoba Archives, Consumers' Association, Margaret Stansfield to Mrs Slimmon, 14 January 1971.
86 Ibid.
87 Ibid., "Do You Belong to the Consumers' Association of Canada?" 1970–1.
88 Conversation with Jean Carson and June Menzies, May 1975.

CHAPTER SIX

1 *Census of Canada 1951*, I, Table 13; Urquhart and Buckley, *Historical Statistics of Canada*, Tables A67–69.
2 Van de Vorst, "History of Farm Women's Work in Manitoba," 229, 8.
3 Buffalohead, "Farmers, Warriors, Traders," 236–44; Peers, "Subsistence, Secondary Literature, and Gender Bias," 39–50.
4 Weist, "Beasts of Burden and Menial Slaves," 31; Peers, "Subsistence, Secondary Literature, and Gender Bias," 39.
5 Carter, "First Nations Women of Prairie Canada in the Early Years," 56.
6 Carter, *Lost Harvests*, 258.
7 Friesen, *Canadian Prairies*, 303, 304.
8 See Jeffrey, *Frontier Women*; Jensen, *Loosening the Bonds*; Moynihan, Armitage, and Dichamp, eds., *So Much to be Done*; Myres, *Westering Women*. For studies of farm women's work in the United States, see these books and Jensen, *Promise to the Land*; Sachs, *Gendered Fields*.

9 Canadian Pacific Railway, *What Women Say about the Canadian North West*, and *Women's Work in Western Canada*.

10 Van de Vorst, "History of Farm Women's Work in Manitoba," 229, 7, 8–9; Strange, *With the West in Her Eyes*, 218–31.

11 Van de Vorst, "History of Farm Women's Work in Manitoba," 9.

12 McCallum, "Prairie Women and Dower Law," 20.

13 Ibid., 29; Cavanaugh, "The Limitations of the Pioneering Partnership," 199.

14 Jackel, "Introduction," xxi.

15 Cohen, *Women's Work, Markets, and Economic Development*, 61.

16 Morton, *Manitoba*, 164–5.

17 Van de Vorst, "History of Farm Women's Work in Manitoba," 59.

18 Owen, "Cost of Farm-Making in Early Manitoba," 4, 7.

19 Van de Vorst, "History of Farm Women's Work in Manitoba," 67, 64.

20 Danysk, *Hired Hands*, 71.

21 Ibid., 9, 65, 67; Cohen, *Women's Work, Markets, and Economic Development*, 66–71.

22 Morton, *Manitoba*, 250–60.

23 McClung, *Clearing in the West*, 126–31; Van de Vorst, "History of Farm Women's Work in Manitoba," 73, 75–7; Cohen, *Women's Work, Markets, and Economic Development*, 71–92.

24 Van de Vorst, "History of Farm Women's Work in Manitoba," 79.

25 Ibid., 80, 81–3.

26 Aberson, *From the Prairies with Hope*.

27 *Grain Growers' Guide*, 29 August 1923, 17.

28 Murchie, *Agricultural Progress on the Prairie Frontier*, 142–3, 186, 209; Dawson and Yonge, *Pioneering in the Prairie Provinces*, 142–3.

29 Haig, *Brave Harvest*, 167.

30 Manitoba Museum of Man and Nature, Oral History Tapes, tape 419, Mrs Ruth Land.

31 Van de Vorst, "History of Farm Women's Work in Manitoba," 97, 98. 101.

32 *Grain Growers' Guide*, 8 September 1915, 10.

33 Broadfoot, *Next-Year Country*, 240–2.

34 Van de Vorst, "History of Farm Women's Work in Manitoba," 156.

35 Ewanchuk, *Pioneer Profiles*, 257–8.

36 Ibid., 171.

37 Thomson, "Diary," 121.

38 Dorsch, " 'You Just Did What Had To Be Done'," 116–30.

39 Altogether 364 questionnaires were completed but only 307 were returned in time to be used for the report. The following percentages were calculated from the total number of 364 questionnaires in the United Farmers of Manitoba archive. For further information, see Kinnear, " 'Do You Want Your Daughter to Marry a Farmer?' " 146, 147.

40 Kinnear, " 'Do You Want Your Daughter to Marry a Farmer?' " 142–6.
41 PAM, United Farmers of Manitoba, "United Farm Women of Manitoba Rural Survey 1922 Report," 3.
42 Kinnear, " 'Do You Want Your Daughter to Marry a Farmer?' " 146, 147.
43 Ibid., 147–8.
44 PAM, Department of Agriculture, *Manitoba Agriculture Year Book*, 1985, 98.
45 Friesen, *Canadian Prairies*, 430–1.
46 Van de Vorst, "History of Farm Women's Work in Manitoba," 225.
47 McClung, *In Times Like These*, 118, 109; Sundberg, "Farm Women on the Canadian Prairie Frontier."
48 *Grain Growers' Guide*, 27 May 1925, 17.
49 Strong-Boag, "Pulling in Double Harness or Hauling a Double Load," 48.
50 Manitoba, *Report of the Manitoba Volunteer Committee on the Status of Women*, 99.
51 Aberson, *From the Prairies with Hope*, 43–7.

CHAPTER SEVEN

1 Ostry, *Female Worker in Canada*, 1.
2 Organization for Economic Co-operation and Development, *Equal Opportunities for Women*, 15–32. See also Frances, Kealey, and Sangster, "Women and Wage Labour," 54–5.
3 Canada, *Report on the Status of Women in Canada*, 53.
4 Skocpol and Ritter, "Gender and the Origin of Modern Social Policies," 36–93; See also Skocpol, *Protecting Soldiers and Mothers*; Koven and Michel, eds., *Mothers of a New World*; Bock and Thane, eds., *Maternity and Gender Politics*; Ladd-Taylor, *Mother-Work*.
5 Ursel, *Private Lives, Public Policy*, 89.
6 Ibid., 98. For a measured view of this divisive issue, see the editors' introduction to Wikander, Kessler-Harris, and Lewis, eds., *Protecting Women*, 1–28.
7 Cott, *Grounding of Modern Feminism*, 115–42.
8 Pugh, *Women and the Women's Movement in Britain*, 43–153; Alberti, "Keeping the Candle Burning," 299.
9 Ursel, *Private Lives, Public Policy*, 93.
10 *Labour Gazette*, July 1918, 537.
11 Kealey, "Women and Labour during World War I," 77–8.
12 *Labour Gazette*, January 1925, 57.
13 Ibid., September 1926, 847.
14 Ibid., September 1927, 926.
15 Ibid., December 1927, 1277.
16 Ibid., December 1928, 1320.
17 Ursel, *Private Lives, Public Policy*, 241.

18 Horodyski, "Women and the Winnipeg General Strike," 32; Angel, "Workers, Picketing and the Winnipeg General Strike," 55.

19 Mochoruk and Webber, "Women in the Winnipeg Garment Trade, 1929–1945," 145.

20 Lindsay, *Clothes Off Our Back*, 27.

21 *Labour Gazette*, 1959, 905.

22 White, *Women and Unions*, 21–7.

23 *Labour Gazette*, 1942, 1230.

24 Ibid., 1946, 447.

25 Ibid., 1956, 654.

26 Sangster, *Earning Respect*, 171.

27 Strange, *Toronto's Girl Problem*, 27.

28 *Census of Canada 1931*, V, Table 25; *Census of Canada 1936*, II, Table 35; *Census of Canada 1941*, VI, Table 5; *Census of Canada 1946*, II, Table 24; *Census of Canada 1951*, V, Tables 14 and 15; *Census of Canada 1961*, Catalogue 94–536, Table 15; *Census of Canada 1971*, Catalogue 94–913, Table 39.

29 Oddson, *Employment of Women in Manitoba*, Appendix A, Table 2.

30 Armstrong and Armstrong, *Double Ghetto*, 34.

31 Oddson, *Employment of Women in Manitoba*, Appendix A, Table 7.

32 Bridenthal, "Something Old, Something New"; Pierson, *'They're Still Women After All'*, 9–94.

33 Armstrong and Armstrong, *Double Ghetto*, 35–41.

34 Statistics Canada, *Historical Compendium of Education Statistics*, CS 81–568.

35 Kinnear, "'Mostly for the Male Members'," 6.

36 *Census of Canada 1946*, II, Table 22; *Census of Canada 1951*, V, Tables 14 and 15; *Census of Canada 1961*, Catalogue 94–536, Tables 15–19; *Census of Canada 1971*, Catalogue 94–713, Table 1.

37 *Census of Canada 1951*, V, Table 6; *Census of Canada 1961*, Catalogue 94–542, Table 31; *Census of Canada 1971*, Catalogue 94–764, Table 12.

38 *Labour Gazette*, 1965, 338.

39 Ostry, *Female Worker in Canada*, 41–3; *Labour Gazette*, 1965, 801.

40 Oddson, *Employment of Women in Manitoba*, Appendix B, Table 18a and Table 21.

41 Carter, "Woman's Sphere."

42 White, "Restructuring the Domestic Sphere," 191; Carter, "First Nations Women of Prairie Canada in the Early Years," 67.

43 Barber, "Servant Problem in Manitoba," 100–19.

44 Ibid., 112.

45 Epp, "Mennonite Girls' Homes of Winnipeg," 16, 18–19.

46 PAM, Manitoba Labour Education Centre, Women's History Project Oral History Collection, tape C 582, Margaret Albrecht.

47 Epp, "Mennonite Girls' Homes of Winnipeg," 26–33.

48 *Freyja* 4 (1901–2): 176–7.

49 Barber, "Servant Problem in Manitoba," 109–12.

50 *Labour Gazette*, March 1921, 398.

51 Canada, Advisory Committee on Reconstruction, *Report of the Subcommittee on the Post-War Problems of Women 1943*, 10–12.

52 Strange, *Toronto's Girl Problem*, 37; Armstrong and Armstrong, *Double Ghetto*, 35. In Toronto the shift away from domestic service occurred earlier: in 1880 "over half of Toronto's female workers were employed as servants, whereas only one-quarter worked in service by 1911." Strange, *Toronto's Girl Problem*, 37.

53 Oddson, *Employment of Women in Manitoba*, Appendix A, Table 2.

54 Benson, *Counter Cultures*, 18.

55 Ibid., 27.

56 PAM, University Women's Club, *Work of Women and Girls*; Kealey, "Women and Labour during World War I."

57 PAM, University Women's Club, *Work of Women and Girls*, 3, 3–5, 5–11.

58 Ibid., 11–13.

59 Woodsworth, "Report on Living Standards 1913," in Artibise, *Winnipeg: A Social History*, 317.

60 Manitoba, Legislative Assembly, *Sessional Paper 27*, 7 February 1918.

61 PAM, University Women's Club, *Work of Women and Girls*, 15.

62 Ibid., 11–18.

63 Ibid., 18–21.

64 PAM, Manitoba Labour Education Centre, Women's History Project Oral History Collection, tape C 587, Helen Peterson.

65 Ibid., tape C 581, anonymous; Jewish Historical Society, Oral History Tapes, tape 365, Clara Charach.

66 PAM, Manitoba Labour Education Centre, Women's History Project Oral History Collection, tape C 585–6, Sheila Mayhew.

67 Ibid., tape C 611, anonymous; tape C 577, Charlotte Lepp; tape C 612, Margaret McTavish.

68 Ibid., tape C 585–6, Sheila Mayhew, and tape C 612, Margaret McTavish.

69 Ibid., tape C 574, Noreen Rooke.

70 Oddson, *Employment of Women in Manitoba*, Appendix B, Table 18b.

71 Lowe, "Mechanization, Feminization, and Managerial Control," 195.

72 Ibid., 184–93.

73 Ibid., 197.

74 Oddson, *Employment of Women in Manitoba*, Appendix A, Tables 3 and 4.

75 Lowe, "Mechanization, Feminization, and Managerial Control," 202.

76 Haig, *Brave Harvest*, 17–18, 43.

77 PAM, Manitoba Labour Education Centre, Women's History Project Oral History Collection, tape C 581, anonymous.

78 Ibid., tape c 573, Ruth Pauls.

79 Ibid., tape c 576, Ruth Melman.

80 Ibid., tape c 692, anonymous.

81 Ibid.

82 Lowe, *Women in the Administrative Revolution*, 179.

83 Hail and Duncan, *Out of the North*, 62.

84 Carter, "First Nations Women of Prairie Canada in the Early Years," 62–3; Schneider, "Women's Work."

85 Oddson, *Employment of Women in Manitoba*, Appendix A, Tables 6 and 7.

86 *Census of Canada 1951*, IV, Table 2; *Census of Canada 1971*, Catalogue 94–716.

87 *Census of Canada 1911*, VI, Table 5; *Census of Canada 1921*, IV, Table 4; *Census of Canada 1931*, VII, Table 56; *Census of Canada 1941*, VII, Table 17; *Census of Canada 1951*, IV, Table 16; *Census of Canada 1961*, Catalogue 94–518, Volume 3.2, Table 1; *Census of Canada 1971*, Catalogue 94–740, Volume 3.4, Table 2.

88 McClung, *The Stream Runs Fast*, 103–6.

89 Kealey, "Women and Labour during World War I," 77.

90 Manitoba, Legislative Assembly, *Sessional Paper 27*, 7 February 1918, Ed McGrath to the Hon. G.A. Grierson, 9 January 1918.

91 Kealey, "Women and Labour during World War I," 78; Smith, *Let Us Rise*, 40–4.

92 Manitoba, Legislative Assembly, *Sessional Paper 27*, 7 February 1918.

93 Kealey, "Women and Labour during World War I," 88, 91.

94 Oddson, *Employment of Women in Manitoba*, 60. PAM, Manitoba Labour Education Centre, Needles Trades Oral History Project 1984, Beatrice Sanden, c 1048, Rose Katz, c 1050, Gertrude Zukowsky, c 1055, Rose Gordon, c 1060. Mochoruk and Webber, "Women in the Winnipeg Garment Trade, 1929–1945," 136.

95 PAM, Manitoba Labour Education Centre, Women's History Project Oral History Collection, tape c 584, anonymous.

96 Smith, *Let Us Rise*, 82–4.

97 Lindsay. *Clothes Off Our Back*, 26.

98 Roberts, Millar, and Lepp, "Women in the Winnipeg Garment Trade, 1950s–1970s," 153.

99 Ibid., 153, 155.

100 For an overview of literature with respect to women in professional work, see Kinnear, *In Subordination*, 3–29.

101 *Census of Canada 1881*, II, Table 14; *Census of Canada 1931*, VII, Table 4; *Census of Canada 1941*, VII, Table 4; *Census of Canada 1951*, IV, Table 4; *Census of Canada 1961*, Catalogue 94–514, Volume 3.1, Table 20; *Census of Canada 1971*, Catalogue 94–716, Volume 3.2, Table 2.

102 Oddson, *Employment of Women in Manitoba*, 39.

103 Prentice, "Feminization of Teaching," 55.

104 Oddson, *Employment of Women in Manitoba*, Appendix A, Tables 3 and 4.

105 Shack, *Two-Thirds Minority*, 11, 12, 17, 58; Kinnear, *In Subordination*, 123–51.

106 *Grain Growers' Guide*, 10 May 1922.

107 Ibid., 17 May 1916.

108 Ibid., 24 February 1926.

109 Shack, *Two-Thirds Minority*, 52; Manitoba Museum of Man and Nature, Oral History, tape 597, Margaret Gow.

110 Thomson, "Diary," 78.

111 *Grain Growers' Guide*, 8 February 1922.

112 Nuffield, *With the West in Her Eyes*, 144, 149.

113 Shack, "Making of a Teacher 1917–1935," 446.

114 Ibid., 458.

115 Gray, *Boy from Winnipeg*, 38–9.

116 University of Winnipeg, Winnipeg School Division, Scrapbooks, 1: 15.

117 Kinnear, "Mostly for the Male Members," 1–20.

118 Manitoba Teachers' Society, Winnipeg Teachers' Association, file 2, Vera Patrick, 1935.

119 Kinnear, "Mostly for the Male Members," 12.

120 Shack, *Two-Thirds Minority*, 29, 35, 40, 43.

121 *Winnipeg Telegram*, 19 May 1904.

122 For a biography of Johns, see Street, *Watchfires on the Mountains*.

123 McPherson, *Bedside Matters*, 115–63.

124 McPherson, "Skilled Service and Women's Work: Canadian Nursing 1920–1939"; Fines, "History of the Manitoba Association of Registered Nurses," 168, 202.

125 Manitoba Museum of Man and Nature, Oral History Tapes 368a, b, Agnes Baird.

126 *Winnipeg Tribune*, 11 July 1950.

127 Fines, "History of the Manitoba Association of Registered Nurses," 42.

128 Ibid., 48.

129 Ibid., 51.

130 Hart, "Public Health in Manitoba," paper prepared for the Annual Meeting of the Canadian Public Health Association, Winnipeg 1979, 7.

131 Fines, "History of the Manitoba Association of Registered Nurses," 168–206.

132 Ruth Evans Papers, Hilda St. Germain, "Tales of a Red Cross Nurse," 1953; Dorothy M. Park, "Remembered Acts of Kindness and of Love," *Family Herald and Weekly Star*, 6 May 1954.

133 Ruth Evans Papers, Margaret Litton Hodgins, "Memoirs of a Red Cross Outpost."

134 Ibid., Ruth Evans, "The Red Cross North of 53," and "Red Cross Outposts in Manitoba," 1988.

135 Fines, "History of the Manitoba Association of Registered Nurses," 120–1.

136 Kinnear, *In Subordination*, 108.

137 Ibid., 112.

138 Ibid., 119.

139 *Census of Canada 1971*, Volume 3.2, Table 2.

140 See, for example, the comments in my *In Subordination*, 152–67.

CHAPTER EIGHT

1 *The Quotarian* 16 (no. 8, October 1938): 8.

2 Phillips, *Democracy and Difference*, 75–90; Christie and Gauvreau, *Full-Orbed Christianity*, 121.

3 Lake, "Between Old Worlds and New," 280.

4 Buffalohead, "Farmers, Warriors, Traders," 243–4; Peers, *Ojibwa of Western Canda*, 56–60, 84; Pettipas, "Severing the Ties that Bind," 50–2; Canada, *Report of the Royal Commission on Aboriginal Peoples*, 2: 125.

5 Canada, *Report of the Royal Commission on Aboriginal Peoples*, 2: 124.

6 See Jamieson, *Indian Women and the Law in Canada: Citizens Minus*; Moss, "Canadian State and Indian Women"; Nahanee, "Indian Women, Sex Equality, and the Charter"; Canada, *Report of the Royal Commission on Aboriginal Peoples*, 4: 21–4.

7 Stowell, *If I Were King of Canada*; Canada, Advisory Committee on Reconstruction, *Report of the Subcommittee on the Post-War Problems of Women*.

8 For a general overview of women's volunteer work in Canada, see Prentice et al, *Canadian Women*. For a close examination of such work in Atlantic Canada, see Fingard, *The Dark Side of Life in Victorian Halifax*.

9 Kinnear, *Margaret McWilliams*, 86–8.

10 *Winnipeg Telegram*, "Women's Paper," 8 May 1907, 24, 32–3.

11 Thomas, "Some Manitoba Women Who Did First Things," 19–20.

12 Lady Schultz, Mrs. J.C. Patterson, Mrs. Hugh John Macdonald, Mrs. Colin Campbell, Mrs. George Bryce.

13 Griffiths, *Splendid Vision*.

14 *Winnipeg Telegram*, "Women's Paper," 38.

15 Ibid.

16 Cook, "Ambiguous Heritage."

17 Rooke and Schnell, *No Bleeding Heart*, 199.

18 PAM, Local Council of Women, 75th Anniversary, 18 April 1969; Heads, "Local Council of Women of Winnipeg."

19 Hébert, "Les grandes gardiennes de la langue et de la foi," 112–13, 326–31.

20 United Church of Canada, St. Stephen's Broadway, "St. Stephen's Silver Jubilee, 1895–1930," 12, 15.

21 Kristjanson, *The Icelandic People in Manitoba*, 177, 194.

22 Kinnear, "Icelandic Connection," 25–8.

23 McClung, *The Stream Runs Fast*, 106–22.

24 Hathaway, "Political Equality League of Manitoba," 8–10.

25 See Bacchi, *Liberation Deferred?* 117–32.

26 PAM, Political Equality League, Minutes, 1912–1914; Cleverdon, *Woman Suffrage Movement in Canada*, 61, 62.

27 NA, Cleverdon Papers, Lillian Beynon Thomas to Catherine Cleverdon, 21 April 1944.

28 *Canadian Men and Women of the Time*, 1912, 922.

29 Winnipeg *Voice*, 6 December 1907.

30 Ibid., 12 November, 20 December 1912.

31 Ibid., 23 July, 17 September 1915.

32 PAM, Lillian Beynon Thomas Papers, "Manitoba Women Voted First," 1959.

33 NA, Cleverdon Papers, Lillian Beynon Thomas to Catherine Cleverdon, 21 April 1944.

34 Molgat, "The *Voice* and the Women of Winnipeg," 37.

35 Gutkin and Gutkin, *Profiles in Dissent*, 213–50.

36 Molgat, "The *Voice* and the Women of Winnipeg," 35–40.

37 Roberts, "Why Do Women Do Nothing to Stop the War?" 6–15, 20–6; Roberts, "Women's Peace Activism in Canada," 282–5; Roberts, *A Reconstructed World*, 162–235.

38 For instance, see *Winnipeg Free Press*, 18 October 1933, on Jessie Maclennan, a successful school board candidate throughout the 1930s.

39 Manitoba Women's Institute, *Great Human Heart*, 31–2.

40 *Grain Growers' Guide*, January 1920.

41 PAM, United Farmers of Manitoba, Secretary's Report to the 1923 Annual Convention, 14; Kinnear, "'Do You Want your Daughter to Marry a Farmer?'" 137–53.

42 Elections Canada, *History of the Vote in Canada*, 61–8, 85–9.

43 Geller, "Wartime Elections Act of 1917 and the Canadian Women's Movement."

44 *Grain Growers' Guide*, 27 December 1916.

45 *Grain Growers' Guide*, 24 January 1917; Savage, *Our Nell*, 126–9.

46 *Grain Growers' Guide*, 18 July 1917; Winnipeg *Voice*, 7 December 1917; Cook, "F.M. Beynon and Christian Reformism."

47 For an analysis of early twentieth-century American feminism, see Cott, *Grounding of Modern Feminism*.

48 PAM, Canadian Women's Press Club, 1917 Scrapbook.

49 Ibid.

50 *Manitoba Free Press*, 13 December 1917.

51 PAM, Political Equality League, Minutes, 29 March 1912.

52 Ibid., Canadian Women's Press Club, 1917 Scrapbook, 15.

53 Ibid., 31.

54 *Grain Growers' Guide*, 20 June 1917.

55 Martha Jane Hample, in whose house the league was founded, was a school trustee towards the end of the war and two former leaguers, Alice Holling and Genevieve Lipsett Skinner, were unsuccessful candidates in the provincial election of 1920. Hample and Alice Munro, another former leaguer, were unsuccessful candidates in the 1922 provincial election.

56 McDowell, "Harriet Dick: A Lady before Her Time?"; Sangster, "Making of a Socialist-Feminist."

57 Thelma Forbes (Progressive Conservative, Cypress), first elected in a by-election in 1959, Carolyne Morrison (Progressive Conservative, Pembina), elected in 1966, and Inez Trueman (Progressive Conservative, Fort Rouge), in 1969. *Canadian Parliamentary Guide*, 1963, 541, and 1967, 568; *Winnipeg Free Press* 26 June 1969.

58 Brian McKillop, "Citizen and Socialist," 51.

59 See Rea, "Politics of Conscience"; Rea, "Politics of Class"; Rea, "Consolidation of Power."

60 Aldermen: Jessie Kirk in 1920 and Margaret McWilliams who served 1933–40. Trustees: Jessie Maclennan, 1925–40, Mary Dyma, 1931–5, and Gloria Queen-Hughes, 1933–40.

61 Hilda Hesson 1940–7, Maude McCreery 1949–57, Lillian Hallonquist 1952–70, Edith Tennant 1957–67, Inez Trueman 1967–9, and June Westbury 1969.

62 *Winnipeg Free Press* 28 October 1950, 26 October 1962, 26 October 1968, 23 October 1969.

63 Labour: Mrs Jock McNeil 1941; Jean Danyleyko 1946; Beatrice Brigden 1956; Mary Kardash 1964. Independent: Gloria Queen-Hughes 1958, 1967; Alice Peterson 1960, 1962; Vera McIlroy 1968.

64 Labour women were elected trustees in 1941 (Jessie Maclennan), 1942 (Mindel Cherniak Sheps), 1947 (Margaret Chunn), 1960 (Mary Kardash), 1964 (Isabel Sudol), 1965 (Kardash), 1966 (Sudol), 1967 (Una B. Decter and Kardash), 1968 (Sudol), and 1969 (Sudol).

65 Jacob Penner, Sam Forkin, Joe Zuken, and William Kardash, the husband of Mary Kardash.

66 *Winnipeg Free Press*, 24 November and 2 December 1920, 19 November 1923.

67 Ibid., 21 November 1930.

68 Ibid., 26 November 1938; *Winnipeg Tribune*, 22 November 1938.

69 *Winnipeg Free Press*, 18 October 1950.

70 Ibid., 6 October 1966.

71 See the brief biographies published in the *Winnipeg Free Press* before each municipal election.

72 Phillips, *Democracy and Difference*, 76.

CHAPTER NINE

1 Ursel, *Private Lives, Public Policy*, 302.
2 Bowker, ed., *Social Criticism of Stephen Leacock*, 60.
3 Crawford, *Legal Status of Women in Manitoba*.
4 Manitoba, *Report of the Manitoba Volunteer Committee on the Status of Women*.
5 Hathaway, "Political Equality League of Manitoba," 8–10.
6 NA, National Council of Women of Canada, volume 151, pamphlet: Henrietta Muir Edwards, "Legal Status of Canadian Women as Shown by Extracts from Dominion and Provincial Laws Relating to Marriage, Property, Dower, Divorce, Descent of Land, Franchise, Crime and other Subjects."
7 Crawford, *Legal Status of Women in Manitoba*, 5.
8 Ibid., 10.
9 McCallum, "Prairie Women and Dower Law," 29.
10 Crawford, *Legal Status of Women in Manitoba*, 15.
11 See the work of Emily Murphy, who "created a series of women-seducing villains, primarily non-white and non-Christian, who threatened the Anglo-Saxon way of life": Robert Solomon in his introduction to Murphy's *Black Candle*, 3. Also, Backhouse, "White Women's Labor Laws," 336–48, 367.
12 *Labour Gazette*, July 1914, 49.
13 For a comprehensive treatment of women and law, see Backhouse, *Petticoats and Prejudice*.
14 Crawford, *Legal Status of Women in Manitoba*, 37.
15 Ibid., 40.
16 Manitoba, *Report of the Manitoba Volunteer Committee on the Status of Women*, 36.
17 Christie and Gauvreau, *Full-Orbed Christianity*, 117.
18 Ibid., 92–7.
19 Sisler, *Partnership of Equals*, 25.
20 Black. "Ripples in the Second Wave," 103–5.
21 Ursel, *Private Lives, Public Policy*, 292.
22 Cohen, "Canadian Women's Movement and Its Efforts to Influence the Canadian Economy," 215–24.
23 Ursel, *Private Lives, Public Policy*, 300.
24 *Labour Gazette*, 1965, 1031.
25 Manitoba, *Report of the Manitoba Volunteer Committee on the Status of Women*, 19.
26 Shields, *Stone Diaries*, 121.
27 Ibid., 282.

$\mathscr{B}$IBLIOGRAPHY

PRIMARY SOURCES

ARCHIVAL

Jewish Historical Society, Winnipeg
Oral History Tapes

Manitoba Museum of Man and Nature, Winnipeg
Oral History Tapes

Mennonite Heritage Centre, Winnipeg
Helena (Penner) Hiebert, "Granny Stories"
Evril Wiebe, "Early Days: An Interview with Mrs Agatha Wiedeman," 2 April
  1977

National Archives of Canada (NA), Ottawa
Canadian Federation of University Women
Catherine Cleverdon Papers
Department of Labour, Employment of Women and Day Care of Children
  [1945]
National Council of Women

Privately Held Papers
Ruth Evans Papers

Provincial Archives of Manitoba (PAM), Winnipeg
Canadian Women's Press Club
Council of Social Agencies

Department of Agriculture, *Manitoba Agriculture Year Book*, 1985
Department of Education, Half Yearly Attendance Reports, Winnipeg, 1942–3
Junior League
Manitoba Labour Education Centre
    Women's History Project Oral History Collection
    Needles Trade Oral History Project, 1984
Political Equality League
Lillian Beynon Thomas Papers
United Farmers of Manitoba
University Women's Club
Women's Canadian Club
Winnipeg Council of Women

United Church of Canada, University of Winnipeg
St. Stephen's Broadway, Parish Records

University of Manitoba Archives, Winnipeg
Consumers' Association
Mary Speechly Papers

Winnipeg School Division, Winnipeg
Scrapbooks

Manitoba Teachers' Society, Winnipeg
Winnipeg Teachers' Association

GOVERNMENT DOCUMENTS

Canada
Advisory Committee on Reconstruction. *Report of the Subcommittee on the Post-War Problems of Women.* 1943.
Report of the Royal Commission on Aboriginal Peoples. 5 volumes. 1996.
Report of the Royal Commission on the Status of Women in Canada. 1970.
Statistics Canada
    Censuses of Canada
    Historical Compendium of Education Statistics
    Vital Statistics

Manitoba
Advisory Committee on the Co-ordination of Post-War Planning. *Report of the Subcommittee on Women's Services.* 1945.
Department of Education
    Annual Reports 1870–1970
    Programme of Studies 1919–1931

Legislative Assembly. *Sessional Paper 17*. 7 February 1918.
Report of the Manitoba Volunteer Committee on the Status of Women. March 1968.
Report of the Royal Commission to Inquire into the Administration of the Child Welfare Division of the Department of Public Health and Welfare. 1928.

NEWSPAPERS AND PERIODICALS

Freyja
Grain Growers' Guide (Winnipeg)
Labour Gazette (Ottawa)
Le Manitoba (Winnipeg)
Manitoba / Winnipeg Free Press (Winnipeg)
Western School Journal (Winnipeg)
Winnipeg Telegram (Winnipeg)
Winnipeg Tribune (Winnipeg)
Voice (Winnipeg)

SECONDARY SOURCES

Aberson, Jane L.S. *From the Prairies with Hope*. Edited by Robert E. Vander Vennon. Regina: Canadian Prairies Research Centre 1991.
Acton, Janice, ed. *Women at Work in Ontario*. Toronto: Canadian Women's Educational Press 1974.
Addams, Jane. *Democracy and Social Ethics*. New York: Macmillan 1916.
– *The Second Twenty Years at Hull-House*. New York: Macmillan 1930.
– *Twenty Years at Hull-House*. New York: Macmillan 1930.
Akenson, D.H., ed. *Canadian Papers in Rural History*, Volume VI. Gananoque ON: Langdale 1988.
Albers, Patricia, and Beatrice Medicine, eds. *The Hidden Half: Studies of Plains Indian Women*. Lanham MD: University Press of America 1983.
Alberti, Johanna. "Keeping the Candle Burning: Some British Feminists between Two Wars." In Daley and Nolan, eds., *Suffrage and Beyond*, 295–312.
Allen, Richard. *The Social Passion: Religion and Social Reform in Canada 1914–28*. Toronto: University of Toronto Press 1971.
Amott, Teresa L., and Julie A Matthaei. *Race, Gender and Work: A Multicultural History of Women in the United States*. Boston: South End Press 1991.
Andrew, Caroline, and Sanda Rodgers, eds. *Women and the Canadian State*. Montreal & Kingston: McGill-Queen's University Press 1997.
Angel, Eric. "Workers, Picketing and the Winnipeg General Strike of 1919." Master's thesis, Queen's University, 1995.
Apter, Terri. *Professional Progress: Why Women Still Don't Have Wives*. London: Macmillan 1983.

Armstrong, Pat, and Hugh Armstrong. "Beyond Sexless Class and Classless Sex: Towards Feminist Marxism." In Luxton, ed., *Feminist Marxism*, 1–38.
- *The Double Ghetto: Canadian Women and Their Segregated Work*. Revised edition. Toronto: McClelland & Stewart 1984.
Arnason, David. *The New Icelanders: A North American Community*. Winnipeg: Turnstone Press 1994.
Artibise, Alan F.J. *Winnipeg: A Social History of Urban Growth, 1874–1914*. Montreal & Kingston: McGill-Queen's University Press 1975.
Bacchi, Carol Lee. *Liberation Deferred? The Ideas of the English-Canadian Suffragists, 1877–1918*. Toronto: University of Toronto Press 1983.
Backhouse, Constance. *Petticoats and Prejudice: Women and Law in Nineteenth Century Canada*. Toronto: Women's Press 1991.
- "The White Women's Labor Laws: Anti-Chinese Racism in Early Twentieth-Century Canada." *Law and History Review* 14 (fall 1996): 315–68.
Backhouse, Constance, and David H. Flaherty, eds. *Challenging Times: The Women's Movement in Canada and the United States*. Kingston & Montreal: McGill-Queen's University Press 1992.
Barber, Marilyn. "The Servant Problem in Manitoba, 1896–1930." In Kinnear, ed., *First Days, Fighting Days*, 100–19.
Baron, Ava, ed. *Work Engendered: Toward a New History of American Labor*. Ithaca NY: Cornell University Press 1991.
Barman, Jean. *The West beyond the West: A History of British Columbia*. Revised edition. Toronto: University of Toronto Press 1996.
Barman, Jean, Yvonne Hébert, and Don McCaskill, "Legacy of the Past." In Barman, Hébert, and McCaskill, eds. *Indian Education in Canada*. 2 volumes. Vancouver: University of British Columbia Press 1986, 1987.
Beardy, Flora, and Robert Coutts, eds. *Voices from Hudson Bay: Cree Stories from York Factory*. Montreal & Kingston: McGill-Queen's University Press 1996.
Benson, Susan Porter. *Counter Cultures: Saleswomen, Managers and Customers in American Department Stores, 1890–1940*. Urbana: University of Illinois Press 1986.
Berger, Carl, and Ramsay Cook, eds. *The West and the Nation*. Toronto: McClelland & Stewart 1976.
Beynon, Francis Marion. *Aleta Dey*. London: Virago 1988. First published 1919.
Binnie Clarke, Georgina. *Wheat and Woman*. Edited by Susan Jackel. Toronto: University of Toronto Press 1979.
Birtles, William. "A Tribute to the Pioneer Nurses of Manitoba: Mary Ellen Birtles," *Nurscene* (May 1989): 5–7.
Black, Naomi. "Ripples in the Second Wave: Comparing the Contemporary Women's Movement in Canada and the United States." In Backhouse and Flaherty, eds., *Challenging Times*, 94–109.
- *Social Feminism*. Ithaca NY: Cornell University Press 1989.

Blake, William. *Jerusalem*. Edited by William Hughes. New York: Barnes & Noble 1964.

Blank, Rebecca M. "What Should Mainstream Economists Learn from Feminist Theory?" In Ferber and Nelson, eds., *Beyond Economic Man*, 133–43.

Bock, Giselda, and Pat Thane, eds. *Maternity and Gender Politics: Women and the Rise of the European Welfare States 1880s–1950s*. London: Routledge 1991.

Bodichon, Barbara L.S. "Women and Work." In Lacey, ed., *Bodichon and the Langham Place Group*, 36–73.

Bonin, Marie. "The Grey Nuns and the Red River Settlement," *Manitoba History* 11 (spring 1986): 12–14.

Boris, Ellen. "Beyond Dichotomy: Recent Books in North American Women's Labor History," *Journal of Women's History* 4 (winter 1993): 162–79.

Bowker, Alan, ed. *The Social Criticism of Stephen Leacock*. Toronto: University of Toronto Press 1973.

Boyd, Monica, Margrit Eichler, and John R. Hofley. "Family: Functions, Formation and Fertility." In Gail Cook, ed., *Opportunity for Choice: A Goal for Women in Canada*, 13–52. Ottawa: Statistics Canada in association with the C.D. Howe Research Institute 1976.

Bradbury, Bettina. *Working Families: Age, Gender and Daily Survival in Industrializing Montreal*. Toronto: McClelland & Stewart 1993.

Brandt, Gail Cuthbert. "'Pigeon-Holed and Forgotten': The Work of the Sub-committee on the Post-War Problems of Women, 1943." *Histoire Sociale / Social History* 15 (1982): 239–59.

– "Postmodern Patchwork: Some Recent Trends in the Writing of Women's History in Canada." *Canadian Historical Review* 72 (December 1991): 441–70.

Bridenthal, Renate. "Something Old, Something New: Women between the Two World Wars." In Bridenthal, Koonz, and Stuard, eds., *Becoming Visible*, 473–88.

Bridenthal, Renate, Claudia Koonz, and Susan Stuard, eds. *Becoming Visible: Women in European History*. 2nd edition. Boston: Houghton Mifflin 1987.

Brittain, Vera. *Testament of Youth*. London: Virago 1978. First published 1933.

– "Women in Industry: Restrictive Legislation Again." In Paul Berry and Alan Bishop, eds., *Testament of a Generation: The Journalism of Vera Brittain and Winifred Holtby*. London: Virago 1988.

Broadfoot, Barry. *Next-Year Country: Voices of Prairie People*. Toronto: McClelland & Stewart 1988.

– *Ten Lost Years, 1929–1939: Memories of Canadians Who Survived the Depression*. Toronto: Doubleday Canada 1973.

Brouwer, Ruth. *New Women for God: Canadian Presbyterian Women and India Missions 1876–1914*. Toronto: University of Toronto Press 1990.

Brown, Jennifer. *Strangers in the Blood: Fur Trade Company Families in Indian Country*. Vancouver: University of British Columbia Press 1980.

Bruley, Sue. *Leninism, Stalinism and the Women's Movement in Britain, 1920–1939*. New York: Garland 1986.

Bruno-Jofré, Rosa del C., ed. *Issues in the History of Education in Manitoba: From the Construction of the Common School to the Politics of Voices*. Lewiston / Queenston / Lampeter: Edwin Mellen Press 1993.

Buffalohead, Priscilla. "Farmers, Warriors, Traders: A Fresh Look at Ojibway Women." *Minnesota History* 48 (summer 1983): 236–44.

Bumsted, J.M. "Developing a Canadian Disaster Relief Policy: The 1950 Manitoba Flood." *Canadian Historical Review* 68 (September 1987): 347–73.

– *The Winnipeg General Strike of 1919: An Illustrated History*. Winnipeg: Watson & Dwyer 1994.

Butler, Elizabeth Beardsley. *Saleswomen in Mercantile Stores, Baltimore 1909*. New York: Charities Publication Committee 1912.

Caine, Barbara. *Victorian Feminists*. Oxford: Oxford University Press 1992.

Campbell, Alison. "Beatrice Brigden: The Formative Years of a Socialist Feminist 1888–1932." Master's thesis, University of Manitoba, 1981.

Canadian Pacific Railway. *What Women Say of the Canadian North West*. Montreal 1886.

– *Women's Work in Western Canada*. Montreal 1906.

Canadian Welfare Council. *Rural Need in Canada*. Ottawa: Canadian Welfare Council 1965.

Carter, Sarah. "First Nations Women of Prairie Canada in the Early Years, the 1870s to the 1920s: A Preliminary Enquiry." In Miller and Chuchryk, eds., *Women of the First Nations*, 51–76.

– *Lost Harvests: Prairie Indian Reserve Farmers and Government Policy*. Montreal & Kingston: McGill-Queen's University Press 1990.

– "The Woman's Sphere: Domestic Life at Riel House and Dalnavert," *Manitoba History* 11 (spring 1986): 55–61.

Cavanaugh, Catherine. "In Search of a Useful Life: Irene Marryat Parlby, 1868–1965." Doctoral thesis, University of Alberta, 1994.

– "The Limitations of the Pioneering Partnership: The Alberta Campaign for Homestead Dower, 1909–25." *Canadian Historical Review* 74 (June 1993): 198–225.

Cavanaugh, Catherine, and Randi Warne, eds. *Standing on New Ground: Women in Alberta*. Edmonton: University of Alberta Press 1993.

Christie, Nancy, and Michael Gauvreau. *A Full-Orbed Christianity: The Protestant Churches and Social Welfare in Canada 1900–1940*. Montreal & Kingston: McGill-Queen's University Press 1996.

Clark, Alice. *The Working Life of Women in the Seventeenth Century*. London: Frank Cass 1968.

Cleverdon, Catherine. *The Woman Suffrage Movement in Canada*. Toronto: University of Toronto Press 1974.

Clio Collective. *Quebec Women: A History*. Translated by Roger Gannon and Rosalind Gill. Toronto: Women's Press 1987.

Coates, Ken, and Fred McGuinness. *Manitoba: The Province and the People.* Edmonton: Hurtig 1987.

Cohen, Marjorie Griffin. "The Canadian Women's Movement and Its Efforts to Influence the Canadian Economy." In Backhouse and Flaherty, eds., *Challenging Times*, 215–24.

– *Women's Work, Markets, and Economic Development in Nineteenth-Century Ontario.* Toronto: University of Toronto Press 1988.

Cook, Ramsay. "Ambiguous Heritage: Wesley College and the Social Gospel Reconsidered." *Manitoba History* 19 (spring 1990): 2–11.

– "Francis Marion Beynon and the Crisis of Christian Reformism." In Berger and Cook, eds., *The West and the Nation*, 187–208.

Cott, Nancy. "Comment on Karen Offen's 'Defining Feminism: A Comparative Historical Approach'." *Signs* 15 (no. 1, 1989): 203–5.

– *The Grounding of Modern Feminism.* New Haven CT: Yale University Press 1987.

Crawford, Mary. *Legal Status of Women in Manitoba.* Winnipeg: Political Equality League 1913.

Creese, Gillian, and Veronica Strong-Boag, eds., *British Columbia Reconsidered: Essays on Women.* Vancouver: Press Gang Publishers 1992.

Culleton, Beatrice. *April Raintree.* Winnipeg: Peguis 1992.

Daley, Caroline, and Melanie Nolan, eds. *Suffrage and Beyond: International Feminist Perspectives.* New York: New York University Press 1994.

Danysk, Cecilia. *Hired Hands: Labour and the Development of Prairie Agriculture 1880–1930.* Toronto: McClelland & Stewart 1995.

Davidson, C.B. *Employment in Manitoba.* Winnipeg: Manitoba Economic Survey Board 1938.

Davidson, C.B., H.C. Grant, and Frank Shefrin. *The Population of Manitoba.* Winnipeg: Manitoba Economic Survey Board 1938.

Davis, Allan F. *American Heroine: The Life and Legend of Jane Addams.* New York: Oxford University Press 1973.

Davis, Angela. "Mary Speechly: A Life of Service." *The Beaver* 74 (no. 5, 1994): 35–9.

– "'Valiant Servants': Women and Technology on the Canadian Prairies 1910–1940." *Manitoba History* 25 (spring 1993): 33–42.

Dawson, C.A. *Group Settlement: Ethnic Communities in Western Canada.* Canadian Frontiers of Settlement VII. Millwood NY: Kraus Reprint 1974.

Dawson, C.A., and Eva R. Yonge. *Pioneering in the Prairie Provinces: The Social Side of the Settlement Process.* Canadian Frontiers of Settlement VIII. Millwood NY: Kraus Reprint 1974.

De Brou, David, and Aileen Moffatt, eds. *"Other" Voices: Historical Essays on Saskatchewan Women.* Regina: Canadian Plains Research Centre 1995.

Degler, Carl. "Introduction." To Gilman, *Women and Economics.*

De Mallie, Raymond. "Male and Female in Traditional Lakota Culture." In Albers and Medicine, eds., *Hidden Half*, 237–66.

Dickason, Olive Patricia. *Canada's First Nations: A History of Founding Peoples from Earliest Times*. Toronto: McClelland & Stewart 1992.

Dorsch, Julie. " 'You Just Did What Had to be Done': Life Histories of Four Saskatchewan 'Farmers' Wives'." In De Brou and Moffatt, eds., *"Other" Voices*, 116–30.

DuBois, Ellen Carol. "Comment on Karen Offen's 'Defining Feminism: A Comparative Historical Approach'." *Signs* 15 (no. 1, 1989): 195–7.

Duverger, Maurice. *The Political Role of Women*. Paris: United Nations Educational, Scientific and Cultural Organization 1955.

Dyhouse, Carol. *Feminism and the Family in England, 1880–1939*. Oxford: Basil Blackwell 1989.

Edge, Fred. *The Iron Rose: The Extraordinary Life of Charlotte Ross M.D.* Winnipeg: University of Manitoba Press 1992.

Eichler, Margrit. *The Double Standard: A Feminist Critique of Feminist Social Science*. New York: St. Martin's Press 1979.

Elias, Peter Douglas. *The Dakota of the Canadian Northwest: Lessons for Survival*. Winnipeg: University of Manitoba Press 1988.

Enns, F.G. *Gretna: Window on the Northwest*. Altona MA: Friesen 1987.

Enns, Gerhard J. "Mennonites and Modernism: The Changing Impact of the Mennonite Collegiate Institute on Mennonite Education and Society in Manitoba, 1888–1948." In Bruno-Jofré, ed., *Issues in the History of Education in Manitoba*, 137–56.

Epp, Marlene. "The Mennonite Girls' Homes of Winnipeg, 1925–1959: A Home Away from Home." Unpublished paper, University of Waterloo, April 1988.

Errington, Elizabeth Jane. *Wives and Mothers, Schoolmistresses and Scullery Maids: Working Women in Upper Canada, 1790–1840*. Montreal & Kingston: McGill-Queen's University Press 1995.

Ewanchuk, Michael. *Pioneer Profiles: Ukrainian Settlers in Manitoba*. Winnipeg: Ewanchuk 1981.

Ferber, Marianne A., and Julie A. Nelson, eds., *Beyond Economic Man: Feminist Theory and Economics*. Chicago: University of Chicago Press 1993.

Ferns, Harry S. *Reading from Left to Right: One Man's Political History*. Toronto: University of Toronto Press 1983.

Fines, Beatrice. "History of the Manitoba Association of Registered Nurses." Typescript in archives of the Association in Winnipeg, 1978.

Fingard, Judith. "College, Career and Community: Dalhousie Co-eds 1881–1921." In Paul Axelrod and John G. Reid, eds. *Youth, University and Canadian Society*, 26–50. Montreal & Kingston: McGill-Queen's University Press 1989.

– *The Dark Side of Life in Victorian Halifax*. Porters Lake: Pottersfield Press 1989.

The First Ukrainian Women Graduates from the University of Manitoba prior to 1940. Winnipeg: Alpha Omega Women's Alumnae 1974.

Flexner, Eleanor. *Mary Wollstonecraft*. Baltimore: Penguin 1973.

Folbré, Nancy. "Socialism, Feminist and Scientific." In Ferber and Nelson, eds., *Beyond Economic Man*, 94–110.

– *Who Pays for the Kids? Gender and the Structures of Restraint*. New York: Routledge 1994.

Foster, John E., ed. *The Developing West: Essays on Canadian History in Honour of Lewis H. Thomas*. Edmonton: University of Alberta Press 1983.

Frances, Raelene, Linda Kealey, and Joan Sangster. "Women and Wage Labour in Australia and Canada 1880–1980." *Labour / Le Travail* 38 (fall 1996): 54–89.

Francis, E.K. *In Search of Utopia: The Mennonites in Manitoba*. Altona MA: Friesen 1955.

Francis, R. Douglas, and Howard Palmer, eds. *The Prairie West: Historical Readings*. 2nd edition. Edmonton: Pica Pica Press 1992.

Fraser, Nancy, and Linda Gordon. "A Genealogy of Dependency: Tracing a Keyword of the U.S. Welfare State," *Signs* 9 (no. 2, 1994): 309–36.

Fraser, William John. *A History of St. John's College, Winnipeg*. Winnipeg: Wallingford 1966.

Friedan, Betty. *The Feminine Mystique*. New York: Norton 1983. First published 1963.

– *The Second Stage*. New York: Summit 1981.

Friesen, Gerald. *The Canadian Prairies: A History*. Toronto: University of Toronto Press 1984.

– *River Road: Essays on Manitoba and Prairie History*. Winnipeg: University of Manitoba Press 1996.

Gagan, Rosemary. *A Sensitive Independence: Canadian Methodist Women Missionaries in Canada and the Orient 1881–1925*. Montreal & Kingston: McGill-Queen's University Press 1992.

Galloway, Margaret. *I Lived in Paradise*. Winnipeg: Bulman 1941.

Gaskell, Jane S., and Arlene Tigar McLaren, eds. *Women and Education: A Canadian Perspective*. Calgary: Detselig 1987.

Gee, Ellen M. "Female Marriage Patterns in Canada: Changes and Differentials." *Journal of Comparative Family Studies* 9 (no. 4, 1980): 457–73.

– "The Life Course of Canadian Women: An Historical and Demographic Analysis." *Social Indicators Research* 18 (1986): 263–83.

– "Marriage in Nineteenth Century Canada." *Canadian Review of Sociology and Anthropology* 19 (no. 3, 1982): 311–25.

Gee, Ellen M., and Meredith Kimball. *Women and Aging*. Toronto: Butterworths 1987.

Gee, Ellen M., and Jean E. Veevers. "Accelerating Sex Differentials in Mortality: An Analysis of Contributing Factors." *Social Biology* 30 (no. 1, 1983): 75–85.

Geller, Gloria. "The Wartime Elections Act of 1917 and the Canadian Women's Movement." *Atlantis* 2 (no. 1, 1976): 88–106.

Gilman, Charlotte Perkins. *Women and Economics*. Edited by Carl Degler. New York: Harper 1966. First published 1898.

Goeres, Michael. "Disorder, Dependency and Fiscal Responsibility: Unemployment Relief in Winnipeg 1907–1942," Master's thesis, University of Manitoba, 1981.

Gollancz, Victor, ed. *The Making of Women: Oxford Essays in Feminism*. London: Gollancz 1917.

Gordon, Linda. *Pitied but not Envied: Single Mothers and the History of Welfare*. New York: Free Press 1994.

Graves, Pamela M. *Labour Women: Women in British Working-Class Politics 1918–1939*. Cambridge: Cambridge University Press 1994.

Gray, James H. *The Boy from Winnipeg*. Toronto: Macmillan 1970.

– *The Winter Years*. Toronto: Macmillan 1966.

Gray, Susan. "Methodist Indian Day Schools and Indian Communities in Northern Manitoba, 1890–1925. *Manitoba History* 30 (autumn 1995): 2–16.

Gregor, Alexander, and Keith Wilson. *History of Education in Manitoba*. 2 volumes. Winnipeg: University of Manitoba Faculty of Education 1983.

Griffiths, N.E.S. *The Splendid Vision: Centennial History of the National Council of Women of Canada 1893–1993*. Ottawa: Carleton University Press 1993.

Guildford, Janet, and Suzanne Morton, eds. *Separate Spheres: Women's Worlds in the 19th Century Maritimes*. Fredericton: Acadiensis Press 1994.

Gutkin, Harry, and Mildred Gutkin. *Profiles in Dissent: The Shaping of Radical Thought in the Canadian West*. Edmonton: NeWest 1997.

– *The Worst of Times, the Best of Times: Growing Up in Winnipeg's North End*. Markham ON: Fitzhenry & Whiteside 1987.

Hacker, Carlotta. *The Indomitable Lady Doctors*. Toronto: Clarke Irwin 1974.

Haig, Kennethe. *Brave Harvest*. Toronto: Allen 1945.

Hail, Barbara, and Kate Duncan, *Out of the North: The Subarctic Collection of the Haffenreffer Museum of Anthropology*. Bristol RI: Haffenreffer Museum of Anthropology 1989.

Hajnal, John. "European Marriage Patterns in Perspective." In D.V. Glass and D.E.C. Eversley, eds., *Population in History: Essays in Historical Demography*, 101–43. London: Weidenfeld and Nicolson 1965.

Hallett, Mary, and Marilyn Davis. *Firing the Heather: The Life and Times of Nellie McClung*. Saskatoon: Fifth House 1994.

Hanawalt, Barbara. *The Ties That Bound: Peasant Families in Medieval England*. New York: Oxford University Press 1986.

– ed. *Women and Work in Preindustrial Europe*. Bloomington: Indiana University Press 1986.

Harris, Alice Kessler. *Out to Work: A History of Wage-Earning Women in the United States*. New York: Oxford University Press 1982.

Harrison, Brian. *Prudent Revolutionaries: Portraits of British Feminists between the Wars*. Oxford: Clarendon 1987.

Harrison, Marjorie. *Go West – Go Wise! A Canadian Revelation*. London: Arnold 1930.

Hart, Margaret E. "Public Health in Manitoba 1909–1979." Paper prepared for the annual meeting of the Canadian Public Health Association, Winnipeg, 19–21 June 1979.

Harvey, Cameron. "Women in Law in Canada." *Manitoba Law Journal* (1970–71): 9–38.

Hathaway, Debbie. "The Political Equality League of Manitoba." *Manitoba History* 3 (spring 1982): 8–10.

Heads, Wendy. "The Local Council of Women of Winnipeg 1894–1920: Tradition and Transformation." Master's thesis, University of Manitoba, 1997.

Healy, W.J. *Women of Red River*. Winnipeg: Peguis 1970. First published 1923.

Hébert, Monique. "Les grandes gardiennes de la langue et de la foi: une histoire des franco-manitobaines de 1916 à 1947." Doctoral thesis, University of Manitoba, 1994.

Helmbold, Lois Rita, and Ann Schofield. "Women's Labor History, 1790–1945," *Reviews in American History* 17 (no. 3, 1989): 501–18.

Henley, Richard. "The School Question Continued: The Issue of Compulsory Schooling in Manitoba." In Bruno-Jofré, ed., *Issues in the History of Education in Manitoba*, 47–72.

Heriot, A.A. "School Inspectors in Manitoba," Typescript.

Heron, Craig, and Robert Storey, eds. *On the Job: Confronting the Labour Process in Canada*. Montreal & Kingston: McGill-Queen's University Press 1986.

Hill, Bridget. *Women, Work and Sexual Politics in Eighteenth Century England*. Oxford: Basil Blackwell 1989.

Hobbs, Margaret. "Rethinking Antifeminism in the 1930s: Gender Crisis or Workplace Justice? A Response to Alice Kessler-Harris." *Gender and History* 5 (spring 1993): 4–15.

Horodyski, Mary. "Women and the Winnipeg General Strike of 1919." *Manitoba History* 11 (spring 1986): 28–37.

Hurl, Lorna. "The Politics of Child Welfare in Manitoba, 1922–3." *Manitoba History* 7 (spring 1984): 2–9.

Hryniuk, Stella, and Neil McDonald. "The Schooling Experience of Ukrainians in Manitoba, 1896–1916." In Francis and Palmer, eds., *The Prairie West*, 289–307.

Iacovetta, Franca, and Mariana Valverde, eds. *Gender Conflicts: New Essays in Women's History*. Toronto: University of Toronto Press 1992.

Jackel, Susan. "First Days, Fighting Days: Prairie Presswomen and Suffrage Activism, 1906–1916." In Kinnear, ed., *First Days, Fighting Days*, 53–75.

– "Introduction." To *Wheat and Woman* by Georgina Binnie Clarke, v–xxxvii.

– ed. *A Flannel Shirt and Liberty*. Vancouver: University of British Columbia Press 1982.

Jamieson, Kathleen. *Indian Women and the Law in Canada: Citizens Minus.* Ottawa: Minister of Supply and Services Canada 1978.

Jeffrey, Julie Roy. *Frontier Women: The Trans-Mississippi West 1840–1880.* New York: Hill and Wang 1979.

Jennings, Ann L. "Public or Private? Institutional Economics and Feminism." In Ferber and Nelson, eds., *Beyond Economic Man*, 111–30.

Jensen, Joan M. *Loosening the Bonds: Mid-Atlantic Farm Women 1750–1850.* New Haven CT: Yale University Press 1986.

– *Promise to the Land: Essays on Rural Women.* Albuquerque: University of New Mexico Press 1991.

Johns, Ethel, and Beatrice Fines. *The Winnipeg General Hospital and Health Sciences School of Nursing 1887–1987.* Winnipeg: Alumnae Association of the WGH and HSC School of Nursing [1990].

Kealey, Linda. "Women and Labour during World War I: Women Workers and the Minimum Wage in Manitoba." In Kinnear, ed., *First Days, Fighting Days*, 76–99.

– ed. *Pursuing Equality: Historical Perspectives on Women in Newfoundland and Labrador.* St. John's: Institute of Social and Economic Research 1993.

Kealey, Linda, and Joan Sangster, eds. *Beyond the Vote: Canadian Women and Politics.* Toronto: University of Toronto Press 1989.

Kelcey, Barbara E., and Angela E. Davis, eds. *A Great Movement Underway: Women and the Grain Growers' Guide.* Winnipeg: Manitoba Record Society 1997.

Kennedy, Ellen, and Susan Mendus, eds. *Women in Western Philosophy: Kant to Nietzsche.* Brighton: Wheatsheaf 1987.

Kerr, D.G.G., ed. *A Historical Atlas of Canada.* 2nd edition. Don Mills ON: T. Nelson 1961.

Kessler-Harris, Alice. *Out to Work: A History of Wage-Earning Women in the United States.* New York: Oxford University Press 1982.

Kinnear, Mary. "Disappointed in Discourse: Women Professors at the University of Manitoba before 1970." *Historical Studies in Education* 4 (no. 2, 1992): 269–87.

– " 'Do You Want Your Daughter to Marry a Farmer?': Women's Work on the Farm, 1922." In Akenson, ed., *Canadian Papers in Rural History*, 137–53.

– "The Icelandic Connection: *Freyja* and the Manitoba Woman Suffrage Movement." *Canadian Woman Studies* 7 (no. 4, 1986): 25–8.

– *In Subordination: Women in the Professions 1870–1970.* Montreal & Kingston: McGill-Queen's University Press 1995.

– *Margaret McWilliams: An Interwar Feminist.* Montreal & Kingston: McGill-Queen's University Press 1991.

– " 'Mostly for the Male Members': Winnipeg Teachers 1933–1966." *Historical Studies in Education* 6 (no. 1, 1994): 1–20.

- "That There Woman Lawyer: Women Lawyers in Manitoba before 1970." *Canadian Journal of Women and the Law* 5 (no. 2, 1992): 411–41.
- "Women and Post-Suffrage Prairie Politics: Female Candidates in Municipal Elections in Winnipeg, 1918–1939." *Prairie Forum* 15 (no. 2, 1991): 41–58.
- ed. *First Days, Fighting Days: Women in Manitoba History.* Regina: Canadian Plains Research Centre 1987.

Kinnear, Mary, and Vera Fast. *Planting the Garden: An Annotated Archival Bibliography of the History of Women in Manitoba.* Winnipeg: University of Manitoba Press 1987.

Knox, Ellen M. *The Girl of the New Day.* Toronto: McClelland & Stewart 1918.

Kobayashi, Audrey, ed. *Women, Work, and Place.* Montreal & Kingston: McGill-Queen's University Press 1994.

Koven, Seth, and Sonya Michel, eds. *Mothers of a New World: Maternalist Politics and the Origins of Welfare States.* New York: Routledge 1993.

Kristjanson, W. *The Icelandic People in Manitoba: A Manitoba Saga.* Winnipeg: Kristjanson 1967.

Kuiper, Edith, and Jolande Sap, eds. *Out of the Margin: Feminist Perspectives on Economics.* London and New York: Routledge 1995.

Lacey, Candida Ann, ed. *Barbara Leigh Smith Bodichon and the Langham Place Group.* New York and London: Routledge & Kegan Paul 1987.

Ladd-Taylor, Molly. *Mother-Work: Women, Child Welfare and the State 1890–1930.* Urbana: University of Illinois Press 1994.

Lake, Marilyn. "Between Old Worlds and New: Feminist Citizenship, Nation and Race, the Destabilisation of Identity." In Daley and Nolan, eds., *Suffrage and Beyond,* 277–94.
- "The Inviolable Woman: Feminist Conceptions of Citizenship in Australia, 1900–1945." *Gender and History* 8 (no. 2, 1996): 197–211.

Laurence, Margaret. *The Diviners.* Toronto: McClelland & Stewart 1974.
- *A Jest of God.* Toronto: McClelland & Stewart 1966.
- *The Stone Angel.* Toronto: McClelland & Stewart 1964.

Lee, Linda. "The Myth of Female Equality in Pioneer Society: The Red River Colony as a Test Case." Master's thesis, University of Manitoba, 1978.

Le Gates, Marlene. *Making Waves: A History of Feminism in Western Society.* Toronto: Copp Clark 1996.

Lerner, Gerda. *The Creation of Feminist Consciousness: From the Middle Ages to 1870.* New York: Oxford University Press 1993.
- *The Creation of Patriarchy.* New York: Oxford University Press 1986.

Lévesque, Andrée. *Making and Breaking the Rules: Women in Quebec, 1919–1929.* Toronto: McClelland & Stewart 1994.

Levine, Susan. *Degrees of Equality: The American Association of University Women and the Challenge of Twentieth Century Feminism.* Philadelphia PA: Temple University Press 1995.

Lewis, Jane. "Eleanor Rathbone and the Family." *New Society*, 27 January 1983, 137.

– *Women in England 1870–1950: Sexual Divisions and Social Change.* Bloomington: Indiana University Press 1984.

Lindsay, Debra. *The Clothes Off Our Back: A History of ACTWU 459.* Winnipeg: Manitoba Labour History Series, ACTWU, 1995.

Longino, Helen E. "Economics for Whom?" In Ferber and Nelson, eds., *Beyond Economic Man*, 158–68.

Lowe, Graham. "Mechanization, Feminization, and Managerial Control in the Early Twentieth Century Office." In Heron and Storey, eds., *On the Job*, 177–209.

– *Women in the Administrative Revolution.* Toronto: University of Toronto Press 1987.

Luciuk, Lubomyr Y., and Bohdan S. Kordan. *Creating a Landscape: A Geography of Ukrainians in Canada.* Toronto: University of Toronto Press 1989.

Luxton, Meg. *More Than a Labour of Love.* Toronto: Women's Press 1980.

– ed. *Feminist Marxism or Marxist Feminism: A Debate.* Toronto: Portcullis 1985.

McCallum, Margaret E. "Prairie Women and the Struggle for a Dower Law, 1905–20." *Prairie Forum* 18 (no. 1, 1993): 19–34.

McCloskey, Donald N. *The Rhetoric of Economics.* Madison: University of Wisconsin Press 1985.

– "Some Consequences of a Conjective Economics." In Ferber and Nelson, eds., *Beyond Economic Man*, 69–93.

McClung, Nellie. *Clearing in the West.* Toronto: Allen 1964. First published 1935.

– *The Stream Runs Fast.* Toronto: Thomas Allen 1965. First published 1945.

– *In Times Like These.* Introduction by Veronica Strong-Boag. Toronto: University of Toronto Press 1972. First published 1915.

McColl, Frances V. *Vignettes of Early Winnipeg.* Winnipeg: Frances McColl 1981.

McCracken, Melinda. *Memories Are Made of This.* Toronto: Lorimer 1975.

McDowell, Linda. "Harriet Dick: A Lady before Her Time?" *Manitoba Pageant* (1975): 11–13.

MacInnis, Grace. *J.S. Woodsworth: A Man to Remember.* Toronto: Macmillan 1953.

McKillop, Brian. "Citizen and Socialist: The Ethos of Political Winnipeg 1919–1935." Master's thesis, University of Manitoba, 1970.

McLaren, Angus, and Arlene Tigar McLaren. *The Bedroom and the State: Changing Practices and Policies of Contraception and Abortion in Canada, 1880–1980.* Toronto: McClelland & Stewart 1986.

McPherson, Kathryn. *Bedside Matters: The Transformation of Canadian Nursing 1900–1990.* Toronto: Oxford University Press 1996.

- "Skilled Service and Women's Work: Canadian Nursing 1920–1939." Doctoral thesis, Simon Fraser University, 1989.

Mander, Christine. *Emily Murphy: Rebel*. Toronto: Simon & Pierre 1985.

Manitoba Women's Institute. *The Great Human Heart: A History of the Manitoba Women's Institute 1910–1980*. Winnipeg: The Institute 1980.

Milkman, Ruth. "New Research in Women's Labor History." *Signs* 18 (winter 1993): 376–88.

Mill, J.S. *Collected Works of John Stuart Mill*. Edited by John M. Robson. Volumes 4 and 21. Toronto: University of Toronto Press 1963, 1984.

Miller, Christine, and Patricia Chuchryk, eds. *Women of the First Nations: Power, Wisdom and Strength*. Winnipeg: University of Manitoba Press 1996.

Miller, Harry B. *The Spirit Lives On: The Washakada Indian Home and the Anglican Indian Residential School, 1888–1949*. Melville, Sask., 1990.

Miller, J.R. *Shingwauk's Vision: A History of Native Residential Schools*. Toronto: University of Toronto Press 1996.

Mink, Gwendolyn. *The Wages of Motherhood: Inequality in the Welfare State 1917–1942*. Ithaca NY: Cornell University Press 1995.

Mochoruk, James D., and Donna Webber. "Women in the Winnipeg Garment Trade, 1929–1945." In Kinnear, ed., *First Days, Fighting Days*, 134–48.

Molgat, Anne. "The *Voice* and the Women of Winnipeg 1894–1918." Master's thesis, University of Ottawa, 1988.

Morton, W.L. *Manitoba: A History*. Toronto: University of Toronto Press 1973.

- "Manitoba Schools and Canadian Nationality, 1890–1923." In R. Craig Brown, ed., *Minorities, Schools, and Politics*, 10–18. Toronto: University of Toronto Press 1969.

- *One University: A History of the University of Manitoba*. Toronto: McClelland & Stewart 1957.

Moss, Wendy. "The Canadian State and Indian Women: The Struggle for Sex Equality under the Indian Act." In Andrew and Rodgers, eds. *Women and the Canadian State*, 79–88.

Moynihan, Ruth B., Susan Armitage, and Christine Fischer Dichamp, eds. *So Much to be Done: Women Settlers on the Mining and Ranching Frontier*. Lincoln: University of Nebraska Press 1990.

Murchie, R.W. *Agricultural Progress on the Prairie Frontier*. Canadian Frontiers of Settlement v. Millwood NY: Kraus Reprint 1974.

Murphy, Emily. *The Black Candle: Canada's First Book on Drug Abuse*. Introduction by Robert Solomon. Toronto: Coles 1973.

- *Janey Canuck in the West*. Toronto: McClelland & Stewart 1975. First published 1910.

Myres, Sandra L. *Westering Women and the Frontier Experience 1800–1915*. Albuquerque: University of New Mexico Press 1991.

Nahanee, Teresa Anne. "Indian Women, Sex Equality, and the Charter." In Andrew and Rodgers, eds., *Women and the Canadian State*, 89–103.

Nelson, Julie A. *Feminism, Objectivity and Economics*. London & New York: Routledge 1996.

– "The Study of Choice or the Study of Provisioning?" In Ferber and Nelson, eds., *Beyond Economic Man*, 23–36.

Nuffield, E.W. *With the West in Her Eyes: Nellie Hislop's Story*. Winnipeg: Hyperion 1987.

Oakley, Ann. *Subject Women*. New York: Pantheon 1981.

Oddson, Asta. *Employment of Women in Manitoba*. Winnipeg: Manitoba Economic Survey Board 1939.

Offen, Karen. "Defining Feminism: A Comparative Historical Approach," *Signs* 14 (no. 1, 1988): 119–57.

Okin, Susan Moller. *Women in Western Political Thought*. Princeton NJ: Princeton University Press 1979.

Organization for Economic Co-operation and Development. *Equal Opportunities for Women*. Paris: OECD 1979.

Osborne, Ken. "Introduction." In Bruno-Jofré, ed., *Issues in the History of Education of Manitoba*, 1–16.

Ostenso, Martha. *Wild Geese*. Toronto: McClelland & Stewart 1971. First published 1925.

Ostry, Sylvia. *The Female Worker in Canada*. Ottawa: Dominion Bureau of Statistics 1968.

Owen, Wendy. "The Cost of Farm-Making in Early Manitoba: The Strategy of Almon James Cotton as a Case Study." *Manitoba History* 18 (autumn 1989): 4–11.

Parr, Joy. *The Gender of Breadwinners: Women, Men and Change in Two Industrial Towns 1880–1950*. Toronto: University of Toronto Press 1990.

– ed. *Childhood and Family in Canadian History*. Toronto: McClelland & Stewart 1982.

Parr, Joy, and Mark Rosenfield, eds. *Gender and History in Canada*. Toronto: Copp Clark 1996.

Pateman, Carol. *The Disorder of Women*. Cambridge: Polity 1989.

– *The Sexual Contract*. Cambridge: Polity 1988.

Pateman, Carol, and Elizabeth Gross, eds. *Feminist Challenges: Social and Political Theory*. Sydney: Allen and Unwin 1986.

Peers, Laura. *The Ojibwa of Western Canada*. Winnipeg: University of Manitoba Press 1994.

– "Subsistence, Secondary Literature, and Gender Bias: The Saulteaux." In Miller and Chuchryk, eds., *Women of the First Nations*, 39–50.

Pentland, H.C. Review of David J. Bercuson, *Confrontation at Winnipeg*. *Red River Valley Historian* (summer 1976): 27.

Perkin, Joan. *Women and Marriage in Nineteenth Century England*. Chicago: Lyceum 1989.

Peters, Victor. *All Things Common: The Hutterian Way of Life*. Minneapolis: University of Minnesota Press 1965.

Peterson, T. "Ethnic and Class Politics in Manitoba." In Martin Robin, ed., *Canadian Provincial Politics: The Party Systems of the Ten Provinces*, 69–115. Scarborough ON: Prentice-Hall 1972.

Pettipas, Katherine. *Severing the Ties that Bind: Government Repression of Indigenous Religious Ceremonies on the Prairies*. Winnipeg: University of Manitoba Press 1994.

Phillips, Anne. *Democracy and Difference*. Cambridge: Polity Press 1993.

– *Divided Loyalties: Dilemmas of Sex and Class*. London: Virago 1987.

– *Hidden Hands: Women and Economic Policies*. London: Pluto 1983.

Phillips, Roderick. *Untying the Knot: A Short History of Divorce*. Cambridge: Cambridge University Press 1991.

Pierson, Ruth Roach. "'Home Aide': A Solution to Women's Unemployment after the Second World War." *Atlantis* 2 (no. 2, 1977): 85–97.

– *'They're Still Women After All': The Second World War and Canadian Womanhood*. Toronto: McClelland & Stewart 1986.

Pinchbeck, Ivy. *Women Workers and the Industrial Revolution 1750–1850*. London: Frank Cass 1968. First published 1930.

Power, Eileen. *Medieval Women*. Edited by M.M. Postan. Cambridge: Cambridge University Press 1975.

Prentice, Alison. "The Feminization of Teaching." In Trofimenkoff and Prentice, eds., *Neglected Majority*, 49–65.

Prentice, Alison, et al. *Canadian Women: A History*. Toronto: Harcourt Brace Jovanovich, 1988; 2nd edition 1996.

Pugh, Martin. *Women and the Women's Movement in Britain 1914–59*. London: Macmillan 1992.

Pujol, Michèle A. *Feminism and Anti-Feminism in Early Economic Thought*. Aldershot, Hants: Edward Elgar 1992.

Rathbone, Eleanor. "The Remuneration of Women." In Gollancz, ed., *Making of Women*, 100–27.

Rea, J.E. "The Consolidation of Power: Winnipeg City Council 1946–1975," Government of Manitoba, Committee of Review, City of Winnipeg Act, 1976, Appendix IV.

– "The Politics of Class: Winnipeg City Council, 1919–1945." In Berger and Cook, eds., *The West and the Nation*, 232–49.

– "The Politics of Conscience: Winnipeg after the Strike." Canadian Historical Association, *Historical Papers* (1971): 276–88.

Rendall, Jane. "Virtue and Commerce: Women in the Making of Adam Smith's Political Economy." In Kennedy and Mendus, eds., *Women in Western Philosophy*, 44–77.

Roberts, Barbara. *A Reconstructed World: A Feminist Biography of Gertrude Richardson*. Montreal & Kingston: McGill-Queen's University Press 1996.

– *"Why Do Women Do Nothing to End the War?": Canadian Feminist Pacifists and the Great War*. CRIAW Papers 13. Ottawa: Canadian Research Institute for the Advancement of Women 1985.

– "Women's Peace Activism in Canada." In Kealey and Sangster, eds., *Beyond the Vote*, 276–308.

Roberts, Barbara, David Millar, and Analee Lepp. "Women in the Winnipeg Garment Trade, 1950s–1970s." In Kinnear, ed., *First Days, Fighting Days*, 149–72.

Rooke, P.T., and R.L. Schnell. *No Bleeding Heart: Charlotte Whitton, A Feminist on the Right*. Vancouver: University of British Columbia Press 1987.

Roy, Gabrielle. *Enchantment and Sorrow: The Autobiography of Gabrielle Roy*. Translated by Patricia Claxton. Toronto: Lester & Orpen Dennys 1987.

Sachs, Carolyn. *Gendered Fields: Rural Women, Agriculture and Environment*. Boulder CO: Westview 1996.

Sangster, Joan. *Dreams of Equality: Women on the Canadian Left, 1920–1950*. Toronto: McClelland & Stewart 1989.

– *Earning Respect: The Lives of Working Women in Small-Town Ontario, 1920–1960*. Toronto: University of Toronto Press 1995.

Sangster, Joan. "The Making of a Socialist-Feminist: The Early Career of Beatrice Brigden." *Atlantis* 13 (no. 1, 1987): 14–28.

Savage, Candace. *Our Nell: A Scrapbook Biography of Nellie McClung*. Saskatoon: Prairie Books 1979.

Schneider, Mary Jane. "Women's Work: An Examination of Women's Roles in Plains Indian Arts and Crafts." In Albers and Medicine, eds., *Hidden Half*, 101–22.

Schreiner, Olive. *Woman and Labour*. Introduction by Jane Graves. London: Virago 1978. First published 1911.

Scott, Joan Wallach. "Introduction." In Joan Wallach Scott, ed., *Feminism and History*, 1–13. Oxford: Oxford University Press 1996.

Sealey, D. Bruce. *The Education of Native Peoples in Manitoba*. Winnipeg: University of Manitoba 1980.

Shack, Sybil. "The Making of a Teacher 1917–1935: One Woman's Perspective." In Bruno-Jofré, ed., *Issues in the History of Education in Manitoba*, 431–70.

– *The Two-Thirds Minority: Women in Canadian Education*. Toronto: Faculty of Education, University of Toronto, 1973.

Sheehan, Nancy M. "National Issues and Curricula Issues: Women and Educational Reform, 1900–1930." In Gaskell and McLaren, eds., *Women and Education*, 233–40.

Shields, Carol. *The Stone Diaries*. London: Fourth Estate 1993.

Shilliday, Gregg, ed. *Manitoba 125: A History*. 3 volumes. Winnipeg: Great Plains Publications 1993, 1994, 1995.

Silverman, Eliane. *The Last Best West: Women on the Alberta Frontier, 1880–1930*. Montreal: Eden Press 1984.

Sisler, Berenice B. *A Partnership of Equals: The Struggle for the Reform of Family Law in Manitoba*. Winnipeg: Watson & Dwyer 1995.

Skocpol, Theda. *Protecting Soldiers and Mothers: The Political Origins of Social Policy in the United States.* Cambridge MA: Harvard University Press 1995.

Skocpol, Theda, and Gretchen Ritter. "Gender and the Origin of Modern Social Policies." *Studies in American Political Development* 5 (no. 1, 1991): 36–93.

Smith, Adam. *The Wealth of Nations.* Edited by R.H. Campbell, A.S. Skinner, and W.B. Todd. Oxford: Clarendon Press 1979.

Smith, Doug. *Let Us Rise: An Illustrated History of the Manitoba Labour Movement.* Winnipeg: New Star Books 1985.

Sprague, Douglas, and R.P. Frye. *The Genealogy of the First Metis Nation.* Winnipeg: Pemmican Publications 1983.

Spry, Irene M. "The 'Private Adventurers' of Rupert's Land." In Foster, ed., *Developing West,* 49–76.

Stewart, Mary Lynn. *Women, Work and the French State: Labour Protection and Social Patriarchy, 1879–1919.* Kingston & Montreal: McGill-Queen's University Press 1989.

Stocks, Mary D. *Eleanor Rathbone: A Biography.* London: Gollancz 1949.

Stowell, Oliver (R.F. McWilliams and Margaret McWilliams). *If I Were King of Canada.* Toronto: J.M. Dent 1931.

Strange, Carolyn. *Toronto's Girl Problem: The Perils and Pleasures of the City 1880–1930.* Toronto: University of Toronto Press 1995.

Strange, Kathleen. *With the West in Her Eyes: The Story of a Modern Pioneer.* Toronto: Geo. McLeod 1937.

Street, Margaret M. *Watchfires on the Mountains: The Life and Writings of Ethel Johns.* Toronto: University of Toronto Press 1973.

Strong-Boag, Veronica. " 'Ever a Crusader': Nellie McClung, First-Wave Feminist." In Strong-Boag and Fellman, eds., *Rethinking Canada* (2nd edition), 308–21.

– "Home Dreams: Women and the Suburban Experiment in Canada, 1945–60." In Strong-Boag and Fellman, eds., *Rethinking Canada* (3rd edition), 375–401.

– "Intruders in the Nursery: Childcare Professionals Reshape the Years One to Five, 1920–1940." In Parr, ed., *Childhood and Family,* 160–78.

– "Keeping House in God's Country: Canadian Women at Work in the Home." In Heron and Storey, eds., *On the Job,* 124–51.

– *The New Day Recalled: Lives of Girls and Women in English Canada 1919–1939.* Toronto: Copp Clark Pitman 1988.

– *The Parliament of Women: The National Council of Women of Canada 1893–1929.* Ottawa: National Museums of Canada 1976.

– "Pulling in Double Harness or Hauling a Double Load: Women, Work and Feminism on the Canadian Prairie." *Journal of Canadian Studies* 21 (no. 3, 1986): 32–52.

– " 'Wages for Housework': Mothers' Allowances and the Beginnings of Social Security in Canada." *Journal of Canadian Studies* 14 (no. 1, 1979): 24–34.

Strong-Boag, Veronica, and Anita Clair Fellman, eds. *Rethinking Canada: The Promise of Women's History.* Toronto: Copp Clark Pitman 1986; 2nd edition 1991; 3rd edition 1997.

Sundberg, Sara Brooks. "Farm Women on the Canadian Prairie Frontier: The Helpmate Image." In Strong-Boag and Fellman, eds., *Rethinking Canada,* 95–106.

Swan River Valley, Manitoba: Rural Survey. [Winnipeg]: Departments of Social Service and Evangelism of the Presbyterian and Methodist Churches, August-September 1914.

Swyripa, Frances. *Wedded to the Cause: Ukrainian-Canadian Women and Ethnic Identity 1891–1991.* Toronto: University of Toronto Press 1993.

Taylor, Barbara. *Eve and the New Jerusalem: Socialism and Feminism in the Nineteenth Century.* London: Virago 1984.

Taylor, Harriet. "On Marriage." In Robson, ed., *Collected Works of John Stuart Mill,* 21:375.

Taylor, Harriet, and John Stuart Mill, "Papers on Women's Rights, 1847–1850." In Robson, ed., *Collected Works of John Stuart Mill,* 21:392.

Thomas, Lillian Beynon. "Some Manitoba Women Who Did First Things," *Transactions of the Historical and Scientific Society of Manitoba* 3 (no. 4, 1947–8): 13–25.

Thomson, Mary Louise Pickering. "Diary." Edited by Norman Williamson. Typescript 1978.

Tilly, Louise, and Joan W. Scott. *Women, Work and Family.* New York: Holt, Rinehart and Winston 1978.

Titley, Brian. "Industrial Education for Manitoba Natives: The Case of Rupert's Land Indian School." In Bruno-Jofré, ed., *Issues in the History of Education in Manitoba,* 371–404.

Tough, Frank. *'As Their Natural Resources Fail': Native Peoples and the Economic History of Northern Manitoba, 1870–1930.* Vancouver: University of British Columbia Press 1996.

Trofimenkoff, Susan, and Alison Prentice, eds. *The Neglected Majority: Essays in Canadian Women's History.* Toronto: McClelland & Stewart 1977.

Turek, Victor. *Poles in Manitoba.* Toronto: Polish Research Institute in Canada 1967.

Turtle Mountain District, Manitoba: Rural Survey. [Winnipeg]: Departments of Social Service and Evangelism of the Presbyterian and Methodist Churches, June-July 1914.

Urquhart, M.C., and K.A.H. Buckley. *Historical Statistics of Canada.* 2nd edition. Ottawa: 1983.

Ursel, Jane. *Private Lives, Public Policy.* Toronto: Women's Press 1992.

Vandervort, Julie. *Tell the Driver: A Biography of Elinor Black M.D.* Winnipeg: University of Manitoba Press 1993.

Van de Vorst, Carolina Antoinetta J.A. "A History of Farm Women's Work in Manitoba." Master's thesis, University of Manitoba, 1988.

Van Kirk, Sylvia. *Many Tender Ties: Women in Fur Trade Society in Western Canada 1670–1830.* Winnipeg: Watson & Dwyer 1980.

– " 'The Reputation of a Lady': Sarah Ballenden and the Foss-Pelly Scandal." *Manitoba History* 11 (spring 1986): 4–11.

– "The Role of Native Women in the Fur Trade Society of Western Canada 1670–1830." In Strong-Boag and Fellman, eds., *Rethinking Canada*, 58–66.

– " 'What if Mama Is an Indian': The Cultural Ambivalence of the Alexander Ross Family." In Foster, ed., *Developing West*, 123–36.

Walsh, Margaret. "Women In or Out of American Economic History." *Women's History Review* 1 (no. 2, 1992): 307–18.

Waring, Marilyn. *If Women Counted: A New Feminist Economics.* New York: Macmillan 1988.

Ward, W. Peter. "Population Growth in Western Canada 1901–1971." In Foster, ed., *Developing West*, 155–78.

Warne, Randi R. *Literature as Pulpit: The Christian Social Activism of Nellie L. McClung.* Waterloo: Wilfrid Laurier University Press 1993.

Warkentin, John, and Richard Ruggles, ed. *Manitoba Historical Atlas.* Winnipeg: The Historical and Scientific Society of Manitoba 1970.

Weist, Katherine. "Beasts of Burden and Menial Slaves: Nineteenth Century Observations of Northern Plains Indian Women." In Albers and Medicine, eds. *The Hidden Half*, 29–52.

Welter, Barbara. "The Cult of True Womanhood, 1820–1860." *American Quarterly* 18 (summer 1966): 151–74.

Wexler, Alice. *Emma Goldman: An Intimate Life.* New York: Pantheon 1984.

– *Emma Goldman in America.* Boston: Beacon Press 1984.

White, Julie. *Women and Unions.* Ottawa: Canadian Advisory Council on the Status of Women 1980.

White, Pamela. "Restructuring the Domestic Sphere – Prairie Indian Women on Reserves: Image, Ideology and State Policy, 1880–1930." Doctoral thesis, McGill University, 1987.

Wikander, Ulla, Alice Kessler-Harris, and Jane Lewis, eds. *Protecting Women: Labor Legislation in Europe, the United States and Australia, 1880–1920.* Urbana: University of Illinois Press 1995.

Wilson, Johanna Gudrun. *A History of Home Economics Education in Manitoba.* Winnipeg: Manitoba Home Economics Association 1969.

Wiseman, Nelson. "The Pattern of Prairie Politics." *Queen's Quarterly* 87 (1981): 298–315.

Wollstonecraft, Mary. *A Vindication of the Rights of Woman.* Edited by Carol H. Poston. New York: Norton 1975.

Woods, D.S. *Education in Manitoba.* 2 volumes. Winnipeg: Manitoba Economic Survey Board 1938.

Woodsworth, J.S. *My Neighbour.* Toronto: Missionary Society of the Methodist Church 1911.

– *Strangers within Our Gates.* Toronto: Frederick Clarke Stephenson 1909.

The Work of Women and Girls in the Department Stores of Winnipeg. Winnipeg: University Women's Club 1914.

Wrigley, E.A., and R.S. Schofield. *The Population History of England 1541–1871*. Cambridge: Cambridge University Press, 1989.

Yuzyk, Paul. *The Ukrainians in Manitoba: A Social History*. Toronto: University of Toronto Press 1953.

Zeilig, Martin. "Emma Goldman in Winnipeg." *Manitoba History* 25 (spring 1993): 23–7.

$\mathcal{I}$NDEX